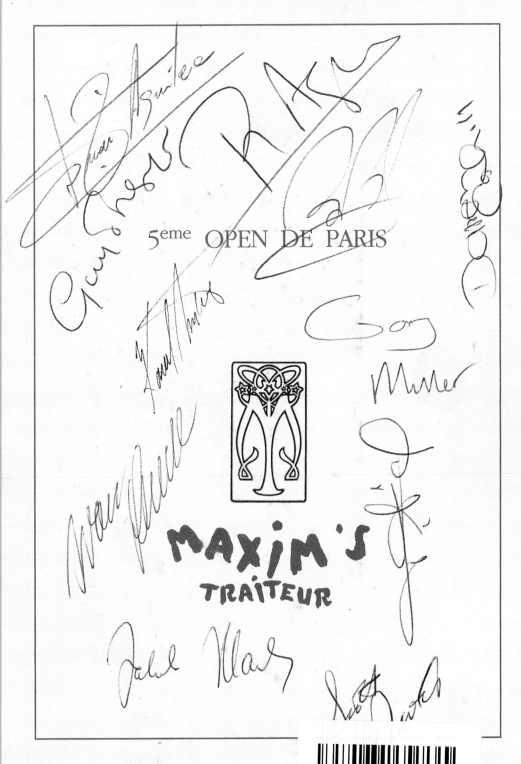

5ᵉᵐᵉ OPEN DE PARIS

MAXiM'S
TRAITEUR

The ATP Tour
Year One - 1990

EDITED BY RICHARD EVANS

The official illustrated
guide to the 77 tournaments
in the new ATP Tour -
with the full results

BLOOMSBURY

First published 1991 by Bloomsbury Publishing Limited,
2 Soho Square, London W1V 5DE

Text copyright © 1991 Association of Tennis Professionals
Design and layout copyright © Bloomsbury Publishing Limited

British Library Cataloguing in Publication Data

A CIP record for this book is available from the British Library

ISBN 0 7475 09123

10 9 8 7 6 5 4 3 2 1

Edited and designed by Toucan Books Limited, London

Originated by Universal Colour Scanning Ltd., Hong Kong

Printed by Butler and Tanner Limited,
Frome, Somerset

*Endpapers: Signatures on Maxim's menu (clockwise from
top left): Juan Aguilera, Ronald Agenor, Boris Becker,
Darren Cahill, Gary Muller, Brad Gilbert, Scott Davis,
Jakob Hlasek, Ivan Lendl, Karel Novacek, Guy Forget.
Signatures on Hotel Gravenbruch Kempinski menu (clockwise
from top left): Kurt Nielsen, Marilyn Fernbergeer,
Bob Green, Charlie Pasarell, Jochen Grosse, Ove Bengtson,
John Feaver, Wilhelm Bungert, Arthur Ashe, Gordon Forbes.*

Acknowledgments

The deadline was absurd but the teamwork magnificent
and I am indebted to Robert Sackville West
and his design team at Toucan who took the brunt of the
workload while Kathy Rooney at Bloomsbury
cracked the whip.
But without the speedy response of the writers and
photographers whose talents made this
book possible nothing would have been achieved. If this is
a worthy record, it is due to them.
Finally, a word of thanks to my assistant editor,
Caroline Hutton who pulled in words and photos
from all over the globe and never flagged in the face of
a daunting task.

Contents

The IBM Story

By Howard Greenwald

In America, baseball fans live and die by statistics: Runs batted in. Earned run averages. Batting averages for left-handed third basemen, during extra-inning home games, with two men on and one out, in May. At night. Only Americans need laugh. Basketball and football fans in the US are only slightly less obsessive, but they too have statistics by the bushel to back up their belief that their hero was the greatest ballplayer of all time. Americans are not alone in their love affair with statistics; it's no different around the rest of the world. Followers of ski racing, track and field, Olympics - all hunger for the statistical detail that tells them which athletes to cheer, celebrate, revere. For 30 years IBM has been helping to amass those statistics, making competitive athletics come alive for fans all over the world, in these and other sports. Now IBM, title sponsor of the ATP Tour, has brought its experience and expertise to the one of the last major sports without statistical parity: professional tennis.

Tennis long ago abandoned heavy wooden rackets and white woollen outfits, but for decades tennis record-keepers had little interest in maintaining a complete historical account of the game. True, umpires scored every match. But the statistics were filed and forgotten. True, the record books did a fine job of listing tournament results, even some major match scores. But none recorded how those matches were played, how those wins were achieved - and virtually none bothered reporting on early round or backcourt matches. Effective 1 January, 1991, it's a whole new ballgame. A new statistical system goes into operation on that date called IBM/ATP Tour MatchFacts, which - by analysing data scanned into computers from new umpire scorecards - captures, stores, updates and distributes to the news media on command the day-to-day performances of tennis professionals in some 3000 tournament matches sponsored annually by the ATP Tour.

Tennis great Arthur Ashe, on hand for the system's unveiling in November 1990 at the ATP Tour World Championship in Frankfurt, called it 'a clear service winner' by IBM. 'It's a milestone in the game,' he told the press. ATP Tour CEO Mark Miles was equally impressed. 'We're just delighted the Information Age has come to tennis. For the tennis fan, this IBM system is going to add a whole new dimension of enjoyment, provide a greater appreciation of the game.'

In addition to tracking wins and losses, MatchFacts routinely produces player statistics on aces served, first-serve percentage, percentage of first and second serve points won, percentage of service games won, break point opportunities and conversions, percentage of points won against an opponent's first and second serves, and percentage of return games won. Printed summaries generated from this scanned data are available to the press at all tournaments, and remotely via computer modem. Match-Facts is part of a broader IBM/ATP Tour sports information system, which provides most of the key statistics traditionally required by professional tennis - for example, current ranking and prize money standings.

'IBM is just doing what comes naturally,' said Jack McMahon, Manager of Corporate Promotions for IBM. 'The company has been doing this sort of thing around the world - sponsoring local, regional, national and international sporting events and supporting them with its technology - since as far back as the 1960 Olympic Winter Games in Squaw Valley. And IBM will continue to be there - for example, at the 1992 Summer Games in Barcelona, the Winter Games in France, and the 1994 Games in Norway. In tennis, you'll continue to see the logo at the French Open, where IBM France provides the information system; at Wimbledon, where IBM UK does the same; and at IBM All Japan Tennis tournaments, sponsored by IBM Japan.'

Why does IBM do this? It's more than just visibility for the IBM name. IBM sees it as a chance both to serve the community, and demonstrate its technology to millions of people it wants to reach. A fair trade, by any measure. Clear beneficiaries of IBM's commitment to sports are the competitors themselves, whose performances are scored, recorded and distributed, assuring them immediate recognition and a place in sports history; sponsoring organisations, which need the operational support; the media, who depend on the data produced; and sports fans, for whom IBM computers provide perspectives on their favourite sports and athletes which would otherwise be impossible.

Mark Miles

Vijay Amritraj

Dear Reader,

Just like the ATP Tour itself, this book combines the talents of many people to bring you a record in words and pictures of a new venture in men's professional tennis.

At the beginning of 1990, players and tournament directors came together to re-structure the existing Grand Prix circuit and create a streamlined, modernised tour for the nineties - one of which, we hope, everyone connected with the game can be proud.

Apart from ensuring that as many pros as possible can earn a good living from this beautiful game, I see it as my responsibility to ensure that the tennis fan derives maximum pleasure from watching our players perform. That means producing stronger tournaments with more top class players competing at the very peak of their ability.

Happily, the first year of the ATP Tour went a long way to achieving that goal and, through the pages of this book, you will be able to re-live the most exciting moments from 81 tournaments around the world - tournaments that provide a cultural kaleidescope of such diversity that no one can fail to be enriched in a manner that reaches out far beyond the confines of a single sport.

At the ATP Tour we will be working harder than ever to ensure that 1991 is even more rewarding for you all.

Yours sincerely,

Mark Miles,
CEO, ATP Tour

Dear Reader,

It has been a great privilege to represent the players during this first, momentous year of the IBM/ATP Tour.

Since the Association of Tennis Professionals was founded in 1972, it has been our dream to have control over our own destiny and present our sport to the public in a manner we felt was best for the game. After the resounding success of the first ATP Tour Championship in Frankfurt, the indications are that we have set off on the right track.

Standards of play and behaviour have shown a dramatic improvement in the first twelve months of the new Tour and, as someone who has always been conscious of the need for the tennis professional to present himself in the best possible light, this has been especially rewarding for me.

I hope you will find this fine record of a year's tennis action the world rewarding, too.

Yours sincerely,

Vijay Amritraj,
President, ATP Tour Players Council

A New Era for Men's Tennis

By Richard Evans

Beating Goran Ivanisevic or losing to Stefan Edberg, Boris Becker is the perfect sportsman.

By the time Andre Agassi held up the blue crystal crown at the end of a thrilling week of tennis at the ATP Tour World Championship in Frankfurt no one was left in any doubt that the game had entered a new era. One look at Andre was confirmation enough. But if the young man from Las Vegas does not meet with universal approval with his attire, his tennis speaks for itself and it spoke louder than all the colours on his back at the Festhalle. Is this the new face of professional tennis? Not necessarily, for Agassi is an original whom people will copy at their peril.

But the ATP Tour is the new face of professional tennis and, judging by the achievements of the first 12 months, it is ready to lead the game into the next century. By any statistical yardstick, the men's circuit in 1990 was an improvement on the old Grand Prix tour. Crowds were up by more than 16%; television coverage was vastly expanded with Eurosport, in particular, becoming a major purveyor of the tennis message in Europe and prize money spiralled despite the pending gloom of a general economic recesssion.

None of this would have been healthy if the product itself had not improved. But it did, dramatically. More players played more tournaments, thanks, largely, to a change in the ATP computerised ranking system which switched from an average system to one that only counted a player's best 14 tournaments. This encouraged players to take the risk of playing more and cut-offs at Championship Series events - the miniumum ranking required to gain direct entry into an event - plunged from 143 in 1989 to 93. But statistics, which are now being stored as never before by our partners, IBM, still only tell part of the story. Much of the other part is brillinatly captured in the pages that follow by some of the game's finest writers and photographers. The reader will find and

account of every tournament on the ATP Tour - all 77 of them them spread over six continents - as well as summaries of the four Grand Slams which, although not strictly part of the tour because they are governed by the Grand Slam committee, nevertheless count for points on the road to Frankfurt.

It turned out to be an extraordinary year in almost every sense. The competition was so fierce that no one was allowed to bestride this mighty world like a Collossus - youth and age having its fling in almost equal measure with Andres Gomez becoming the oldest Grand Slam winner for twenty years when he won in Paris and Pete Sampras becoming the youngest US Open champion in history at Flushing Meadow. Ivan Lendl won in Australia; Stefan Edberg at Wimbledon and Agassi in Frankfurt. For the entire year it was a battle to the death but, somehow sportsmanship survived. The mood one detected on the new tour was the best I could remember since the days of Rod Laver and John Newcombe; not as close in comradeship, to be sure, but sporting, nonetheless. No one epitomised this better than the man who played some of the best tennis of the year and ended up without a Grand Slam title to show for it. Boris Becker may have had enough by the time he finally lost to Agassi in Frankfurt but basically he remained the same in victory and defeat - as these pictures show.

There were many unsung heroes of the inaugural ATP Tour, road managers, trainers, headquarters staff and media personell who worked long hours at tournaments all over the world. But perhaps the ATP Tour umpires should take a special bow. Gayle Bradshaw, the senior supervisor and his team took officiating up to a new level and with it came a better standard of behaviour. It was another plus as the ATP Tour set off optimistically into the new decade.

The Young Tigers

By John Barrett

Pete Sampras

The American dream came true in 1990 for the immensely popular Pete Sampras.

Appropriately, he wears on his shirt the picture of an archer who has just loosed an arrow from his bow. It is a fitting symbol for, during the course of the 1990 US Open, Pete Sampras, the shy and reserved No. 12 seed, fired a quiverful of arrows - 100 piercing service aces and countless flashing returns and passes - that brought down in succession Dan Goldie, Peter Lundgren, Jakob Hlasek, Thomas Muster (seeded 6), Ivan Lendl (3), John McEnroe and Andre Agassi (4). It was the most remarkable performance these championships had ever seen and earned for the modest Californian the distinction of becoming the youngest ever to hold the title at 19 years and 28 days.

Pete's parents, Sam and Georgia, were not at Flushing Meadow to watch this historic moment. 'We get too nervous,' admits Sam, the son of Greek immigrants. 'And anyway we've brought up Pete to understand that he must make it on his own.'

During his junior years when Pete was noted for his talent but not for his application, it was not always apparent that he would make anything much in life. The man who believed he might was Dr. Pete Fischer, a friend of the family who acted as Pete's unofficial (and unpaid) coach for nine years. 'He had such wonderful natural timing and with his double-handed backhand was so good from the baseline he could beat all the other kids.' But he couldn't beat Chang or Agassi, his rivals for national honours. 'National junior titles were not the targets,' remembers Fischer. 'We were looking further ahead than that.'

After doing particularly badly in a tournament when he was 14, Pete turned for advice to Fischer. 'I'd realised I would have to do something about my game. I couldn't serve and I had no real idea of how to volley. I was just trying to play the way all the kids played - counter-punching from the baseline. I was getting nowhere, I simply wasn't improving. I asked him if I should give up my two-handed backhand. After much discussion that's what we decided to do.'

Friends in the game told him he was mad but, like Pete, they were probably unaware that there had been a perfect precedent for such a decision. When Stefan Edberg was a junior he, too, had had a double-handed backhand. His Swedish coach, Percy Rosberg, the man who started Bjorn Borg on his way, knew all about the value of such a shot. But he also knew of its limitations. Recognising Stefan's great potential as a volleyer, Percy had persuaded him to make the change to a single-handed backhand. With four Grand Slam titles to his name, plus the current No. 1 world ranking, Stefan is glad he listened. So is Pete. 'It wasn't easy at first. After six months of hitting the fence and losing my temper with frustration, a few started to go in. It was a great relief!'

The role model for young Pete was the legendary Australian Rod Laver who had won the second of his two Grand Slams in 1969, two years before Pete was born. Dr. Fischer had video tapes of some of Laver's great matches and the youngster never tired of watching them. 'I admire the way the game was played in those days,' he says. 'They just got on with the game without any fuss and seemed to respect each other. Laver was so fast, too, and he had such a variety of shots - and all with those wooden rackets!' With such examples before him, it is not surprising that Pete is something of a throwback. He shows the same respect for the game and its traditions as Laver. In an age of flamboyance in dress and behaviour, he shows admirable restraint. It is all very refreshing.

Pete's game, too, is uncomplicated. The fast wrist action produces tremendous racket-head speed on his fluent whiplash serve which has been timed at 124 miles per hour. It also makes the direction of delivery very hard to read, as both Lendl and McEnroe discovered. Exceptionally fast reflexes allow him to hit his returns of serve so soon after the bounce that the server is often passed before he has had time to recover from his service swing. It is the same on the passing shots. Not for Pete the semi-Western topspins beloved of so many of his contemporaries. He swings through flat and fast, meeting the ball on the rise and controlling the angle of the racket face with sure instinct. For a man who claimed he could not volley as a junior he has come a long way. Like all the great volleyers, he sees the ball early enough to meet it well out in front of him and punches it or caresses it with the precision of a surgeon.

The improvement from a ranking of 81 in January 1990 to a position of No. 6 at the end of the year was the result of months of hard work on and off the court with his coach Joe Brandi. When Dr. Fischer decided he no longer wanted to help Pete because he was not working as hard as he should have been, Sampras was jolted out of his lethargy. He went to Nick Bollettieri's academy in Florida. It was there that Joe was assigned to Pete - much to the relief of Pete's brother Gus who had filled the necessary role of travelling companion for two years and wanted to pursue his own interests.

The first breakthrough came in February at the US Pro Indoor in Philadelphia where Pete won his first title on the tour. After losing in the final Andres Gomez, the big Ecuadorean left-hander, said, 'I believe that Pete is the best of the crop of fine young Americans who are making such an impact on the game.'

Just how good Pete Sampras might become no one can say. His win on grass at Manchester showed an ability to modify his shots to new conditions. But the first round loss at Wimbledon the following week showed how much there is still to learn. There are so many imponderables - like the pressure of living up to his bubble reputation, the injuries to his shins that hampered the last part of 1990, the competition from his contemporaries, the need to learn the arts of clay court play and the commercial pressures of suddenly being wanted by everybody for endorsements. If Pete can survive these testing times, and there is every reason to suppose that he has the character and the will to do so, then there is no limit to what he might achieve. It is a matter of setting realistic goals. Then, like the good marksman he is, he should hit the target.

Goran Ivanisevic

'Unbelievable!' Goran Ivanisevic's favourite word sums up this young man's remarkable natural talent.

It has all happened so quickly that we have hardly had time to assimilate the news. But it is true. According to the omnipotent computer, the tall 19-year-old Yugoslav Goran Ivanisevic is the ninth best player in the world. If you are surprised by the fact, Boris Becker is not. For Boris simply stood and gaped as this lanky 6' 5" beanpole of a lad delivered 18 thunderous aces in their first round match at the French Open last year to eliminate the official World Champion ignominiously in four sets. Afterwards Boris said he had never faced a better serve - praise indeed from someone who had regularly measured the deliveries of Ivan Lendl, Stefan Edberg and John McEnroe. As if to underline the truth of Becker's assessment, Goran swept on to the quarter finals at the expense of Jarryd, Kuhnen and Kroon before the tough little Austrian, Thomas Muster, ended his run in four sets.

Goran believes that the foundation for those impressive performances had been laid the previous week in Dusseldorf. There, with Goran Prpic and Slobodan Zivojinovic, he had been part of the successful Yugoslav team that had won the World Team Cup for the first time. Goran's 3-6, 7-5, 6-1 win over Jim Courier on the last day had paved the way for a 2-1 victory over the Americans in the final. 'It was a great feeling to be part of a winning team,' he said. 'It made me realise that even on clay I was as good as the best guys.'

Ever since his father Srjdan had put a racket into his hand when he was five years old, Goran has felt a natural affinity for the game. The swinging left-handed serve was always a natural shot, as was the double-handed backhand which has become such a destructive weapon on all surfaces. During the early years in his home town of Split on the Adriatic coast, Goran was coached by Ladislav Kachar who saw his protégé claim every age group title that was open to him in Yugoslavia, year after year. He watched him, too, as the growing boy started to make an impression internationally. There was understandable pride as Goran won the US Open junior doubles with Diego Nargiso in 1987 and equal satisfaction the following year as he reached the doubles final in Paris with Coratti of Italy. Perhaps Goran did not always work as hard as he might have done. There were times when he dreamed of playing soccer for his home town club in Split, the national champions.

There were worries, too, about Goran's fiery temperament. Unable at times to control himself, he was frequently in trouble with umpires and linesmen as he threw his rackets about and queried calls. During the European Junior Championships one year he was actually disqualified and had to serve a three-month suspension. 'Yes, that was a difficult time in my life,' he remembers. 'I am such an intense competitor that I would get very angry with myself if I was not winning. It has been hard to learn to control this part of my game but as I have got older it has improved.' The man who has done most to help Goran in this department is the former Hungarian No. 1 Balazs Taroczy. Since July 1989 this former French and Wimbledon doubles champion has been coaching and calming, cajoling and encouraging this ambitious, intense young man, trying to release the latent talent.

It all came right at Wimbledon. Making the most of the fast conditions which are ideal for his attacking game, Goran unleashed a stream of aces and winning serves that demolished Leach, Delaitre, Rostagno (McEnroe's conqueror), Koevermans and the 1985 finalist Kevin Curren, on his way to the semi-finals. There the holder, Becker, faced him once again. When the champion lost the opening set 4-6 and was broken again in the 11th game of the second set, it seemed we might be witnessing one of those special moments of Wimbledon history when a future champion first dons the mantle the greatness. As Becker said afterwards 'He was serving so hard and with such youthful enthusiasm it made me think of another young man who had stood on that same

court in 1985.' But Ivanisevic was facing Becker, not Jarryd, the man whom the German had beaten in that year's semi-final.

With Ivanisevic serving at 6-5, the Centre Court crowd was hushed. Double fault. 'Love-fifteen,' intoned the umpire as a collective sigh engulfed the stadium. The champion knew how to steady himself in such circumstances. Make a nervous opponent play the ball. As the server came in on the second point he made a quick stab at a backhand volley and the ball dropped into the net. 'Love-thirty'. A ripple of excitement, then silence. Now applause for a fine crosscourt backhand volley and cheers for another winning serve. 'Thirty all'. Surely, this time he would finish it off. But as Ivanisevic went to play a backhand on the next point he slipped and dragged the ball into the net. 'Thirty-forty'. Several times the Yugoslav bounced the ball and measured the distance. Up it went, a high toss and 'thwack' - another unreturnable delivery. An explosion of applause and cheers drowned the umpire's call of 'Deuce'. But now it was time for Becker to show his mettle. Two dipping returns forced two volleying errors and through the clapping and the shouting he heard the umpire call 'Game to Becker. Six games all. Tie-break.'

Three-love to Ivanisevic became three-all. One more good serve gave the Yugoslav a 4-3 lead. It was the last point he saw. With a run of four points Becker wrapped up the tie-break 7-4. It was virtually the end. In 17 minutes Becker had swept through the next six games as Ivanisevic reacted to the opportunity lost. The young man had recovered his poise by the fourth set but he was forced to concede it on another tie-break, 7-5 this time.

It had been a memorable match, one that stamped Goran Ivanisevic as a possible future champion - as did a first Tour title in Stuttgart a few weeks later. Possible? Well, yes. That love set was rather worrying, as was the 0-6 final set that Goran lost at the US Open to Darren Cahill in the third round. Afterwards he admitted that he had not been trying. 'It was so hot and I had sweated so much I had nothing left,' he had said afterwards. 'I was simply too tired to try. I guess I'll have to get a lot fitter and stronger.' It was much the same story in the Basel final when Goran won the first two sets against John McEnroe but allowed the 31-year-old American to escape at 6-4 in the fifth.

These are the difficulties that Goran and Balazs must face together. If, as I am sure they will, they solve them and continue to work on technique, especially the forehand volley, then you need look no further for the next Wimbledon champion. And that is not my view; it is the considered opinion of as astute an observer as Ion Tiriac. Remember who he discovered?

Edberg Reaches the Summit

By Robert Philip

Stefan Edberg, the third Swede to become No. 1 in the world, after his win in Cincinnati.

ome things,' muttered Sir Peter Ustinov, gazing out over the All England Club to the church spire shimmering in the far off distance among the mighty oaks on Wimbledon Hill, 'do not need changing. English summer afternoons like this do not need changing, birdsong does not need changing, Van Gogh's sunflowers do not need changing, Stefan Edberg's backhand does not need changing.'

Sir Peter, like many a wise tennis critic, had Stefan Edberg marked down for true greatness from 1983 when the Swede, then but a callow youth of 17, completed a teenage 'Grand Slam' by winning the junior singles events at all four major championships on three different surfaces.

Seven years on, Edberg has since claimed two Wimbledon and two Australian Open titles, twice played on triumphant Swedish Davis Cup teams, and amassed over $8 million in prize money, while becoming only the eighth player ever to be ranked world number one on the ATP Tour computer. The third Swede to succeed to the throne, Edberg is the latest incumbent in a regal lineage stretching back through Ivan Lendl, Mats Wilander, John McEnroe, Jimmy Connors, Bjorn Borg and John Newcombe to Ilie Nastase.

The Lean Machine, as he is known to that sexist band in the women's locker-room, officially replaced Lendl at the top of the computer printout by virtue of his quarter-final victory over Michael Chang in the ATP Tour Championship of Cincinnati on 13 August, but had been, in effect, the new undisputed king since the second Sunday in July when he defeated Becker in four sets to win his second Wimbledon title.

Though many have claimed credit, it was Chicago Cubs' baseball manager Leo Durocher who took out a copyright on the phrase 'Nice guys finish last'. He never met Stefan Edberg. In a 'sporting' era of pompous, petulant, posturing personalities, Edberg is a throwback to the Corinthian days of yore; close your eyes and it is easy to picture the Swede in sepia tones, leaping the net to congratulate Tilden, Budge or Laver.

Nor does he cultivate a colourful off-court image, let others patronize the current 'in' place in London, Paris or Rome; while the so-called 'tennis set' heads for the *Quilted Giraffe* off Madison Avenue during the U.S. Open, each September Edberg renews acquaintance with *Il Vagabondo* on East 62nd Street, a tiny trattoria where the New York paparazzi are unknown but both the chef and his Bucatini all'Amatriciana are genuine Venetian.

It is not surprising, therefore, that Edberg chooses to live in London rather than Monte Carlo - fast turning into the largest conurbation on the sporting globe - where he can eat, shop or practise in sublime anonymity. 'He is, without any doubt, the nicest sportsman I have ever met,' is the opinion of Swedish golfer Mats Lanner. 'You would never know Edberg is a world champion, he is just so modest and courteous.

'I have only met him on a couple of occasions, but he has always been more interested in talking about the day Sweden produces its first Ryder Cup golfer than in discussing his own wonderful achievements.'

But despite his gentle nature, like all champions in any sport, Edberg has a spine of tungsten steel (or graphite) to go with his fabulous talent. 'He's the man in the iron mask,' says the Swede's British coach Tony Pickard. 'Everyone thinks they have Stefan sussed out ... they don't. People talk about Jimmy Connors being the ultimate 'street fighter', they obviously don't know this one.'

Edberg also just happens to be one of the most beautiful players of this, or any other, generation; some dismiss him as a strict serve-volleyer, wilfully choosing to ignore the fact some of his greatest Davis Cup victories came on slow, red clay and that he was somewhat unfortunate to lose to Michael Chang in the final of the 1989 French Open, when only the frailties of his forehand let him down.

That notorious weakness apart, the 25-year-old Swede is a glorious sight to behold, as smooth as Nat King Cole, as effortless as Sugar Ray Leonard, as athletically graceful as Michael Jackson. The man who made serve-volley an art form.

Significantly, the coach who discovered the youngster from Vastervik, always predicted his mental approach would be the key to his future. 'I worked with Edberg until he was 19 and when he left me I told him he had everything - serve, volley, backhand,' said Percy Rosberg in his little workshop in Bastaad. 'But to be a champion, I told him he had to improve his mind. He had to be more aggressive in his head. He had to learn to fight.

Rosberg had an equally significant role to play in ensuring Edberg did not develop into a Wilander II or Boris III clone.

'When he became European junior champion at the age of 16 Stefan had a two-fisted backhand, just like Borg; but I reckoned he should change it and it took him just eight months to be playing the shot with confidence. Now I think it is the best one-handed backhand in the world. It is certainly the most beautiful to watch ... though I may be a little bit biased.'

When it comes to the world No. 1, aren't we all?

BP National Championships

By Joseph Romanos

Wellington, 1-7 January
Tournament Director: Ian Wells

Emilio Sanchez, Magnus Gustafsson and Kelly Evernden are just three of the players who would have special cause to remember the 1990 BP Nationals in Wellington, the first tournament of the new ATP Tour.

Sanchez missed the New Year's Day tournament opening because he was otherwise occupied in Perth helping his sister Arantxa earn Spain victory over the United States in the final of the Hopman Cup. After beating John McEnroe to seal victory for Spain, Sanchez hopped on a plane and headed for New Zealand. After an unexpectedly long stop-off in Melbourne, Sanchez finally got to Wellington at 4.30 pm on Tuesday, 90 minutes before he would have been defaulted. He walked straight on court against home-town favourite Steve Guy and scraped by 6-4 in the third.

By the following Sunday the escapades of Traumatic Tuesday had been put well behind him. He came back from 1-2 and 2-4 down in the fourth set to Richey Reneburg 6-7, 6-4, 4-6, 6-4, 6-1 in a see-sawing 200-minute final. 'This has been a dream week for me. To beat McEnroe to help Spain win the Hopman Cup. Then to come here and win the first tournament of our new tour. I never expected such things so soon,' said Sanchez later. He explained that after some serious injuries

the previous year, he was on the comeback trail, fit but not confident. In one magic week he'd recaptured his best form. Gustafsson arrived in Wellington fresh from having taken part in the Davis Cup final for Sweden against Boris Becker and the rest of the West German team. Seeded third, Gustafsson was bundled out in the first round by Gilad Bloom and looked a little glum for a day or two. His spirits picked up on the Wednesday though when he became the special guest at the players' barbecue. His twenty-third birthday fell on the Wednesday and he was presented with a huge cake. Gustafsson was clearly delighted with the gesture and showed only mild concern when he found he couldn't blow out the candles, which he belatedly discovered were of the relighting variety.

Evernden, a special hero in Wellington, where he has three times won the national title, didn't get past the first round in the singles. He ran into Lars Wahlgren, who did a good impression of a Swedish backboard and proved too steady for the brilliant but erratic New Zealander. Evernden led by a set and a break, but eventually lost 3-6, 7-6, 7-6. 'I thought it was going to be a week to forget,' said the popular Kiwi, 'but fortunately there's always the doubles.' Evernden had intended teaming with Australian Mark Kratzmann, but when Kratz decided not to play in Wellington, a scratch pairing of Evernden

Emilio Sanchez, the title winner, gets the year and the ATP Tour off to a fine start.

and Venezuelan Nicolas Pereira was formed. 'Kelly did me a favour by playing with me,' said Pereira. 'I wouldn't have been able to get into the doubles on my ranking. We agreed if we were still alive in the semi-finals, I would miss trying to qualify for the Auckland singles the next week.' That's what happened as Evernden and Pereira blasted their way past two of the world's best doubles teams, Tim Pawsat and Laurie Warder, and Emilio Sanchez and Sergio Casal, to claim the doubles. There were some things about the BP Nationals which made it a tournament to be remembered, and some others which should be forgotten quickly. Because New Zealand leads the world in time zones the Wellington event kicked off a couple of hours before the Adelaide tournament.

To mark the birth of the ATP tour, Evernden made a short speech at the opening ceremony and a group of players and officials, including tournament director Graeme Sims, hit some balls in front of the crowd. The ATP were out in some force and there were balloons, souvenir T-shirts and other gifts.

On the better-forgotten side, inevitably, was Wellington's weather. New Zealand's capital is reputed to be as windy as any city in the world. Windy Wellington lived up to its tag during the BP Nationals. Early in the week play was forced indoors, not because of rain, but because of gale-force winds. Some players felt this reaction was a little radical, until they saw the trees around the tennis complex swaying ominously.

Australian Men's Hardcourt Championships

By Bruce Matthews

Adelaide, 1-7 January
Tournament Director: Ron Green

With grit that typifies the manner he tackles tennis and life in general, Austrian Thomas Muster laid another cornerstone in the restoration of his career by winning the Australian hardcourt singles crown in Adelaide.

The 3-6, 6-2, 7-5 triumph over Jimmy Arias of the US carried far more significance for Muster than merely his sixth singles title. It was a timely example at the start of the new ATP tour of what can be achieved by sheer hard work. Another triumph over pain for a young man whose life, let alone his livelihood, lay in tatters on a Florida parking lot nine months earlier. Muster's victory on the Rebound Ace at Memorial Drive was his first final since March 1989 when he was forced to default the Lipton International after being rammed by a drunk driver as he climbed from his car to get a sandwich. You've heard of the sandwich that cost an arm and a leg .... well,

Sunny South Australian skies provide the canopy for this shot of the famous Memorial Drive Courts.

Under the lights, Thomas Muster celebrates his return to full fitness with a cup, a cheque and a title.

John Fitzgerald suggested playing conditions were 'life threatening' following a slogging three sets win in the first round. Paul Annacone leapt to Fitzgerald's defence after a straight sets opening victory. Three hours after the match, Annacone's body core was still overheated. He admitted to being scared as he draped damp towels over his body and legs in his hotel room that night to stem the perspiration flow.

Even in the cool of night matches, some still got hot under the collar. Top seed Sergi Bruguera's angry father confronted chair umpire Chris O'Brien following a marathon semi-final against Muster. Luis Bruguera shook a finger at the startled O'Brien as he left centre court and ATP tour supervisor Ed Hartisty defused a potentially explosive incident when he stepped in to place restraining hands on the shouting Spaniard's shoulders. O'Brien enraged the Bruguera family when he penalised Sergi for a coaching violation in the deciding set tie break. Young Bruguera, almost out on his feet with exhaustion after the three-hour battle, was warned for coaching from his father in the stand when trailing 0-3 in the tie break. The teenager stood beneath the umpire's chair pleading his case and was eventually docked a penalty point following an earlier time-wasting infringement. He lost concentration and the first six points of the tie break to concede the match to Muster 2-6, 6-2, 7-6 - an unfortunate end to the

this one nearly did as the rugged Austrian suffered ruptured cruciate and medial ligaments in his left knee. The hunger and ambition which sustained the bullocking left-hander through the crisis was mirrored by a remarkable recovery in the third set. Arias, searching for the elusive title to purge a six-year stretch of self-doubt, strode to 3-0 and held a point on serve for a 4-1 lead before the grunting Muster launched a counter-attack. Several times Muster called ATP trainer Rob Hanna to courtside for treatment at the change of

With typical grit, Thomas Muster lays another cornerstone in the restoration of his career.

finest match of the tournament. Andrew Castle and Nduka Odizor knew their luck was in long before they beat qualifiers Alexander Mronz and Michiel Schapers 7-6, 6-2 in the doubles final. Castle and Odizor were due to

ends and his reconstructed left knee was encased in ice-packs after the match.

Muster wasn't alone with his discomfort during a red-hot start to the new tour. On the day of the grand opening, temperatures of 60.5 degrees Celsius (145 Fahrenheit) were recorded on centre court. Controversy erupted after home state hero

play young Australians Jason Stoltenberg and Todd Woodbridge in the first round, but were confronted by lucky losers Niclas Kroon and Magnus Larsson after Stoltenberg tore ligaments in his ankle during a first-round singles match. At least Mronz and Schapers created history - they became the first doubles team in the history of the open era to reach the final from the qualifying rounds.

New South Wales Open Championships

By Tim Prentice

Sydney, 8-14 January
Tournament Directors: Barry K. Masters, Rod Read

Tennis form books were turned upside down in three balmy hours on quarter finals day at the Holden New South Wales Open at Sydney's White City Stadium last January. Both Ivan Lendl and Boris Becker, ranked one and two on the computer at the time, were outplayed and eliminated by Yannick Noah and Carl-Uwe Steeb before a stunned gallery of 6500 spectators. Noah's stylish 6-1, 6-4 defeat of Lendl gave him the impetus to annexe the singles title while Steeb's 7-6, 6-3 triumph over Becker saw him become the first German to defeat Becker since King Boris scored his maiden Wimbledon success in 1985. Frenchman Noah was at his charismatic best throughout the week-long event which boasted its strongest field in more than two decades with eight of the world's top 20 in attendance.

He treated the bumper summer crowds to impromptu acrobatic displays, charmed the press with some of the most entertaining conferences in years, while on court his powerful serve and uncanny touch cut a swathe through the all-star field. In the final, the brilliant left-hander dropped the first set to Steeb on the Rebound Ace surface but recovered superbly for a 5-7, 6-3, 6-4 victory. It was Noah's first singles title in two years and he dedicated his success to his 'best friend' Erica and his new coach, Dennis Ralston.

'I've got my fire back,' the tournament's seventh seed said later, 'I was going to retire three or four months ago because I thought I could never come back from where I was. Erica gave me the support I needed especially when I considered retiring; she sparked my career. It's such a wonderful feeling to win again and I want to enjoy it.' (Noah's Sydney form was no flash in the pan. He sustained it over the next two weeks, reaching the semi-finals of the Ford Australian Open at Melbourne's Flinders Park Stadium.)

> *Tennis form books were turned upside down in three balmy hours on quarter finals day*

Rising American stars Pete Sampras and David Wheaton scored highly impressive wins over seeded players in the NSW event, which began in poor weather but climaxed in glorious sunshine. Big-serving Sampras blew away the fourth seed Tim Mayotte 7-6, 6-2, and Wheaton outplayed Ecuador's Andres Gomez, seeded six, 7-5, 6-4. Showing the benefits of having played the tournament's qualifying rounds, Sampras went on to feature in the best match of the Open - a gripping quarter final against the former world No. 1 Mats Wilander. Wilander had to summon his vast experience to subdue the lanky American teenager 6-7, 7-5, 6-0 in a highly entertaining two-hour contest.

Sampras overcame a 1-3 deficit in the first set tie-break to win 7-4, and had the Swede in deep trouble throughout the second set. The unflappable Wilander diligently saved twelve break points before breaking Sampras in the twelfth game to level the match. The pendulum then swung markedly. Sampras, having been practically shot for shot level in the first two sets, could take no more of the strategy battle in the sauna-like conditions, and folded in the third set.

Pat Cash made a triumphant return to competitive tennis, teaming with countryman Mark Kratzmann to win the doubles title at the New South Wales Open. It was Cash's first tournament since April 1988 when he injured his Achilles tendon at the Tokyo Seiko. In the semis, the duo upset No. 3 seeds Goran Ivanisevic and Petr Korda, before capping off the run with a victory over top seeds Pieter Aldrich and Danie Visser 6-4, 7-6 in the final.

The NSW Open again served as the perfect warm-up event for the Ford Australian Open with the players and fans revelling in the sunshine and top-class facilities. White City also unveiled the Australian Tennis Museum during the Open, which is destined to develop into one of the finest of its type on the tennis globe.

A spectacular study of a spectacular performer - Yannick Noah flies towards the NSW Open title.

Benson and Hedges New Zealand Open

By Joseph Romanos

Auckland, 8-14 January
Tournament Director: Tom Kiely

New Zealand has never seen a tennis tournament like the 1990 Benson and Hedges Open in Auckland. For controversy and excitement, it was tops, and not surprisingly the crowds were the biggest in the 22 years of the tournament's history. The tournament finished with two dramatic singles semi-finals and a high-quality final in which Scott Davis beat Andrei Chesnokov 4-6, 6-3, 6-3. That was the excitement. The controversy happened earlier in the week.

First on the rack was Amos Mansdorf, the dark-eyed Israeli who won in Auckland in 1988 and was runner-up the following year. Mansdorf was floating happily through one of those interminable press conferences after his first-round victory over Karel Novacek when a Reuters journalist threw in a curly one. The conversation had turned, as it does all too often in New Zealand, to sport and politics. South Africa seems to be the bête noire of New Zealand society and Mansdorf, because he plays in South Africa, is always the subject of anti-apartheid protests.

It never seems to worry him and he told the assembled journalists that he was a tennis player and that in his view sport and politics don't mix. A routine answer and fair enough. 'Then,' said the Reuters newshound, 'would you have played tennis in Nazi Germany?' Mansdorf was taken aback. After a moment's thought, he said, 'If I could have, I would have.' He meant it innocently, but the comment proved to be explosive. For a day or two, he seemed to be Israel's least favourite son as his quote was sent home. Happily the furore died down.

Tour veteran Scott Davis won another singles title to kick his year off in the right gear.

As a true fisherman Miloslav Mecir can't help liking New Zealand. Unfortunately he spent more and more time with line and tackle back home in Czechoslovakia as the year went by. A back operation may have terminated his professional career.

Mansdorf claimed he'd been misquoted, his countrymen forgave him and by the week's end he was back in their good books. He played as well as ever too, reaching the semi-final where Chesnokov beat him 7-6, 6-2.

Next into the lion's den was second-seeded Czech Miloslav Mecir. Now Mecir won the Benson and Hedges title in 1987 and what a popular player he was that week in Auckland. He never lost a set, he took a day off to go fishing ... the people loved him. It was different this time. Mecir was paid to play in Auckland. He arrived in the country carrying an ankle injury and went fishing in Taupo for a few days while it got better. Then he returned to the ASB Centre courts and turned in what can fairly be described as a sub-par effort, losing 6-3, 6-3 to Steve Guy, who is ranked several hundred places below him. Tournament director, Tom Kiely, was less than impressed to lose his big drawcard in

the first round, even if it did mean New Zealander Guy advanced. So over the first few days, the tournament write-ups were to be found not only on the back pages but also on the front pages. This controversy was most unusual for the Benson and Hedges event, which is normally one of the happiest on the calendar. The players are taken on harbour cruises, they get the chance to go windsurfing and swimming, they can fish ... and they play some tennis too. Over the years countless players have tested the hospitality and returned.

One man who left Auckland with specially fond memories of the 1990 Open was Russian Andrei Chesnokov. After an inglorious early exit the previous week in Wellington, Chesnokov was wearing that worried, hunched look that players get when they're on the brink of a slump. One day he walked into the pro shop at the centre and picked up a Prince racquet. Chesnokov spoke of how he hadn't been happy with his game since switching to Prince, but he liked the look of the one he'd picked up. It was slightly thinner in the head. 'I'll take it,' he told the astounded shop assistant. Then he tucked it in his bag and marched out to centre court where he beat Richey Reneberg, who'd eliminated him the week before. Chesnokov kept using his lucky racquet and advanced all the way to the final, winning a memorable semi-final over defending champion Ramesh Krishnan 5-7, 6-3, 6-4. In the final Davis, looking to break a tournament drought, used his hustling serve-and-volley tactics to good effect to wear down Chesnokov in a gripping match that had the capacity crowds humming with admiration. The doubles went to Americans Kelly Jones and Robert Van't Hof who beat Gilad Bloom and Paul Haarhuis 7-6, 6-0.

As the players packed up and headed off to Australia for the first Grand Slam of the year, tournament director Kiely couldn't help but smile as he reflected on the week. 'In all the years I've been involved, I've never known a tournament to attract so much attention,' he said. 'We lost our big drawcards, Mecir and Kelly Evernden in the first round, yet we had massive crowds. You can't complain about that.'

Ford Australian Open

By Richard Evans

Melbourne, 15-28 January
Tournament Director: Colin Stubs

Ivan Lendl won the first Grand Slam of the new decade when he retained his Australian Open title in a less than satisfactory manner at Flinders Park. Both the tournament, growing in stature year by year in its splendidly futuristic setting, and the packed capacity crowd of 15,000, deserved something better than a prematurely terminated final in which Stefan Edberg was forced to default at 4-6, 7-6, 5-2 with a pulled stomach muscle. The injury was the unfortunate legacy of one of the most spectacular performances of Edberg's career. In the semi-final he had felt the muscle pull right at the end of his 6-1, 6-1, 6-2 demolition of Mats Wilander. It was one of those days when the man on the other side of the net becomes an irrelevance. Edberg was simply unstoppable.

No one enjoyed Stefan's classic performance more than Ted Tinling who, the week before, had celebrated 66 active years of service to the game beginning with the first match he umpired for Suzanne Lenglen on the Côte d'Azur. 'That was such a beautiful display,' Tinling enthused. 'It was pure joy to watch. I have rarely seen anything so lovely.' It was destined to be Tinling's last Grand Slam

as style and deportment meant everything to this remarkable figure, it was an accolade Edberg should treasure. He might have felt even better about it but for the injury because,

Yannick Noah battled his way to the semi-final of the Australian Open, on and off court.

even with the pain in his side, he was still able to win the first set against Lendl in the final before a fear of doing some permanent damage forced him to retire. That in itself gave the tournament the unwanted distinction of being the first Grand Slam of the Open era to have an uncompleted final. The previous occasion had been in 1931 when Frank Shields was forced to give Sydney Wood a walkover at Wimbledon. But the tournament had already logged another 'first' when John McEnroe was defaulted while leading Mikael Pernfors by two sets to one in the fourth round. Although there were those who felt McEnroe should have been defaulted on numerous other occasions over the years, this, too, had never happened since the game went Open in 1968.

The default came about as a result of a tightening of the rules for the new ATP Tour which the players themselves had voted in and which had been adopted by the ITF for the Grand Slams. The four-step route to default had been reduced to three and when McEnroe swore at Supervisor Ken Farrar, Britain's Gerry Armstrong, an ATP Tour umpire, had no hesitation in calling out 'Default Mr McEnroe' - a declaration that left the huge pro-McEnroe crowd shrieking abuse at officialdom. But as Armstrong had already warned the American twice, the rules, which McEnroe professed not to understand, were clear. It was an absurd way for McEnroe to go out of the tournament because he had been playing with a calm, self-assured brilliance in the early rounds. But that was until the feisty Pernfors started to unsettle those brittle nerves. Pernfors, who had looked stunned by his sudden passage into the quarter finals, found himself unable to capitalise upon it, however.

Yannick Noah, rampant after his fine victory in the New South Wales Open, swept the Swede aside in straight sets to reach the semi-final of a Grand Slam for the first time since his victory at the French Open in 1983. Had he not let a dubious call upset him in the very first game of his match against

With soaring temperatures at Flinders Park, Ivan Lendl was back in his Foreign Legion headgear.

Lendl the Frenchman might have gone further still but once Ivan had an early break under his belt he proved, once again, how remorseless he becomes when in front.

Kicking off a year that would see them become the most effective doubles team in the world, Danie Visser and Piet Aldrich took the title with a four set victory over Grant Connell and Glenn Michibata.

With rain a rarity, the great sliding roof was only called into play on a couple of occasions during a week that re-emphasised the splendour of an old championship that has been re-born in its new surroundings on the banks of the River Yarra - an annual festival in a sports-mad city.

Stella Artois Indoor

By Ubaldo Scanagatta

Milan, 5-11 March
Tournament Director: Sergio Palmieri

If they had been able to imagine anything so inconceivable, IMG and Cino Marchese might have saved a large part of the Stella Artois advertising budget. Not even Merlin the Magician could have predicted such an astonishing result: a Davis Cup victory for the 'down and out' Italian team (only British tennis is worse than ours) over the great Swedish team captained by Mats Wilander and including Sjogren and Svensson. The surprising first-round Davis Cup win came on the very eve of the Milan Indoor. The last and decisive match in Cagliari, between Paolo Cane and

Wilander, ended on Monday, when many of the competitors for the Milan event were already in Italy. Even John McEnroe admitted he had never enjoyed tennis so much as he did that morning sitting in his hotel room watching such an exciting fifth set.

Thanks to the Cagliari outcome, local scalpers suddenly became interested in tennis again, for the first time since the days of Panatta the Great. During the dark days that followed that heady time, they had survived by exploiting the Italian-Dutch Milan soccer team including Gullit,

Tournament director Sergio Palmieri, IMG's Cino Marchese and ace Italian sports promoter Carlo della Vida celebrate the inauguration of the ATP Tour in Europe flanked by players including young American stars Pete Sampras (left) and Jim Courier (right).

Rijkaard and Van Basten, the Italian-German Inter (soccer team) of Brehme, Matthaeus and Klinsmann, Pavarotti's high notes at the Scala Theatre and the muffled shouts of a few rock groups at the Palatrussardi. 'The golden days are back,' they cried happily, 'this Cane is a good one to sell, but will he last?'

In the event, their fears were confirmed: he did not last long - no more than a couple of evenings at the Palatrussardi. His first opponent was Bruno Oresar. Luckily for Cane, Oresar was suffering from jet lag too (having played the Davis Cup in New Zealand) and the Yugoslav only managed to keep himself awake with ten cups of coffee - he ended up in hospital after the match! And in his second match, he was up against a McEnroe who, that night at least, was back on his best, 1984 form. There was no way Paolo could beat him, and after that he packed his bags, along with the scalpers.

Cane had, none the less, made his contribution to the event's total earnings: over $1.5 million from 55,000 'paying' spectators. In Italy one always has to add the word 'paying' because of all the complimentary tickets that are given out. The number of these is quite extraordinary, though in Milan, the centre of economic power in Italy, organisers distribute only half the number that are given out in Rome, centre of political power. With any luck, things will get better in 1991, because the tournament will leave the big circus tent at the Palatrussardi and move to the marvellous Forum of Assago (a Milan suburb), a complex that is very similar to the Omnisport at Bercy. It will have room for 13,000 people, instead of the present 5000.

The 1990 tournament was not, in fact, very exciting, even though four of the top ten ranked players, as well as Jimmy Connors and Tim Mayotte, were among the entries. Neither the best Ivan Lendl nor the best McEnroe showed up. Both the players were at 70 per cent of their best form. But a Lendl at 70 per cent is still just about good enough to win a middle-ranking event, while a Mac who is not 'Supermac' cannot get beyond the semi-finals. This is exactly what happened.

I have a high esteem for Gentleman Tim, but when he beat 'Minimac' in the semis to join Lendl in the final, I almost pulled out the few remaining strands of hair I still have. Lendl has always stunned Mayotte and this time he did so once more - in just one hour and 26 minutes. Crowd and players alike would have gone home extremely disappointed had the Italians Omar Camporese and Diego Nargiso not won the doubles title by defeating Tom Niussen and Udo Riglewski 6-4, 6-4. This result, at least, lifted the fans' spirits (though not Mayotte's).

But what about the early rounds of the tournament? These proved disappointing for at least one player, Yannick Noah. He went out early, having come from a Davis Cup loss in Australia, and thus opened the way for the Englishman Jeremy Bates, who passed him on ... the right lane, to score his best win of the year.

Another player was eliminated with little more to show for his pains than the first round prize money: Connors. It was here in Milan that 'Jimbo' injured his wrist playing against Markus Zoecke of Germany, an injury that was to torture him for the rest of the season.

In the second round, Milan Srejber had an unexpected win over Aaron Krickstein. The quarters saw easy victories for Lendl and McEnroe, but marathon matches for Pete Sampras and Mayotte who overcame respectively Srejber and Jakob Hlasek. For Sampras it was his second straight win over a basketball-like player (before Srejber, it was Zoecke). Who knows if the great Bob McAdoo, former NBA all-star and now with Philips Milan, was in the crowd cheering for his 'colleagues' or for his young countryman? Sampras played an excellent match against Lendl, even managing to take a set - though at that point very few people (except maybe Sergio Tacchini, who would later have him draw the 'T-shirt with the archer') could have guessed that they would see Sampras triumph at the US Open over six months later. This semi-final was, in fact, the one that was worth watching. Minimac, in the other, was no more than a ghost of his former self.

Volvo Tennis San Francisco

By Linda Pentz

San Francisco, 5-11 February
Tournament Director: Barry Mackay

Money was the word on the lips of many when the new 1990 ATP Tour made its North American debut at the Volvo Tennis/San Francisco tournament under the affable helm of tournament director Barry Mackay. While the focus of the new Tour was the $1 million Championship Series tournaments, the inaugural event in the United States was of a more humble stature. Offering just $225,000 in total prize money, the San Francisco tournament, a World Series event, was entitled to 'buy' players under the new permissable guarantees rule.

Mackay secured Andre Agassi and Brad Gilbert as his top two seeds and, as is often the case, there were some early upsets. One of these was Gilbert, who was dismissed in the first round by Gary Muller, 6-4, 7-6.

Of course there were plenty of good reasons for this, most notably that Muller played a flawless match of immaculate power tennis and Gilbert had arrived in town too late to adjust to the indoor court surface and played erratically and without feel. Even so, the match was close, but of course the issue of the money was instantly seized upon. The fee Gilbert had been paid, it was said, had only served to blunt his interest. Why would Gilbert try when the cheque was already in the bank?

Anyone who really watched the match, knows anything about Gilbert, or the respect in which Mackay is universally held by players, would recognise this theory as patently absurd. But it wasn't until Sunday, when Agassi, the other 'payee', won the tournament, that the scribes and the thus influenced public would believe that a down payment in advance does not result in a reneging of the contract.

Agassi had had such a rough year in 1989, with criticism screaming all around his ears, that he took himself off in the winter months to work on his head and his physique. Both were dramatically improved in San Francisco, and Agassi went into quite a bit of honest self-appraisal before polishing off the likes of Ramesh Krishnan, Dan Goldie, Jim Grabb and Todd Witsken to win his first title on Supreme and the ninth of his career. 'It's been time for me to renew everything - spiritually, emotionally and physically,' said Agassi of his six-week winter lay off. 'My goal in life is always to learn from everything. If things start coming down on me again, I'm ready for it.'

Witsken had the best week of his still young career but got pummelled in the final, never once holding his serve and losing to Agassi 6-1, 6-3 in 66 minutes. Agassi allowed Witsken just 12 points against his own serve and added a $32,400 winner's cheque to the reputed $100,000 Mackay had already paid him. Witsken had spoiled Muller's tournament in the second round with a straight-set win, while Joey Rive took out third-seeded Kevin Curren in the first round and then went on to reach the semi-finals before bowing out to Witsken. Jim Grabb beat fourth seeded Christo van Rensburg in a third-set tie-breaker to reach the semi-finals.

As in the singles, the final four participants in the doubles competition also carried the stars and stripes flag. Kelly Jones and Robert Van't Hof continued their winning ways in San Francisco by taking their second doubles title of 1990 in as many weeks with a 2-6, 7-6, 6-3 victory over Glenn Layendecker and Richey Reneberg in the final. The top three doubles seeds went scattering in the first round - but this time no one suggested that money might be the reason.

Nineteen-year-old Andre Agassi 'spiritually, emotionally and physically' in top form in San Francisco after a six-week winter rest from competitive tennis.

Chevrolet Classic

By Chiquinho Leite Moreira and Fernando Goulart

Guaruja, Brazil, 5-11 Febraury
Tournament Directors: Marco Bismarchi, Ricardo Bernd

Brazil's Chevrolet Classic went down in history as the first tournament of the recently created ATP Tour to be contested in South America. The championship took place at Pernambuco Beach in Guaruja - just one hour from Sao Paulo - in hot and balmy summer weather. A beautiful beach, fabulous weather - all combined to turn the championship into one big party, both on and off the courts. This year's Guaruja tournament, with US$150,000 in prizes on offer, was one of the most exciting in the event's ten year history. The competition attracted two out of the top twenty players: the American Jay Berger, eleventh in the ATP Tour ranking, and the Argentinian Martin Jaite, world thirteenth. Their presence proved beyond doubt the enthusiasm of professionals for the ATP Tour.

This year's Guaruja tournament was one of the most exciting in the event's ten year history.

Tournament organisers were willing to raise their prizes, and they could expect the presence of top players from the international circuit. All was excitement, and the ATP Tour organisers responded by taking a lot of extra luggage to Guaruja: plenty of flags, T-shirts, buttons and other knick-knacks to celebrate the event - all designed to make the new ATP logo known internationally. Everything conspired to make the tournament memorable. During the championship, there was some good news for Elizabeth Laval, the former Dentsu executive who now heads up the ATP Tour's international group office in Sydney. Elizabeth's 'parish' includes South America and it was while she was in Guaruja that she heard of the agreement with IBM to become the Tour's title sponsor. With such a prestigious international company now aligned with the new venture, the ATP Tour looked set fair.

Ricardo Bernd, who was managing the tournament, decided to mark the occasion in typically Brazilian style, with samba schools and 'lambada'. He organised a beach party with players, organisers, many other guests and the press, all sporting ATP T-shirts. The lambada, a sensual and cheerful dance, was a particular success with the players - it requires just the kind of physical suppleness that they all have. The Argentinian Horacio de la Pena and his wife, Heidi Emerson, went their different ways during the dancing, so that each could learn it. Jay Berger proved himself already familiar with the lambada -

Argentina's Horacio de la Pena and Jay Berger of the United States find a heart-breaker, Brazilian style, but look pretty happy about it at the tournament party thrown by Ricardo Bernd and his co-promoters.

and with Brazilian dancers. So he wasted no time in making himself at home, and was very successful. And, of course, there was talent on the courts as well. The Argentinian Martin Jaite, the No. 2 seed, who had always dreamed of a place in the top ten, became the tournament champion, after coming from behing to beat the Brazilian Luiz Mattar, in a tough three-set match 3-6, 6-4, 6-3. Mattar had won the tournament for the past three years, but Jaite was determined to avenge the defeat he suffered last year at the hands of the Brazilian in the final at Rio de Janeiro.

Berger, the No. 1 seed, was not so lucky, and was eliminated in the second round by the classic style of the Argentinian Eduardo Bengoechea in two sets. Bengoechea went on to reach the semi-finals. The Peruvian Jaime Yzaga, known in Brazil as 'Little Master', disappointed the public by losing the opening game to the Cuban Mario Tabares, in two tie- breaks. But the fans had the unexpected pleasure of seeing Brazilian wild card entrant Alexandre Hocevar, ranked a lowly 236, make a run to the semi-finals before being outsted by Jaite. Hocevar rose to 169 in the ATP Tour rankings the following week and, like Bengoechea, enjoyed his finest performance of 1990 in Guaruja.

The champions in the doubles were Javier Frana and Gustavo Luza (of Argentina's Davis Cup team) who beat the two best-known Brazilian players, Cassio Motta and Luiz Mattar, in two hard sets of 7-6 and 7-6.

SkyDome World Tennis

By Tom Mayenknecht

Toronto, 12-18 February
Tournament Director: Peter Fleming

Canadian tennis officials ushered in their 100th Anniversary campaign with some high-tech tennis and the first million-dollar event on the new ATP Tour in February at Toronto's SkyDome, the world's largest retractable roof stadium. Ivan Lendl did in February at SkyDome World Tennis what he had become accustomed to doing in Canada for the better part of the 1980s. He won. For the seventh time, Lendl captured top honours at a major men's professional event in Canada, so it was very much a case of new tour, new venue, familiar champion! Thanks to a convincing 6-3, 6-0 victory over classy American Tim Mayotte, the world's No. 1 added the SkyDome World Tennis trophy to a showcase which already features six Canadian Open men's singles titles won at Players Ltd. Internationals held in Toronto and Montreal. The dominating performance by Lendl - which took just 64 minutes - earned him $155,000 of the total $1.2 million purse put up by Carlsberg Light, the Canadian Imperial Bank of Commerce (CIBC) and Players Ltd.

The 29-year-old Mayotte, 0-16 in previous career appearances against Lendl, said the match mirrored that of the final in Milan the previous week. 'I'm geared up at the start and ready to take it to him, but he just ends up hitting shots that are without answer,' said Mayotte. 'I'm one of a number of guys who just can't figure out how to beat him.' Mayotte admitted any hopes he had of stopping the Lendl juggernaut evaporated with his first serve late in the first set. He began to struggle at 30-30 in the seventh game of the first set, where Lendl posted his first of two consecutive service breaks. 'I felt I was starting to return his serve better,' Lendl said. 'I hit a couple of good returns in the seventh game and I started getting on top of the ball much more.' Lendl said the toughest part of the match was the beginning. 'In the first two or three of his service games I wasn't making anything. That's why he was able to put pressure on me. That's always the key against players like him: you have to return their serve so they can't just swing at everything on your serve; they have to play to win some of your serves.'

Mayotte committed three straight unforced errors in a third consecutive service break which gave Lendl a 2-0 second-set lead. Lendl was near-perfect the rest of the way. Mayotte admitted Lendl had upgraded his game since the last tight match between the two, a five-set Wimbledon marathon in 1986 which went down to a 9-7 final set. 'His game has improved quite a bit more than mine,' Mayotte said. 'That's frustrating because I feel I'm a better player, solidly in the top ten, and not even getting close to beating him.'

Lendl played like a man on a mission throughout the SkyDome tournament, dropping only one set and handing third-seeded John McEnroe a 6-4, 6-0 semi-final setback. Leading 4-3, Lendl rang up 15 straight points to break McEnroe's serve in the eighth game of the first set and the opening game of the second. It was Lendl's second decisive win over McEnroe in as many meetings in Canada. The Czechoslovak-born right-hander defeated McEnroe in the Canadian Open final at the 1989 Players Ltd. International in Montreal. The SkyDome win was Lendl's 18th in 33 meetings against the former No. 1. 'I felt John was not that confident in his game,' said Lendl. 'Sooner or later he may make some mistakes that will help me. Six, seven years ago, that wouldn't have happened. I would have had to rely just on myself. Now I can rely on him helping me a little bit.'

Lendl was in trouble only once at SkyDome, but it was deep trouble in the quarter finals against hard-serving Kevin Curren of the USA. Lendl had to reach back for all he could muster in saving seven match points in a dramatic second-set tie-breaker which made the quarter final the match of the SkyDome tournament. At one point, Lendl looked up the incline of a 1-5 deficit against Curren. But he fought back, received the break on a close line call on match point at 9-10 and hit two devastating lobs to square the match at one set apiece. Curren was tough in his own right. He ousted Andrew Sznajder of Toronto, a member of Canada's Davis Cup team, 6-0, 6-2, in the third round. The top-ranked Canadian playing under the 'Dome, Sznajder opened with a win over qualifier Ola Jonsson of Sweden. The Canadian story was, however, Grant Connell of North Vancouver, another Davis Cupper coming into his own in the top-100 on the ATP Tour rankings. Connell served and volleyed his way to an upset win over Dan Goldie of the USA, 6-4, 2-6, 6-3, and then went on to oust top-20 ranked Jim Courier of the USA, 6-3, 7-5. Connell finally met his match against Curren, bowing out 7-6, 2-6, 6-1.

In doubles Connell and Glenn Michibata - the Australian Open finalists - were not as fortunate. They suffered a 7-6, 6-3 second-round loss against Bret Garnett and John Sobel of the US. The doubles crown ultimately went to Patrick Galbraith of the USA and David MacPherson of Australia, 2-6, 6-4, 6-3 winners over Curren and Neil Broad. Overall, SkyDome World Tennis was a big winner with the players. Lendl said it made for the world's finest indoor tennis event. And John Fitzgerald rated the SkyDome set-up as second only to Wimbledon.

The giant-size image of Tim Mayotte appears on the screen high above the SkyDome court.

Belgian Indoor Championship

By Craig Gabriel

Brussels, 12-18 February
Tournament Director: Adrien Vanden Eede

Brussels, the capital of the Kingdom of Belgium, is famous for delicious chocolates, beautiful glassware, intricate lace work and as the home of the European Economic Community. It is a place steeped in history and the arts. Museums abound with priceless treasures from Reubens to Picasso, and the architecture leaves one marvelling at the brilliance of an era that will never return. Cobbled roads lead a pathway to city squares where fresh flowers are alive with colour. Or there is the antique market with wonderful knick-knacks to tempt many a hip pocket.

Ice hockey and soccer are probably more the norm when it comes to sport, but for a week in mid-February Brussels was more interested in tennis as 30,500 fans turned out for the Belgian Indoor Championship played at the Forest National Stadium in one of the city's suburbs. It was a crisp and chilly week in which the latter stages of winter made their mark. Light winds kept the mercury in the lower regions of the thermometer, but still it was a wonderful feeling to be in Europe in winter as the soft morning sun started each day.

Tournament director Adrien Vanden Eede and his staff transformed the Forest National, which is about twenty years old, into an underground corporate entertainment village which

certainly brought in a social atmosphere. Boris Becker, Stefan Edberg and Jimmy Connors were supposed to head up the field for the $6,000 event, but unfortunately Edberg was still suffering from the strained stomach muscles that had forced him to retire from the final of the Australian Open just three weeks before, while Connors' wrist was still in a bad way following the injury he sustained in Milan the week before in the first round.

Emilio Sanchez and Carl-Uwe Steeb came in at short notice to replace the two absent players and became the second and third seeds respectively behind Becker. Sanchez struck Miloslav Mecir in the first round; a match that provided some of the best tennis of the week. The Czech player, who was travelling with his family, scored a three-set win and went through to the semi-finals where Steeb won in straight sets.

However, without doubt, the two most enthralling matches of the week both involved Jonas Svensson, a genuine nice guy on the Tour. The first was his second round match with the Swiss Jakob Hlasek that ended 11-9 in a third set tie-breaker and was sheer champagne. The second was a quarter-final clash against Svensson's close friend and fellow countryman Svensson and Magnus Gustafsson. The duo played some

SAT 1, host broadcaster for the ATP Tour World Championship at the end of the year, interview Becker after his victory at the Belgian Indoor Championship while a glum Steeb looks on.

wonderful tennis, full of angles, winners and athleticism. Gustafsson eventually came through after being match point down in the second set to win 6-7, 7-6, 6-3.

But if the players were not too keen about close shaves on court, they were quite happy to be clipped and cropped by the leading hairdresser in Brussels. Many also enjoyed the close calls on the video games, and video movies kept others occupied.

The Belgian fans had something to cheer about when young Bart Wuyts, still doing his National Service, defeated his countryman Xavier Daufrense in the first round, 6-1 in the final set. But he then bowed out to Ronald Agenor.

When it came to the championship match, Becker was all geared up by the fact that his opponent was countryman Steeb. Not only did it mark the first time since 1973 that two Germans had reached the final of a major tournament, but Steeb had become the first German in four-and-a-half years to beat his more illustrious friend

at the NSW Open a month earlier. This was their first meeting since then, and Becker had been going through a ten-week title drought period. His determination this time was unmistakable - he charged through 7-5, 6-2, 6-2. Although admitting to being a little 'rusty' this early in the year, Becker agreed that his tennis picked up as the week progressed. 'I feel at home indoors and on Supreme courts,' he said, 'My game really improved during the week. I was helped by some close matches too,' (he defeated Guy Forget 3-6, 6-3, 7-6 in the second round). 'Anyway it's a nice feeling to win a tournament even when you're not playing your best tennis.' Four of Becker's five titles in 1990, including Stuttgart the week after Brussels, were won indoors and his win/loss record at the end of the year for matches played on carpet was to be an incredible 31/3.

The doubles title went to the fourth seeded Spanish-Yugoslav pairing of Sanchez and Slobodan Zivojinovic, who was also travelling with his family. They accounted for the third seeds, Goran Ivanisevic and his coach of five months Balazs Taroczy, 7-5, 6-3.

Ebel US Pro Indoor Tennis Championships

By Mike Dickson

Philadelphia, 19-25 February
Tournament Director: Marilyn and Edward Fernberger

When Ed Fernberger, joint tournament director for the Ebel US Pro Indoor, announced to the crowd that they had just witnessed the first major title victory of a future Hall of Famer, he managed to raise a few eyebrows. None more so than the dark, bushy pair that belonged to the modest young man in question, Pete Sampras. The Californian teenager, long since tipped as a name to watch, had only arrived in Philadelphia as the No. 13 seed with a world ranking of 34. It seemed an ambitious prediction, even for someone with such obvious gifts, yet less than seven months later Mr Fernberger, whose opinion was supported by Fred Perry among others, could comfortably rest his case.

Sampras had just run away with the $1 million title, and was standing in the middle of the court as the closing speeches were being made looking slightly bemused, as did his opponent in the final Andres Gomez, who had just gone down 7-6, 7-5, 6-2. Philadelphia may then be looked back upon as a landmark, or at least a major signpost, in what could prove to be a long-lasting career at the top. At the time it also seemed that it might have represented a very different sort of landmark or signpost for John McEnroe. The fiery veteran arrived on the East coast after a year that had seen his expulsion from the Australian Open

and disappointing defeats in Milan and Toronto. He was the top seed in Philadelphia but immediately went out 6-7, 6-3, 6-3 to compatriot Richey Reneberg, much to his own disgust. 'The sands of time are slipping away faster than ever before. It's frustrating when you're not as good as you were,' said McEnroe. 'What happened in Melbourne is really beginning to sink in now. It's like a wake-up call.' In fact McEnroe went into a lengthy hibernation to re-emerge in London four months later and go on to turn his year around.

By the end of the third round, the tournament was looking wide open. Brad Gilbert, ranked fourth in the world, had succumbed to the kind of gutsy display he himself had become known for when Holland's Paul Haarhuis knocked him out 7-6, 5-7, 6-4.

Every champion needs his share of luck and perhaps fortune smiled on Sampras when he met Andre Agassi in the round of 16. With his dandy pink undershorts and flamboyant style, Agassi was very much the leader of the American Brat Pack, with the likes of Sampras and Courier very content to progress their careers in the slipstream. By the end of the year that was not possible for Sampras but he entered their late night encounter very much the underdog. Agassi hid the

Rick Leach is serenaded by banjo players after he and doubles partner, Jim Pugh, won the doubles competition. Rick's racquet made sweeter music on court.
Overleaf: The Blue Supreme Carpet used for the Ebel US Pro Indoor Tennis Championships at The Spectrum.

discomfort that was revealed later during the first set which he took 7-5. It transpired that he was suffering a touch of Montezuma's Revenge and when Sampras managed to edge the second set 7-5, Agassi took his leave very quickly, forced to retire with stomach problems caused by eating some unfriendly pasta earlier in the evening. Two other less familiar names also caught the eye en route to the semi-finals. Czechoslovakia's Petr Korda, a pleasing left-hander with flowing ground strokes, and his 7-6, 6-1 quarter-final defeat of fourth seed Jay Berger was a joy to watch.

Mark Kratzmann had spent much of the previous five years desperately trying to live up to the extravagant billing given to him as a teenager. Under the wing of new coach Gavin Hopper, this was the week when prolonged hard work started to pay off. It seemed as if he might go all the way to the final when he snatched the first set of his semi-final against Sampras, before he ran out of steam to lose the next two 6-1, 6-4.

Korda came down to earth with a resounding thud when Andres Gomez defeated him 6-2, 6-0 to set up an intriguing clash against Sampras. Rounding off a week of upsets Gomez never looked in the match; he served and volleyed off the court, giving Sampras the title worth $135,000 and a winning start for his new partnership with coach Joe Brandi. The victory, which pushing his ranking to 17, was met with the same shrug of the shoulders that greeted his Flushing Meadow triumph. Philadelphia turned out to be part one of the rise that took place in a year which had started with having to qualify for the Australian Men's Hardcourt Championships in Adelaide.

The doubles event, which attracted one of the strongest fields of the year, ended with American Davis Cuppers Rick Leach and Jim Pugh avenging their Australian Open semi-final defeat by Grant Connell and Glenn Michibata with a 3-6, 6-4, 6-2 victory - their first doubles title of the year - worth $54,750.

Stuttgart Classics

By Andrew Longmore

Stuttgart, 19-25 February
Tournament Director: Ion Tiriac

In the deeply ordered park which runs alongside the River Neckar in Stuttgart, a huge statue of a prancing horse reminds citizens of the real origins of their town. The skyline might be dominated by the three-pointed star of Mercedes-Benz, who have their headquarters in the city, but the real meaning of Stuttgart or Stuttgarten as it was originally known is 'Mare's Garden'. Ironic then that the prancing horse is the symbol of Ferrari. The city, the capital of Swabia, one of the most prosperous regions in Germany, is run with benevolent authority and great wit by Herr Manfred Rommel, Mayor of Stuttgart and son of the great German general. Ask him about his father and he will tell you about his own rather more modest military exploits. 'I only reached the rank of major. I think my father would have been disappointed,' he says. Herr Rommel might not have an army to command but, in partnership with local businessmen, he has grand plans for his city to become what he calls the 'sportspalace' of Germany and, early next century, host city for the Olympic Games. Under the equally tough and benevolent guidance of Ion Tiriac, Stuttgart has already begun to rival Munich and Frankfurt as the

'It is an honour to win so close to my home town and in a tournament organised by my manager.'

tennis capital of Germany. The Davis Cup finals were held in Stuttgart for the first time at the end of 1989 and, after two years as an exhibition event, the Eurocard Classics graduated to the full ATP Tour, with prize money of $1m. The field of 32 was headed by Boris Becker, who had almost single-handedly lifted the Germans to victory over Sweden in that final. Becker had shown his well-being by winning his first title of the year in Brussels early in February, but there was a lingering fear in those close to him that, after the exertions of the previous year, the world, Wimbledon and US Open champion had temporarily lost his appetite for the game.

A performance of enormous power and confidence against Ivan Lendl in the finals of the Eurocard Classics dispelled such doubts and, surprisingly, brought Becker his first tour title in his own country. 'It is an honour to win so close to my home town (Leimen) and in a tournament organised by Ion Tiriac, my manager,' said Becker afterwards. Poor Lendl had won his last two tournaments in Milan and Toronto, but knew his chances of a third were slim as soon as he lost an early break.

A pair of Swabian white horses for doubles champions Guy Forget and Jakob Hlasek, presented by the Mayor.

As Becker powered down a series of hefty first serves, Lendl's spirit wilted and he resorted to a vague serve-and-volley game which perplexed Becker as much as anyone. 'I'm not quite sure why he did that', said the new champion. Lendl did not seem quite sure either. 'The conditions were very fast,' he said. 'But if you don't play well and the other guy does, that's what is going to happen.' Particularly when the other guy is Becker. The following day Lendl was due to make a sentimental journey back to his native Czechoslovakia for the first time in many years to see his family and to play an exhibition match against Miloslav Mecir, so perhaps his mind was on other things. Becker's 6-2, 6-2 victory erased the memory of two disappointments earlier in the week. One was the withdrawal of Stefan Edberg, who was forced to pull out because his stomach muscle, the cause of his retirement in the final of the Australian Open in January, had not healed fully. The other was a first-round defeat for Carl-Uwe Steeb, the No. 4 seed who was born and bred in Stuttgart. 'Charlie' could find none of the belligerence or inspiration which had characterised

his rise into the top 20 and was beaten by the tough little Israeli Amos Mansdorf. Worse nearly followed, as Becker came to within a syllable of default against the qualifier Brod Dyke. Becker was initially warned by umpire Richard Ings for hitting a ball into the crowd. When he protested about the code violation, he received another warning which, under the new three-step code introduced by the ATP, took him two-thirds of the way to disqualification. Only then did Becker calm down and get on with his tennis, which proved too good for Dyke and, after a three-set struggle, for the talented but enigmatic Soviet Alex Volkov in the second.

Lendl's progress through the top half of the draw had been rather more serene. He beat the Italian Omar Camporese in the first round and, with more trouble, Goran Prpic of Yugoslavia, in the second. But the week's surprise package was Aki Rahunen, an impossibly slight Finn, who looked like a refugee from the local school playground and played like a wizened veteran. Having fought his way through qualifying, he beat

The power of the Becker serve is evident as he hurls himself towards the Stuttgart Classics title.

Australian left-hander Brod Dyke didn't look like this when he played Boris Becker in Stuttgart. Lashings of sun-protection cream are hardly necessary indoors, but Dyke still managed to scare his opponent who came within one step of default before staving off a second career loss to Dyke (the South Australian beat Becker in Brussels in 1986) to win a tough battle in three sets.

Javier Sanchez in the first round and then Mansdorf before pushing the stronger and more powerful Magnus Gustafsson from Sweden to three sets.

The Swede, in his turn, refused to be bullied by Lendl in an absorbing semi-final. He won the second set tie-break and only lacked a touch of experience when the moment came to reach out for victory. In the other semi-final, Jonas Svensson, who is blessed with as much talent as anyone on the tour when he cares to use it, matched Becker for most of the first set before falling in a heap. Like Gustafsson, the willowy Swede had chances to take the first set, but through a combination of Becker's solidity and his own infuriating lack of conviction, they escaped, leaving the way clear for the top two seeds to continue their own private battle. The victory gave Becker an 8-7 lead in matches against Lendl, but the war is yet to be won.

The doubles title went to the left-handed and right-handed combination of Guy Forget and Jakob Hlasek, who beat Michael Mortensen and Tom Nijssen comfortably 6-3, 6-2 - the first of four titles for the French-Swiss partnership through the year. Their path to the final had been eased by the fall of two other seeded teams and the default of Boris Becker and Eric Jelen.

Volvo Tennis Indoor

By George Rubenstein

Memphis, 26 February-4 March
Tournament Director: Tommy Buford

America's South has a deep and warm heritage, combining literary, musical and culinary creations which have been at the root of American popular culture. Memphis has been the cradle and weaning point of a number of disciplines and ideas, including the very expressionistic form of music known as the blues. The ability to express one's sincere and inner thoughts, touching chords with pain and struggle, in sometimes haunting lyrical forms, is what makes the blues such a unique art form. The homeliness of the Racquet Club of Memphis is unmatchable anywhere else on the ATP Tour. There is an incredibly warm sense of belonging that nestles invisibly around each of the entrants into the confines of the Club. There are no exceptions, and it goes straight from the top down. Tommy Buford, the tournament director, and his family have nurtured these relationships, and set up the guidelines. Even Tennessee Governor Ned McWherter was showing his high-spirited allegiance to the tournament, as he attended, having been a close colleague of Hamilton Jordan.

Phil Chamberlin, assistant tournament director, Michael Stich and his doubles partner Udo Riglewski, line up with doubles champions Darren Cahill and Mark Kratzmann, and tournament director Tommy Buford.

The family man - doubles expert Ken Flach and his wife Sandra celebrate with their son Dylan on the youngster's second birthday during the Volvo Tennis Indoor.

All types of events were incorporated into the tournament, including an auction at which some former stars, Ilie Nastase and Vitas Gerulaitis, were auctioned off for the benefit of the Boys and Girls Clubs of Memphis. Both were worth $2,000 to someone. Imagine?

There were more surprises than the seeds would like to remember in 1990. First, due to injury, John McEnroe was forced to withdraw, with a strained upper groin injury. Next Stefan Edberg and Michael Chang were defeated by Gary Muller and Glenn Layendecker, respectively in second-round play after first-round byes. In fact, the top eight seeds were out by the third round. Displaying signs of the depth of the Tour that was most interesting and unnerving this year, 21-year-old Michael Stich of Germany proved that he had the biggest surprise in store for the tournament, as he edged Australian veteran Wally Masur in a thrilling third-set tie breaker to capture the $32,000 award. The early victories spurred Stich on to

greater achievements, as he stated, 'When I see these guys go down, I feel like "okay, I can try." In your head, you know you can beat most of these guys,' said the second consecutive first-time winner of a Tour event in 1990 (after Sampras in Philadelphia). Stich and Udo Riglewski, a compatriot, finished as the No. 10 doubles team for the year in the pairs competition on the ATP Tour computer, winning two titles together this year.

But the title was to go to the Australian duo of Darren Cahill and Mark Kratzmann, who earned their sixth title together, and the first of three titles as a unit in 1990, propelling them on their way towards the eighth and final berth in the ATP World Doubles Final in Sanctuary Cove.

Construction is nearly completed on the 20,000+ seat Pyramid, which will house the event for the future. There are strong wishes that the charm and flavour of the Racquet Club won't be lost in the size of the new facility.

ABN Wereld Tennis Toernooi

By Frans Van Der Staay

Rotterdam, 26 February-4 March
Tournament Director: Wim Buitendijk

When Jimmy Connors rang tournament director Wim Buitendijk at the Ahoy Stadium he had to inform the Dutchman that the wrist injury he had suffered in Milan at the start of the month prevented him from participating in Rotterdam. Although obviously a disappointment to him, Buitendijk was not to know that the player who took Connor's place, Michael Tauson of Denmark, was to prove the surprise success at the ABN Wereld Tennis Tournooi.

Top ten players Brad Gilbert and Alberto Mancini headed the 32-strong field and were joined by six other seeds, Yannick Noah, Carl-Uwe Steeb, Magnus Gustafsson, defending champion Jakob Hlasek, Jonas Svensson and Amos Mansdorf. To the delight of the fans and for the first time in the history of the tournament, there were also four Dutchmen in the main draw. Paul Haarhuis, Mark Koevermans, Michiel Schapers and Tom Nijssen had the honour of carrying their country's flag and it was Haarhuis who had the public's greatest support. No one will ever forget how Haarhuis first shot to fame when in 1989 he shocked the tennis world with a second round in the US Open of national hero and four-time champion, John McEnroe. Of his fellow countrymen, only Haarhuis was to survive the first round. Schapers, the 6-foot, 7-inch giant who was

for years the number one player in the Netherlands, lost to Tauson after being upset by a line call at set point. Losing that first set, Schapers never recovered. Haarhuis had put out Noah in straight sets but the Frenchman was mentally and physically tired and was still recovering from the enormous amount of energy he had expended in Australia.

The No. 1 seed Gilbert conceded his only set of the week in the first round to the up-and-coming Soviet player Andrei Cherkasov while the No. 2 seed Mancini lost to qualifier Thomas Hogstedt. It was only Mancini's second match in three months and the Argentinian clay court specialist admitted that the indoor carpet was not compatible with his game. Unfortunately for Mancini first round exits were to become an all too familiar occurrence throughout 1990, and the 1989 Monte Carlo and Italian Open champion slumped out the the top 100 ranking by the year's end.

Tauson temporarily lost favour in the spectators' eyes when he put out their only national hope, Haarhuis, in the second round. Haarhuis' coach of nine years, Henk van Hulst, blamed lack of concentration but Tauson, the highest ranked Danish player since Torben Ulrich in the 1970s, had produced some formidable serving to clinch the match.

One of the most reliable players on the Tour, Brad Gilbert has won titles every year since 1984. 1990 was no exception.

As Buitendijk so rightly noted, 'Except for perhaps Lendl, Becker and Edberg it is a fact that the standard of professional tennis is so high nowadays that anybody can beat anyone else on a good day. That makes for interesting, competitive matches and the public is aware of this.' Indeed the public in Rotterdam don't buy tickets solely to see the biggest stars - they appreciate watching excellent tennis regardless. The record figures that the ABN Wereld Tennis Tournooi attracted this year, 72,000, is testimony to the enthusiasm of the people of the Netherlands.

Tauson continued his winning streak in the quarter finals with a third set tie-break against Gustafsson. As the last man in the main draw, and ranked 144 at the time, Tauson had certainly seized the chance that Connors' withdrawal had given him. He finally met his match in the semis against Gilbert so that the American secured a place in the final. Svensson was his opponent.

The Swede, who had been forced into tie-breakers in three of his four victories, had dashed Hlasek's hopes of retaining the title when he ousted the Swiss in straight sets in the semi-finals. It was the best match of the tournament and Svensson played some marvellous passing shots, including an incredible winner off a seemingly unreturnable high-bouncing volley from Hlasek.

But the final was straightforward. Gilbert's ruthlessly efficient game took him to his 18th career title with a 6-1, 6-3 defeat of his blond opponent. $65,000 richer, Gilbert returned to America a contented man.

Throughout the week the stadium restaurants had served 40,000 bread rolls, 11,000 litres of beer, 700 bottles of champagne, 1000 bottles of wine, 4000 oysters as well as caviar, salmon, lobsters and exquisite deserts. No doubt Gilbert accounted for at least one of the bottles of champagne!

Newsweek Champions Cup

By Richard Evans

Indian Wells, 5-11 March
Tournament Director: Charles Pasarell, Jr.

Steeling himself to overcome gusting desert winds and a determined challenge from Andre Agassi, Stefan Edberg won his first title on the two-month-old ATP Tour when he claimed the Newsweek Cup at the Hyatt Grand Champions by a score of 6-4, 5-7, 7-6, 7-6. Psychologically the victory was an important one for Edberg.

By coming through such a stern test, the Swede cleared his mind of any lingering doubts about his fitness following the pulled stomach muscle that had forced him to default to Ivan Lendl in the final of the Australian Open in January. It was possible that he had not gone all out on the serve to avoid any unnecessary stretching of the abdominals but, by the end of his 3 hour 32 minute duel with Agassi, Edberg had no doubts as to just what kind of shape his legs were in. Seldom could he have run further during a match as Agassi's raking ground strokes had him racing from one side of the court to the other. For a match played under difficult conditions, it was something of a classic of its kind. Both players rose above the problems posed by a wind that was

Donna Mills and Linda Evans, stars of Knotts Landing and Dynasty, bring some blond glamour into the arms of tournament director Charlie Pasarell

'Where did it go?' Doubles winners, Boris Becker and Guy Forget let one pass them by.
Overleaf: An ariel view of Charlie Pasarell's brainchild: The Hyatt Grand Champions Hotel and 10,500 seat stadium near Palm Springs.

stadium in the Californian desert - Pasarell had turned the new Grand Champions site at Indian Wells into one of the most luxurious and popular stops on the Tour.

It had not taken much persuasion for Boris Becker to sign up as touring pro and accept the offer of a house at nearby PGA West and even if he failed to recapture the title he had won in 1987 and '88 - going down to Agassi in the semi-final in straight sets - he still enjoyed himself sufficiently to drive back down Highway 111 the next day to win the doubles title with Guy Forget.

It was on an outside court during the qualifying in 1988 that Pasarell and Grand Champions Tennis Director Ray Moore had first noticed the streamlined talent of Pete Sampras and immediately predicted big things for the youngster. Sampras returned this year as the new US Pro Indoor champion after his triumph in Philadelphia but unfortunately he could not repeat that success for his local southern Californian fans. Richey Reneberg beat him in the second round before going down himself to Aaron Krickstein. It was, in fact, another American youngster of high promise who emerged from that section of the draw: Jim Courier blasted his way past Krickstein with his powerful back court game to set up a semi-final clash with Edberg. That, however, proved one step too far for Courier who was outplayed by the fluency of Stefan's serve and volley game and lost 6-4, 6-1.

swirling around the large bowl of the stadium court as well as a sudden drop in temperature that had people rushing off to their cars in search of blankets. The drama, however, simply got hotter by the hour. At 6-6 in the third set, both players had won 117 points but Edberg soon surged ahead to take the tie-break by 7-1. By the time the second tie-break arrived, Agassi was fighting tooth and nail to prove that his winter training had provided him with sufficient stamina to contest a fifth set but the Swede never allowed him to get that far, clinching the decisive breaker 8-6 after nine of the first 11 points had gone against the serve.

So once again the capacity 10,500 crowd had been entertained by the quality of tennis that Charlie Pasarell had always dreamed of bringing to his desert domain. Since moving his tournament from the beautiful La Quinta Racquet Club four years before - defying the expert opinion that ridiculed his decision to build such a big tennis

During the week a tradition Pasarell had started several years before was continued when Arthur Ashe was honoured at a dinner attended as always by a close coterie of players and friends who form the core of southern Californian tennis. In previous years the likes of Pancho Gonzales, Jack Kramer, Roy Emerson and Rod Laver have been the beneficiaries. This time the dinner was especially poignant for Pasarell. Ashe, who was forced to retire from the game with heart trouble, was Charlie's room-mate at UCLA and the bond between them has never been broken. As usual it was a special occasion for the tennis fraternity just as the Newsweek Cup has become a special sort of tournament for players.

Trophée Hasan II

By Craig Gabriel

Casablanca, 5-11 March
Tournament Director: Larbi Outaleb

There was no Rick's Cafe and precious little romance when the ATP Tour arrived in this sprawling, industrialised Moroccan city for its first event on red clay. But if the world's movie-goers still insist on equating Casablanca with Humphrey Bogart, Ingrid Bergman and a tinkling piano then at least Thomas Muster could have been excused for whistling 'As Time Goes By' once the rain had cleared to leave him with the Trophee Hassan ll singles title after a 6-1, 6-7, 6-2 victory over Guillermo Perez-Roldan. Only 12 months before the 22-year-old Austrian had not been given a very good chance of returning to the game after suffering a severe knee injury in a freak road accident in downtown Miami during the Lipton Players Championships.

But Muster, who would have given Bogart a good run for his money in the tough guy stakes, had put himself through a gruelling re-habilitation programme and the inspired tennis he produced to overwhelm his normally durable Argentine opponent in just under two hours was a testament to his driving determination to regain his position as a member of the world's top ten. The victory here gave a nice little boost to those ambitions, moving him to No.23 from No.30 on the ATP Tour computer and by the end of the year he had climbed all the way back into the top ten.

The gleaming Trophee Hasan II singles cup won by the rejuvenated Austrian Thomas Muster.

Australians Simon Youll and Todd Woodbridge (left) beat the Dutch pair of Paul Haarhuis and Mark Koevermans an the doubles final to win their first title together on the ATP Tour.

The rain, which poured down in mid week, delayed the schedule by more than a day and even the matches had to be switched from the new Complex Federal to the old courts nearby where the father of Moroccan tennis, Monsieur Mjid, used to host amateur events in the pre-Open days. Thanks to Sat 1's satellite feed from West Germany, the players were able, at least, to watch the action from the Newsweek Cup in sunny Indian Wells. When the rain finally stopped, layers of sodden clay were removed from the court and the surface was then set on fire to speed up the drying out process. These drastic measures at least ensured that the new stadium could be used for the final which was watched by Prince Moulay Rachid and a capacity crowd of 3500.

After the extraordinary effort that went into building the impresive new complex, it would have been a shame had it not been used. The actual seating around the court and and the two storey building that now acts as the home of the Royal Moroccan Tennis Federation had been constructed from scratch in just three months. There was a surprisingly large contingent of Australians in the 32-man draw but, despite Johan Anderson's appearance in the quarter-finals, where he lost to No. 3 seed Goran Prpic, their sucess was confined to the doubles. Todd Woodbridge and Simon Youll, playing together for only the second time, emerged as what they themselves described 'unexpected champions' following their 6-3, 6-1 defeat of the Dutch pair Paul Haarhuis and Mark Koevermans in the final. The Aussies earned their success with a decisive 6-1, 6-4 victory over the No. 2 seeds Josef Cihak and Cyril Suk in the quarter finals. 'It feels pretty good to win my first tournament,' said Woodbridge. 'I have won Challenger events and seven junior Grand Slam doubles titles but never a title at the senior level and this is a great way for me to start the ATP Tour.'

> *Layers of sodden clay were removed from the court and the surface was then set on fire.*

Lipton International Players Championships

By Richard Evans

Key Biscayne, 16-25 March
Tournament Director: Cliff Buchholz

It is possible that South Florida was not quite ready for the brothers Buchholz. Not quite ready for the potent mixture of charm, experience and cussed mid-Western determination that is the Buchholz hallmark. To say that it has not been easy for Butch Buchholz and his brother Cliff since they first decided to create one of the world's premier tennis events in Florida would be something of an understatement. Beginning at Laver's near Delray Beach and moving on through Boca West to Key Biscayne, the tournament had three venues in its first three years and only now does a permanent home seem a possibility. Despite a lasting relationship with Lipton's Gerry Boyks, who turned out to be the most understanding of sponsors, Buchholz was still having to consider another move as late as the spring of 1990 because of problems with a small but vocal section of the Key Biscayne community. The politics became fierce at times and Lipton gained the dubious honour of becoming the first tennis tournament to be picketed, not for something contentious like South Africa,

Amos Mansdorf discovered there were other things to do on Key Biscayne. There were cockatoos galore as the Israeli posed for Nick Kennerley's TWI Highlights film.

Tanned and smiling: Rick Leach and Jim Pugh took the doubles trophies at Key Biscayne.

but, merely for existing. Eventually, late in 1990, a thirty year deal was signed with Metro Dade County whose officials had realised all along that the Lipton was a financial, sporting and artistic asset that no sane local government would want to lose. As a result the permanent stadium that has always been part of the Buchholz dream will now be built and the beautiful island of Key Biscayne will become the tournament's permanent home.

One of the unique features of the Lipton is that it provides one of the few weeks of the year when the boys and girls of the ATP Tour and WTA get a chance to mingle in the same players' lounge. And boys and girls a lot of them were, too, with 13-year-old Jennifer Capriati stealing headlines and 16-year-old Monica Seles running off with the women's title while Andre Agassi, all of 19, reversed the previous week's result at Indian Wells by beating Stefan Edberg in the men's final 6-1, 6-4, 0-6, 6-2. It was ironic that Agassi should come through finally to win a big five-set match because, for the first time this year, the tournament format, played over ten days instead of two weeks, had switched to best of three sets up to the final. Although it is impossible to prove, this might have

had more than a little to do with the upsets that soon began to reverberate through the draw. The players had wanted their workload reduced but for some top stars it was reduced a little too drastically for their liking. Yannick Noah, who had pulled himself out of all manner of impossible positions in five-set battles the year before, went down 7-6 in the third to the Aussie southpaw Mark Kratzmann. But that surprise paled by the time Boris Becker went out in the third round to the muscular 24-year-old Frenchman Jean Fleurian 7-6, 6-1. And when Emilio Sanchez wore down Ivan Lendl 6-3, 6-7, 6-4 the tournament would find itself without its No. 1 seed in the final for the first time since its inception in 1985. Would these upsets have occurred over the best of five sets, a format that usually gives the higher ranked player time to impose himself on the match? It is a question worth pondering.

The match of the tournament was undoubtedly that between Edberg and the Swiss No. 1, Jakob Hlasek, in the quarter final which ended in the Swede's favour by a score of 6-7, 7-6, 7-6. And it might so easily have been different. Having missed one match point in the deciding tie-break,

The picture says it all as Andre Agassi wins the most prestigious title of his career.

Hlasek found himself perfectly positioned to put away a winning forehand volley on the second. Connecting as he would have wished, Hlasek punched the ball onto the sideline right underneath the umpire's chair and, after a leap of delight, held out his hand. But the ball was called out and Gerry Armstrong refused to overrule. Hlasek promptly double faulted and then hit a backhand wide to lose the decider by eight points to six. 'It was so close you couldn't really tell,' Edberg admitted afterwards. 'It's terrible when something like that happens. It's happened to me and it's just really bad luck.' Edberg's luck ran out in the final because Agassi was simply too good for him. A stunning display of power hitting between Agassi and Jim Courier in the quarter final had provided ample evidence of just how well tuned Andre's game was and, despite the loss of a love set to Stefan, there was never much doubt that a hard winter's training regime was providing the power and stamina Agassi needed to seize the most prestigious title of his young career.

The packed crowds who enjoyed Florida weather at its best for most of the tournament were rewarded by the rare sight of Becker on a doubles court as he and his Brazilian partner Cassio Motta powered their way through to the final without the loss of a set. Doubles expertise paid off in the end, however, as the US Davis Cup pair of Jim Pugh and Rick Leach claimed their second victory of the year with a 6-4, 3-6, 6-3 win.

A familiar sight as Stefan Edberg adopts the Lawrence of Arabia look during change overs.

Prudential-Bache Securities Classic

By Meg Donovan

Orlando, 2-8 April
Tournament Director: Richard Adler

Minutes away from The Magic Kingdom, 28-year-old Brad Gilbert worked a bit of magic of his own to earn his second 1990 ATP Tour title in the space of one month. Gilbert, a winner in Rotterdam in late February, defeated South African Christo Van Rensburg in the title match 6-2, 6-1. The tournament's No. 1 seed, Gilbert waltzed his way through the draw dropping only 27 games in five matches. His unblemished record in singles for the week was bolstered by an impressive performance of serve; he was broken only three times in the tournament, once in the final three rounds. 'I'm winning the nine-to-five matches,' Gilbert commented, 'the matches I need to win.'

Van Rensburg was a suitable contender in the finals as the popular pro is famous on the ciruit for superb magic tricks of his own which he performs in the locker rooms and at parties round the world. He was no less magical during the week than Gilbert notching hard-fought wins over Slobodan Zivojinovic, Nicolas Pereira, Jason Stoltenberg and David Pate in his best performance of the year. Van Rensburg would jump seven spots in the world ranking poll after his week in Orlando. His run was marred only by debilitating cramps and heat-dehydration in the finals, making him easy prey to the Gilbert onslaught.

The tournament - held for the first time at a new venue, the Heathrow Racquet Club - also saw strong performances by wildcard entrants John Ross, Malivai Washington and Alexis Hombrecher. Ross, who was playing in his first tour event of the year, ousted No. 6 seed Jimmy Arias in the

Venezuals's Nicolas Pereira learns the tricks of the trade to ensure the tension in his strings is just right.

Brad Gibert with his number one fan, son Zachary. Gilbert's wife Kim brings Zachary to many events of the ATP Tour.

opening round before falling to an impressive Washington in straight sets. For Washington, who would go on to reach the semi-finals, it was easily the best performance of his professional tennis career.

After earning a spot in the main draw through the qualifying competition, Washington knocked off Kelly Jones, John Ross and Scott Davis in successive rounds before falling to Gilbert. The Michigan native, whose spends most of the year working with ATP Tour Director of Tennis Brian Gottfried, rose to a career high 119 on the ranking list, after his run in Orlando. Hombrecher - a 19-year-old freshman at Stanford University, tied for last spot on the world ranking list - became a surprise quarter finalist when No. 2 seed Aaron Krickstein was forced to withdraw

from the tournament with a pulled hamstring. Hombrecherthen managed to take Pate to a tie-break in the second set in the semis proving once again that the lowest ranked players can be difficult opposition for the more famous names on the Tour.

The doubles competition in Orlando also saw the emergence of new stars. The second-time tandem of Alfonso Mora and Brian Page extended the No. 1 seeds Scott Davis and David Pate to a second-set tie-break before losing 6-3, 7-6 in the final. It was to be the first of five wins in 1990 for the duo who qualified for the ATP Tour World Doubles Championship at Sanctuary Cove. Davis, who in 1989 teamed with Tim Pawsat for the crown, recorded his second consecutive doubles title in Orlando.

Banespa Open

By Chiquino Leite Moreira

Rio de Janeiro, 2-8 April
Tournament Director: Ricardo Bernd

The ATP Tour event in Rio de Janeiro, which took place on the world-famous Copacabana beach, was a triumph of courage for Brazilian tennis. Brazil, one of the countries which has always promoted a large number of tennis tournaments, has recently suffered from the effects of economic reform with cut-backs that have threatened the existence of many championships. In an attempt to control inflation, the government withdrew most of the money in circulation. Despite this problem, TAWARIC, the organisation promoting the event, decided to rise to the challenge and, with the ATP Tour agreeing to defer the $250,000 prize money payment, the tournament actually took place and was extremely successful. The organisation of the Banespa Open, the 1990 ATP Tour event in Rio de Janeiro - the only tournament actually played on a beach, with tennis courts laid out on the sand - required a bold approach.

The first test was one for the engineers, who had to think of a way of staging the sport in a public place - all beaches are public in Brazil. They came up with a simple solution for building four courts on the sand: the wooden floor was placed over hydraulic hoists, which corrected the unevenness of the sand, and then covered by a Supreme carpet. The rows of seats were held up by metal structures.

The Banespa Open is the only tournament to be played on a beach, with courts laid out on the sand.

The beauty of the Copacabana beach, and the fascination of a city like Rio de Janeiro, brought pros from ten countries to the tournament. Many of them, such as the Americans Bryan Shelton and Brad Pearce, had never played in Brazil before. Experts on fast courts, they enrolled in this championship because of the Supreme carpet. During the week, however, none of these players managed to beat the favourites, and the final game was disputed by the No. 1 seed, the Brazilian Luiz Mattar, and the No. 2, the Canadian Andrew Sznajder. The Brazilian public could still remember the Davis Cup games in Vancouver, where Sznajder defeated the Brazilian team, with two victories against Luiz Mattar and Danilo Marcelino. Therefore, the 7000 seats of the central court were all sold for the final. The people, who were cheering and encouraging Mattar, were very excited by the time match-point arrived.

Upstaging nearby Ipanema, Copacabana can boast an entire tennis tournament for one week of the year. The world's only Centre Court built on a beach - which, in Brazil, is a case of taking the tournament to where the crowds are. The Supreme court was laid on boards over the golden sands.

'Nico', as Mattar is known in Brazil, rewarded the cheers of the people by offering Dartagnan, a sort of cheer-leader, the shirt he had worn. Dartagnan - playing a horn - had encouraged Mattar in the most difficult moments of the game.

In the doubles, the winners were two American university students, who had never been to Brazil before and had never done so well in an ATP Tour tournament. Sven Salumaa and Brian Garrow defeated the Brazilian partnership of Nelson Aerts and Fernando Roese 7-7, 6-3 in an unseeded final. Salumaa and Garrow must have doubted their chances in the second round. They scraped an exciting three-set victory over Nick Brown of England and Steve Guy of New Zealand 7-5, 6-7, 7-5 before their run to the final and eventual triumph. Salumaa and Garrow celebrated their success with other players in a party named 'The White Night'. All the guests were dressed in white for the dinner, which was served in the Copacabana Palace Hotel. The guests, entrepreneurs, industrialists, artists and socialites, made donations to charities in Rio de Janeiro.

Estoril Open

By Caroline Hutton

Estoril, 2-8 April
Tournament Director: Joao Lagos

April was the month of 'Double Takes' on the ATP Tour. In the space of four weeks, three players took both the singles and doubles titles at their tournaments. Emilio Sanchez started the roll at the Estoril Open, Andres Gomez carried it on the following week in Barcelona and Pat Cash completed the hat-trick in Hong Kong. Throughout the rest of 1990 the feat was never accomplished again. Ironically, it had been Sanchez himself who had last held the record when, back in August of 1989, he won the singles and doubles competitions in Kitzbuhel. He had paired up with his younger brother Javier in Austria but in Estoril he was reunited with his former partner and fellow Spaniard, Sergio Casal. They had won the 1988 US Open together but had not played much as a team in 1989. But the duo worked like magic on the court and took the Estoril Open doubles title from Omar Camporese and Paolo Cane 7-5, 4-6, 7-5. 'This is our first victory of the year together,' noted Casal, 'but I don't think it will be our last.' Indeed, the duo were to notch up another five before the year was out, including their win at the French Open.

The Estoril Open may have taken place in neighbouring Portugal, but it was dominated by superb performances from the Spaniards. Juan Aguilera, Jordi Arrese and Sanchez made it through to the semi-finals and Aguilera's opponent Franco Davin, although not a resident in Barcelona like the other three, certainly speaks the same language - he lives in Buenos Aires.

Sanchez, supremely confident, moved past Arrese 6-2, 6-1 to the final while the diminutive Davin took out Aguilera with a fine show of clay court expertise, playing a heavy topspin baseline game. But no-one was going to stop Sanchez. Seemingly in a hurry to win the doubles crown immediately after the singles final, Sanchez disposed of Davin 6-3, 6-1 in a mere 66 minutes and, with $32,400 safely in his pocket, took just 15 minutes to get back his breath back before returning to court with Casal. The light may have faded by the time he lifted his second trophy of the day above his head, but his tennis was as strong as it had been at the beginning of the week.

Although Sanchez wasn't to win another singles title in 1990, consistent performances, including seven semi-final spots, meant that he was the only player to finish inside the top eight in both singles and doubles and thus qualify for a place in the ATP Tour World Championship for singles and doubles at the end of the year. In fact, his victories at Estoril were to prove a mirror image of the rewards he reaped seven months later.

A gleam of victory is evident in Emilio Sanchez's eye as he lifts the trophy after defeating Franco Davin.

The Estoril Open made its first appearance on the ATP Tour and opened the European clay court season. Tournament director Joao Lagos put on a superbly organised event but there was one thing he could not control: the traditional April showers were replaced by thunderstorms and torrential downpours which disrupted play every day. But nothing could have dampened the spirits of Estoril's champion, who prophesied at the end of the week, 'I think this is going to be my year.'

Suntory Japan Open Tennis Championship

By Craig Gabriel

Tokyo, 9-15 April
Tournament Director: Toshiro Sakai

Normally one would think of the Japanese people as having a gentle disposition - well just forget it when one player in particular holds court in Tokyo. There are not too many players on the IBM/ATP Tour that can boast the following Stefan Edberg has in Japan. It is almost frenetic. The Swede's blonde hair, good looks and quiet, reserved demeanour is what appeals to the people there. And they certainly let their feelings be known. The teenyboppers squeeze into every nook and cranny just to get a glimpse of their hero, and if he stops to sign an autograph or pose for a photograph there can almost be a stampede.

The Suntory Japan Open, played at Ariake Stadium, allows Edberg's legion of admirers to get just that bit closer to him, but the effort of keeping the fans at arm's length is a job that Sumo wrestlers would have found daunting. The barricades and security people are tested with the strain of human beings pressing to try and touch him. The Suntory Japan Open was the first tournament in Asia to offer prize money of $1 million and that was a feat that made former Japanese touring pro, now tournament director, Toshiro Sakai very proud. The stadium itself is a bit of distance from the centre of town. It is a 35-minute coach ride that dived through tunnels under the harbour or passed the more speedy Bullet Train on its way to or from the ancient capital of Kyoto. The ride is almost like a day's excursion out of town because there is plenty of chatter from the players and Western rock music is played over the speaker system.

At night during the event, it's the neon-lit Roppongi area for the tennis crowd. It is probably the most western part of the city and two favourite haunts are the Hard Rock Cafe and Tony Roma's Place for Ribs.

It is no secret that Japan has an acute shortage of land. The Ginza in downtown Tokyo will profess to that when one hears about the cost of space. So on getting to the area where Ariake is located, one has to marvel at Japanese determination. All this part of Tokyo is reclaimed land that has been developed to include everything from light industry to a golf driving range. In this day of professional tennis, the Suntory Japan Open is a rare breed of tournament. With the exception of the four Grand Slam events, this is one of only four events on the ATP Tour (the others being the NSW Open in Sydney, the Lipton International at Key Biscayne and the OTB International at Schenectady) that plays host to both sexes. In fact there is even a junior section played at Ariake. This really is a complete tournament.

Strapped up but still moving happily towards the final, Aaron Krickstein is all smiles.

Aaron Krickstein and Stefan Edberg toast the tournament's health at the traditional Suntory party.

In the presence of Crown Prince Hiro, on a cool and windy day that did not lend itself to great tennis, Edberg was embraced in 'that championship feeling' as he clinched and retained the title, this time against Aaron Krickstein, by the score of 6-4, 7-5. The Swede could not get the grin off his face and later commented: 'I love this game tennis and I feel very good. I hate to lose finals and I really wanted to win that one.' The Edberg cheer squad, which was almost the entire stadium of 8,000, went as wild as Japanese fans get and later almost pulled down a barrier trying to touch him.

> *In the presence of Crown Prince Hiro, Stefan Edberg enjoyed 'that championship feeling'.*

goods in the final even though he scored early service breaks in both sets against Edberg. Chang meanwhile is starting to threaten Edberg's popularity in the Land of the Rising Sun and the teenager was moved to comment that 'Japanese girls were quite forward'. They were thrusting gifts into his hands and trying to have their photographs taken with him. This tennis tournament had been plagued by bad weather over the last three days. This is not expected to be a factor in the years to come because a retractable roof is in the process of being installed over the centre court.

For Krickstein it was a memorable week, for he scored his first career win over Ivan Lendl in the semi-finals, while in the quarter finals he had ended any hopes that Michael Chang might have had. The American played some inspired tennis in that match but he was not able to reproduce the

The doubles final was delayed a day because of the weather but Mark Kratzmann and Wally Masur were able to rally back, after losing the first set and then being down a service break in the second, to defeat Americans Kent Kinnear and Brad Pearce 3-6, 6-3, 6-4.

Pat Cash, who was defeated in the first round, steps out with his wife Emily for a night on the town.

Trofeo Conde de Godo

By Pedro Hernandez

Barcelona, 9-15 April
Tournament Director: Sixto Cambra Sanchez

Spring or autumn, it makes no odds. Red clay is always good to Andres Gomez. For the second time in seven months, the Ecuadorean won the title at the Real Tennis Club of Barcelona. In 1989 he had ended the red clay season by beating Ivan Lendl in the semi-finals and Horst Skoff in the final. In 1990 he defeated the Argentinian Guillermo Perez-Roldan 6-0, 7-6, 3-6, 0-6 and 6-2, climbing to No. 9 in the ATP Tour computer rankings - his highest position in over two years. But the occasions were very different. After the tournament in 1989, Gomez had said 'At this point in my career, I am feeling my age and it is hard to play well; but beating Lendl and adding to my singles titles give me a special satisfaction.'

In 1990 he had every reason to feel more positive. 'This victory is more important than last year's, you know, because it moves me into the top ten,' he said. No one knows how much he was thinking of Roland Garros at this stage of the season. But the 1990 victory was extremely difficult. In the opening round, Gomez came back from match point against Michiel Schapers and finally fought a three-hour battle with Perez-Roldan in the final. Following his victory in Barcelona, Andres Gomez said that he was donating $7,000 to the homeless children of Ecuador. 'I dedicate this victory to the people of my country,' he claimed. The week before Barcelona, Gomez, his wife Ana Maria, and son Juan Andres, were in Estoril, where Gomez lost the first round. While there, the Gomez family

Gomez with the first of his two Barcelona trophies.

Javier Sanchez, who teamed up with Gomez to win the doubles title. They defeated Javier's elder brother Emilio and Sergio Casal.

visited the Catholic Statuary of Fatima. 'We are a Catholic family,' he said 'and I made a promise to the Virgin Mary when I asked her to help a family member and to give me strength to win the tournament. I will keep my promise and give $7,000 to homeless children in my country.'

Andres Gomez sweetened his singles success with a sterling doubles run as he teamed up with Javier Sanchez to win the doubles title against Sergio Casal and Emilio Sanchez, 7-6, 7-5. 'This was the only doubles title - among the top clay court titles - that I hadn't won,' he said. 'It was a good week.'

The tournament was very important for the Spanish players. Red clay is good to them - and the Argentines, too. Spain put six players in the round of 16: Emilio Sanchez, Sergi Bruguera, Javier Sanchez, Carlos Costa, German Lopez and Jordi Arrese. But Guillermo Perez-Roldan

extinguished the hopes of the Spanish fans in the semi-finals by stopping Emilio Sanchez, 7-5, 7-6. 'I was disappointed because it was a match in which I missed many opportunities,' said Sanchez. 'I was motivated to win in my club.' The Sanchez family had grown up playing in the Real Tennis Club of Barcelona, and Emilio had won a week earlier at Estoril - a victory which placed him in the top ten for the first time. 'I was expecting a lot from this tournament,' he confirmed.

Sixto Cambra, the tournament director, was also very happy after the tournament. 'Tennis is really important in Barcelona and we had very good crowds,' he said. The tournament suffered from the withdrawal of Boris Becker, however, who had injured his left knee. 'People were looking forward to see Boris play, but they understood his injury - especially when he flew from Germany to explain his knee problem,' continued Cambra.

Philips Open

By Philippe Bouin

Nice, 16-22 April
Tournament Directors: Dominique Bedel, Pascal Portes

Juan Aguilera doesn't run; he floats. Light and nimble of foot, he slides over the ochre clay and paints indecipherable patterns as he maps out the fate of his opponent. Juan Aguilera, the sinister tango dancer, won the Philips open in Nice, with his slender figure, his head held high. Juan the Hidalgo would have been as handsome a winner in the last century as he was this year. He would have celebrated his success in the casino, waltzing all night with beautiful women in his arms.

A hundred years ago a group of young English gentlemen, wintering on the Cote d'Azur, decided to establish a tennis club. The English already had a promenade named after them in Nice, the Promenade des Anglais, lined with palm trees and mimosa on the edge of the Mediterranean. They were soon to have their own tennis club as well. A hundred years later the venue of the 1990 Philips Open still retains the symbolic title 'Nice Lawn Tennis Club', although there is not a single blade of grass to be seen; clay reigns in a climate where tennis is played all year round.

The first Nice LTC had only four courts. The Mayor of Nice, Alziary de Malaussena, had given land in the middle of the city, so that the young from upper class families could occupy their time playing a sport that had become the height of fashion. Of course, he was not to know that this noble gesture would give birth to a tradition which has made Nice one of the oldest tennis cities in the world. Those courts, in the Place Mozart, were soon to be frequented by the champions of the day, invited to the Cote d'Azur by the well-heeled English. At the first tournament in 1898, the Doherty brothers, Laurie and Reggie, brought to the Mediterranean shores the supremacy that they had already started to establish at Wimbledon. It was also on these courts that a very young Suzanne Lenglen played some of the first shots of her career. So, when it was decided in 1919 to move the courts of the Nice LTC to the Parc Imperial, bordering the former residence of Emperor Napoleon III, the Lenglen family were offered the opportunity to settle in the Villa Ariem, right next to the club.

When, more recently, the French Federation decided to open its first Tennis and Studies Training Centre, in the Palace of the Parc Imperial (transformed many years before that into a lycée), the courts that Noah, Bedel, Moretton, Haillet, Gauvin, Leconte and Santoro looked out upon from their dormitory windows were the courts of the Nice LTC. This is where they dreamt of emulating the exploits of the great champions who had won the Nice tournament which, thanks to the efforts of a young and dynamic president Pierre

Paccard, had been part of the Grand Prix since 1971: Nastase (1971, 1972), Orantes (1973) and Borg (1977, 1980). It was also on the centre court of the Nice LTC that we witnessed Borg bursting out laughing, probably for the first and last time, after a winning shot from his opponent. On the day of the 1980 final, the losing Orantes succeeded in making a retro-drop shot which, by the time Borg's lightning legs had brought him to the net, had already bounced the ball back to Orantes's court.

In 1988 Pierre Paccard handed over the organisation of the event to two young ex-Davis Cup players: Dominique Bedel and Pascal Portes. At their initiative, the Philips Open joined the ATP Tour with the intention of becoming one of the prestigious opening tournaments at the start of the European clay court season. Juan Aguilera was this year's very gifted winner, thereby celebrating his comeback after five difficult years during which he had been plagued by injuries. Forget was the French representative in the final, having endured a three-hour semi-final against Andrei Cherkasov. But the most significant achievements probably came from the tall 19-year-old Swiss Marc Rosset, who beat Yannick Noah, and Fabrice Santoro, the diminutive French teenager who himself had put out Chesnokov, the winner in Monte Carlo the following week. Once again, new talents were born in Nice.

A jubilant Spaniard, Juan Aguilera raises his arms in triumph after beating Guy Forget.

KAL Cup Korea

By Craig Gabriel

Seoul, 16-22 April
Tournament Director: Moon-Il Kim

It has been said of Seoul, and indeed of all the Republic of Korea, that this is the awakening giant in the industrial world. So it should come as no surprise that this developing land of 40 million people hosts a world series event on the ATP Tour. Just eighteen months before, during the summer of 1988, Seoul had played host to only the second Olympic Games to be held in Asia. Those Games catapulted Seoul, the world's fifth largest city, into the forefront of global attention. People were talking about kim chi, Korean BBQ and shopping in It'aewon. Not too much has changed.

Tournament director Moon-Il Kim set up the event in the tennis stadium used at the Olympics. The surrounds were a lot quieter this time, almost eerie, as the high-rise apartment blocks from across the street, that was the Olympic Village, continue to look down over the walls on the action.

The KAL Cup was a success story for two players in particular, Alex Antonitsch from Austria and Australian Pat Cash, for it was they who contested the final, brought forward a day because severe weather had been forecast for what should have been finals day.

Another booming serve carries Austria's Alex Antonitsch to the title on the Olympic Stadium Centre Court in Seoul.

70

A big cheque and another doubles title for those prolific Canadians, Grant Connell and Glenn Michibata.

When Antonitsch started his run on the spring Asian circuit he thought it was going to be a 'nightmare'. Tokyo the week before was his first tournament, but he nearly didn't make it. He had forgotten to obtain an entry visa and only after some swift talking was he able to begin what was to become the most profitable run of his career. In Seoul he delivered his first winner's speech after defeating Cash 7-6, 6-3 and collected $20,160. 'I have never been so consistent to win a tournament before,' said Antonitsch. 'I have beaten Noah, Curren, Steeb and Sanchez, but I have never kept up that consistency through the whole tournament.'

For Cash it had been a remarkable effort. Just twelve months before to the week, in Tokyo, he had ruptured his Achilles tendon during a match against Bill Scanlon, and was totally out of tennis for nine months. He was given a wild card into the

'I have never been so consistent to win a tournament before,' says Alex Antonitsch.

qualifying at Seoul and surprised even himself by making the final. 'I did better than I expected,' he said. 'It is not often that a player comes through qualifying and reaches the final.' Cash came into the tournament ranked 590 and he wrote himself into the record books as the lowest-ranked player to reach a final.

The doubles title went to the Australian Open finalists Grant Connell and Glenn Michibata of Canada who defeated Australians Jason Stoltenberg and Todd Woodbridge 7-6, 6-4. Only Kelly Evernden and Nicolas Pereira managed to take a set off Connell and Michibata, who reached this year's Australian Open final. Stoltenberg and Woodbridge had a tougher task on their way to the final, needing three sets to beat seeds Kelly Jones and Robert Van't Hof, and Alex Antonitsch and Tom Nijssen in the semi-finals. It was an especially satisfying victory for Michibata's wife Angie, who is a native Korean.

Volvo Monte Carlo Open

By Richard Evans

Monte Carlo, 23-29 April
Tournament Director: Bernard Noat

Prince Albert of Monaco, who works hard to foster the principality's sporting image, hands over the cup to the new champion, Andrei Chesnokov.

On the very day that *Tass* announced that the Soviet economy was behaving like a bear with very little brain, Andrei Chesnokov dipped his hand very firmly into the honey pot at the Volvo Monte Carlo Open and came up with $125,000 for beating Thomas Muster 7-5, 6-3, 6-3. This sum alone will not solve President Gorbachev's economic crisis but it won't hinder it either. The Soviet Tennis Federation, which has done very nicely out of Chesnokov's sweat and toil in recent years, need not get too excited, however. Speaking on French television, Chesnokov said,

'No, I am not giving money to the Federation. Instead I will buy medicine for people who need.' It was fitting that the popular Russian should bring down the curtain on a highly successful week with a note of concern for his fellow man because this had been a recurring theme throughout seven days of cool but brilliant sunshine at the Monte Carlo Country Club - one of the most spectacularly beautiful tennis venues in the world. Players were seen to clasp each other warmly at the net after hard-fought encounters and even during matches the same spirit prevailed.

Horst Skoff overruled the umpire in Henri Leconte's favour while losing to the Frenchman in the quarter final while Boris Becker could hardly have reacted faster when Emilio Sanchez collapsed with what looked like a twisted ankle in the second set of their quarter final. Becker leapt over the net and raced to where Emilio was lying behind the baseline. Then the celebrated German ran over to the drinks container and brought back an ice pack for Sanchez. All this for an opponent who recovered sufficiently well to go on to win the match. Sanchez made a point of apologising to Becker afterwards, but Boris was not at all put out. 'I have had ankle problems myself and I know how bad they can be,' Becker said. 'Emilio and I are quite close and what I did was quite natural. No big deal.'

I am sure tournament director Bernard Noat appreciated this kind of spirit from athletes who, as ATP members, are all now honorary members of the Monte Carlo Country Club.

A spirit of good will and glasnost prevails as Chesnokov wins the Volvo Monte Carlo Open.

However, Noat was probably rather less pleased with the wholesale demise of the biggest names in a draw that saw none of the top six seeds reach the semi-finals.

Top seed Stefan Edberg, trying to make the switch from the cement of Toyko's Ariake Stadium to red clay, lost two tie-breakers to Spain's experienced Juan Aguilera in the third round while a happily rejuvenated Leconte dethroned the reigning champion Alberto Mancini before dismissing Andres Gomez and Skoff. Muster, another player who had undergone surgery in 1989, then overpowered him in the semi-final.

Nevertheless Leconte's performance offered wonderful entertainment for the huge crowds. So often Henri's play has been a question of much swash and no buckle. But a serious back operation and the need to mend a few fences with a less than loving French tennis public had convinced this flamboyant character of the need to buckle down to the task in hand.

The ATP Tour European Headquarters was opened just before the Monte Carlo Open got under way so former champions Manolo Orantes (extreme left) and Ilie Nastase (second from right) joined Stefan Edberg, Boris Becker Prince Albert and ATP Tour CEO Mark Miles for a little picture taking.

It was also a satisfying week for Muster. Despite missing too many forehands on big points against the relentless Chesnokov, the Austrian left-hander's victories over such tough clay court opposition as Martin Jaite, Jim Courier and Aguilera proved that he had recovered fully from his horrendous road accident in Miami just over a year before.

Chesnokov's win lifted him to a career-high of No. 12 on the ATP Tour computer, emphasising his claim to be regarded as the greatest Soviet player in history alongside the former Wimbledon finalist Alex Metreveli. Andrei, whose dreamy demeanour off court conceals a droll wit was, nonetheless, being serious when he dedicated his victory to his coach Tatiana Naoumko. 'I don't think I would have won if Tatiana had not been with me,' he said. 'She had me work very hard after I lost in Nice so I was well prepared here.'

In doubles Petr Korda had that wise old pro Tomas Smid alongside him during a week that saw them lose only one set before beating Andres Gomez and Javier Sanchez in the final. Back in 1978 I seem to remember finding Smid a partner called Peter Fleming for Monte Carlo and, not surprisingly, they won the title. Since then Smid has returned to win with Pavel Slozil in 1985 and Mark Woodforde in 1989. It is hard to keep a good man down.

The advent of the ATP Tour has had a special impact on tennis in Monte Carlo because the Tour's European headquarters is situated just across the street from the club in the Monte Carlo Sun building. It is there that the former French No. 1 Pierre Darmon heads a staff of more than a dozen full time employees who co-ordinate over forty ATP tournaments played each year in the European Zone. Like Darmon, ATP Marketing Director Zeljko Franulovic has been familiar with the beautiful red clay courts of the Country Club throughout his days as one of Europe's leading players, and this pair forged a direct link between the current modernisation of the professional game and Monte Carlo's long tradition as a centre for European tennis.

As Philippe Bouin relates in his report on the Nice Open, the English were very prominent in the organisation of the game on the Cote d'Azur in the twenties but by the time the first stone was laid for the majestic clubhouse in 1928, the strength of French tennis, personified by the Four Musketeers, was undeniable. Jean Borotra, Henri Cochet, Rene Lacoste, and Jacques Brugnon were amongst the first legends of the game to grace the tiered courts that overlook the glistening waters of the Mediterranean, and soon marble plaques were

The splendour of the Monte Carlo Country Club is captured in this aerial view, taken from the Menton side. The tower block on the right houses the European headquarters of the ATP Tour.

appearing on the clubhouse walls to commemorate winners of tournaments stretching back to the beginning of the century before the present facilities were built.

Now, thanks to the vision of Bernard Noat, today's travel-weary pros will have a home base at which to re-charge their batteries and fine-tune their games before heading out again on the world circuit. With over 30 ATP members resident in Monaco, the location could hardly be more convenient. The Monte Carlo Country Club has lost none of yesteryear's charm but is now firmly geared for the expanding future of a multi-million dollar sport. This is something that Jean Borotra and Rene Lacoste could barely have dreamed of in the those faraway days of flappers, Bugattis and foxtrots at tea time.

The Salem Open '90

By Leo Schlink

Hong Kong, 23-29 April
Tournament Directors: Lincoln Venancio, David Baukol

The career-threatening obstacles that had impeded Pat Cash for almost two years were authoritatively and inspirationally dismantled with his stunning victory in the $210,000 Salem Open at Victoria Park. In overwhelming aquiline Austrian Alex Antonitsch 6-3, 6-4 in a spirited final played in high humidity and draining heat, Cash registered his first tournament triumph since the South African Open at Johannesburg in 1987 - the same year, of course, the muscular Victorian had won Wimbledon - and his sixth title since 1981.

Capping a truly stellar return from the threshold of injury-induced retirement and a wretchedly barren rehabilitation, Cash combined with compatriot Wally Masur to win the doubles, 6-3, 6-3 against Kevin Curren and Joey Rive. For all of Cash's renowned athleticism, bullish desire and determination, such a scenario appeared distinctly fantastic during much of 1989 when he struggled to overcome a crippling Achilles tendon problem. There was also the not inconsiderable matter of mentally climbing a personal Everest - with no guarantees of success, only fear of failure and a professional's pride that dictated one must strive once more to compete with and against the best. In the afterglow of a heady dual triumph, Cash admitted the seeds of doubts that threatened to grow into debilitating impediments had played

strongly on his mind during a ten-month hiatus. 'When I first started training after the injury, there were some doubts,' the 25-year-old lawyer's son said. 'Any sportsman who goes through a bad patch experiences the same thing. You feel like throwing it in. It's been very, very tough and there's going to be a few ups and downs yet. I'm not putting any time limits on myself. Look at Wally Masur, he's playing his best tennis at 27.'

For those fortunate enough to see the Cash Phoenix rise in one of the world's best-appointed stadia - Victoria Park - there was overwhelming evidence that little had changed. Nevertheless, it was with some trepidation that the hero of two Australian Davis Cup victories learned that that the wily 32-year-old veteran, Kevin Curren, a former Wimbledon finalist, would be his first-round assignment. 'I expected to make a quick exit because I had to play Kevin in the first round,' Cash noted afterwards. A straight-sets victory, which came after three days of disruptive rain that had tested, but failed to defeat, the sparkling enthusiasm of tournament directors Lincoln Venancio and David Baukol provided Cash with the necessary incentive to roll through talented German Eric Jelen. The gritty Canadian Grant Connell was next, lifting his steady, if unspectacular, game to admirable levels as Emily Bendit, soon to become Emily Cash, watched on approvingly as great slabs of rust fell from Cash's favoured serve-volley approach. Then came another German, the redoubtable Patrick Kuhnen, whose first-set display, particularly on return and, to a lesser extent on service, was nothing short of outstanding in the semi-final round. Typically, Cash dug deep and eventually prevailed while a cramping Antonitsch clambered past resurgent Jonathan Canter in the bottom half of the draw. Cash's chance to avenge defeat at Seoul had come more quickly than was expected.

Victory was never simple. Forced to save break points in the third game of the first set, and again in the second and fourth games of the second set, Cash's *sang-froid* and capacity to respond were critical factors. Admitting to 'feeling almost dead', Antonitsch could not force the issue as Cash continued to unbalance the stocky right-hander with facile volleying and incisive ground strokes, particularly from the backhand wing. In the end, the stronger personality prevailed and one of the most exciting talents in tennis resurfaced, leaving the sport somewhat richer and less predictable.

A triumphant return to the victory stand for Pat Cash who had been sidelined for almost a year by a serious Achilles tendon injury.

XIX Grand Prix Villa de Madrid

By Pedro Hernandez

Madrid, 30 April-6 May
Tournament Directors: Manolo Santana

Three weeks after his second victory in Barcelona, the Ecuadorean Andres Gomez proved that Spain is very good for his tennis. Gomez, seeded No. 2, won at the Grand Prix Villa de Madrid after defeating the Swiss Marc Rosset 6-3, 7-6 in the final.

Gomez had enjoyed a great run on Spain's red clay courts, winning the tournament in Barcelona in both singles and doubles and then crowning his success in Madrid. 'I feel that my tennis is fresh. And I enjoy playing a lot, and that's very important,' Gomez said after his victory in Madrid. With his win over Rosset, Gomez climbed to the No. 7 spot on the ATP Tour computer singles ranking - his highest position since 22 July 1985.

'We think that Madrid has every chance of regaining the position it held during the last decade.'

As in Barcelona, victory did not come easily to Gomez. He had no problems in the opening round against the Canadian Andrew Sznajder, but the Uruguayan Diego Perez and the Dutchman Mark Koevermans forced him to a third set. 'I was very confident all week, and I always regain my concentration in the third set,' said Gomez.

Eleven Spanish players got a place in the main draw, but Sergi Bruguera had to withdraw due to a gastro-intestinal disorder that caused him to lose five kilos. Bruguera and Emilio Sanchez were favourites with the public, but it was Emilio's brother, Javier, who took a place in the semi-finals. Emilio himself was knocked out of the tournament very early. In the biggest surprise of the week, Marc Rosset beat Emilio 4-6, 6-4, 6-4 in the second round. 'I missed many chances, and Rosset's serve was very good. He broke my rhythm every second,' said Emilio. Rosset grew in confidence, reaching the final and shattering the illusions of the Spaniards. After beating Emilio, Rosset stopped lucky-loser Marco Aurelio Gorriz in the quarter finals and Javier Sanchez in the semi-finals. 'I was certain I was going to beat Rosset and save the honour of my family, but he played better than I did,' said Javier after his match against the tall teenager.

Although they did not know each other personally, the Spaniard Juan Carlos Baguena and the Italian Omar Camporese both knew enough about playing doubles to defeat Andres

Gomez and Javier Sanchez 6-4, 3-6, 6-3 and to end the week as champions. They thus prevented Gomez from having a mirror tournament to that in Barcelona.

Tournament director Manolo Santana was delighted at the end of the week. 'Even though we lost Bruguera and Emilio in three days, the crowds grew bigger throughout the week.

We are very confident about the future. Our sponsors are happy with the tournament, and we think that Madrid has every chance of regaining the position it held during the last decade,' said Santana, who was assisted by Edison Mandarino, the former Brazilian Davis Cup star. Over the years, Mandarino has helped Santana run numerous events, both in Madrid and down on Costa del Sol where Manolo is director of his own club at Punte Romano.

The ever-popular Andres Gomez triumphed in Madrid; it was his second singles title in Spain within the space of a month and helped lay the foundations for his triumph in Paris.

BMW Open

By Alain Deflassieux

Munich, 30 April-6 May
Tournament Director: Lothar Lanz

Germany is the country in Europe where people work the most. The reward for their work is a high standard of living and an economic wealth which is the envy of all. In the BMW Open, two of the most courageous players on the tour, Karel Novacek and Thomas Muster, were rewarded for their hard work. The biggest reward went to Novacek, who defeated Muster 6-4, 6-2 to claim the title and a cheque for $32,400.

After reaching the final in Monte Carlo, Muster had the right to be tired when he had to face Guillermo Perez-Roldan in the first round. But he played with his usual determination and won in two sets, setting the tone for the rest of the tournament. On the other side of the court, Novacek destroyed his opponents in succession, and only lost one set, inadvertently, to Jonas Svensson in the semi-finals. 'There is really nothing one can do against an opponent who plays this well with such a heavy ball,' said Muster, honestly. 'From the beginning of the match I felt that I was hitting the ball well and that I could therefore play with confidence.'

The night before in a semi-final match against Petr Korda, Muster succeeded in breaking Korda's game by playing high balls on his backhand to win 6-3, 6-1. But in Munich, Korda

and his incomparable talents were more fragile than those of his fellow Czech, Novacek. It was the Czechs above all who succeeded on the courts of Iphitos Stadium as they eliminated the three highest-seeded players: Martin Strelba repeated his victory of last year by beating Stefan Edberg (6-4, 6-1) in the second round, then had to retire with pains in his side at 4-3 against Muster; Novacek upset the No. 2 seed Aaron Krickstein (6-2, 7-6) in the second round; and Korda won against Michael Chang (6-7, 7-5, 7-6) in the first round after Chang had accepted a wildcard to play in this particular tournament.

A disappointed Yannick Noah, whom the spectators had been waiting to see, was ousted in the first round by German Jens Woehrmann. Noah left quickly to train with Dennis Ralston before playing Rome. Meanwhile, Novacek, on the other hand, decided against a short break and left Munich the night of his victory in order to drive by car to Hamburg. When asked if he planned to play every week until the year's end, he replied: 'Of course I will play every week. I am fascinated with the organisation of the ATP Tour, so why should I stop now?' Novacek did eventually take a short rest several months later but, by the time he left Munich, the big Czech had played all fifteen weeks of the year. Even then it constituted a heavy workload, but Novacek's attitude only proved that the revised ATP Tour computer ranking system, which had switched to a 'best of fourteen' format, was doing precisely what it had been designed for - namely to encourage everyone to play more. The old system, whereby a player's total points from all tournaments played was divided by fourteen, had tended to penalise those willing to put themselves on the line week after week. By the end of the year, Novacek, with 31 tournaments on the computer, was still able to maintain a ranking of 35 - higher than would have been possible under the old system.

In the doubles Tomas Smid and Petr Korda reached the final for the second consecutive week but this time the title remained beyond their grasp. The emerging German duo of Udo Riglewski and Michael Stich won the second doubles title of their career as a pair - with a straight set win over the Czechs, which completed an impressive week's play in front of an appreciative Bavarian crowd. Only the experienced pair of Kevin Curren and Laurie Warder had managed to take a set off them and it came as no surprise when Riglewski and Stich proved to be one of the most consistent teams of the year.

Epson Singapore Super Tennis

By Craig Gabriel

Singapore, 30 April-6 May
Tournament Director: Graeme Plum

Singapore has been referred to as the 'most amazing island on earth'. It never ceases to surprise with its exotic melee of race, religion, customs and culture. Singapore is Asia-in-cameo. From strange Chinese potions, to spotless streets and five star hotels, Singapore is something else. Everything is more than civilised in Singapore. Whether one wants to shop for gadgetry or the finest silks, this place is a haven for the consumer and plenty of international tennis players took advantage of the situation.

Australian promoter Graeme Plum saw the potential for men's tennis in this tropical paradise, where east meets west, and has created a relaxed week of professional tennis at the Kallang Tennis Centre on Stadium Road. 'I'm sure that all tennis fans in Singapore were delighted that the Epson Singapore Super Tennis was played there once again,' said Plum, 'the support of Epson and the Singapore Tourist Promotion Board has been tremendous and very appreciated.'

Singapore is situated just a few miles north of the Equator which makes for very hot, humid days. With that in mind it really is not feasible for matches to start before the late afternoon, which gave the players and all those connected with the tournament plenty of time to explore this unique

and fascinating island-state. There was time to visit magnificent temples, taste the national drink the 'Singapore Sling' or experiment with foods that would tempt the taste buds of any gourmet.

The Epson Singapore Super Tennis has been on the circuit for just two years but there has only been one player who has won the singles, American Kelly Jones. In 1990, however, it was Australians that dominated the finals and held down every place bar that one. Jones defeated 20-year-old Richard Fromberg, who was playing his first career final, and the American admitted after the match that he was fighting two battles on court in retaining his title 6-4, 2-6, 7-6. The first was Fromberg, one of the outstanding prospects in Australian tennis with his big serve and long reach and the second was the stifling humidity. 'This is really amazing,' said Jones, who thought he would pass out during the match. '1989 was a major victory, but this is just great ... this is personal. I went out and played the best match I could and won.'

There were moments when I didn't think I could go on,' said the former Pepperdine University star after the match. 'The conditions were taking their toll and I was starting to feel twinges of cramp. I think I just played my best match, even feeling tired.' In fact during the presentation

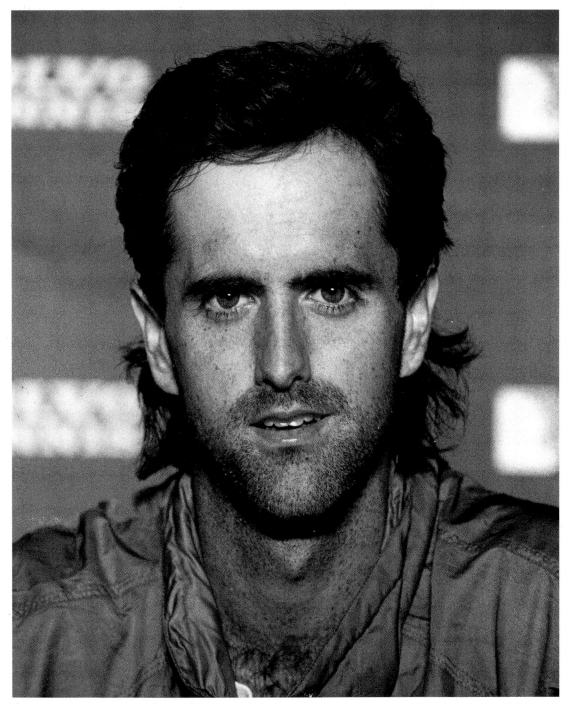

Former Pepperdine University star, Kelly Jones revealed his liking for Singapore by retaining the title he won in 1989. Strangely, Jones, after seven years on the tour, has yet to win a tournament anywhere else.

ceremony Jones had to leave the court because his body was so fatigued that he was close to cramping severely all over. Fromberg, who had caused early upsets by beating top seed Wally Masur and fifth seed Dan Goldie on his way to the final, admitted he did not play as well as he had done most of the week. His serve let him down and he was just a bit unlucky in the tie-break. As he said afterwards, 'I just wasn't good enough on the right points.'

In the doubles Mark Kratzmann won his fourth doubles title of the year with as many partners, thus proving himself to be one of the most versatile doubles players on the Tour. The blonde left-hander this time teamed with Jason Stoltenberg to dismiss Brad Drewett, one of the most senior players on the Tour, and Todd Woodbridge, still one of the most junior. The score was a lop-sided 6-1, 6-0 and it gave Stoltenberg the first doubles title of his career.

BMW German Open

By Ulrich Kaiser

Hamburg, 7-13 May
Tournament Director: Gunter Sanders

It was late in the evening when Juan Aguilera arrived in Hamburg. It took a while for him to find one of the cars that was used for transporting the players. 'What is your name? Juan who?' asked the driver who finally agreed to take him to the town. They drove to a hotel near the station, where players who had to qualify were staying. Juan Aguilera didn't get out. He told the driver he wanted to go direct to the Club an der Alster.

There he met the tournament director, Gunter Sanders, who had good news for him. Because some players had cried off, Aguilera got a direct entry - and he could move into a better hotel.

Nine days later nobody in Hamburg was asking 'Juan who?' For the 28-year-old Spaniard not only won the German Open, he played in the final at times like a tennis teacher

The corporate view - sponsored boxes enable patrons to enjoy the tennis over a meal and behind glass.

A floral tribute and an elegant piece of silver for Juan Aguilera who re-claimed the title he first won in 1984.

showing a pupil how to play. And what hurt the German spectators most was that the pupil was Boris Becker. Juan Aguilera led the German 6-1, 6-0, 5-0 in the final. Not since his junior days had Becker looked so helpless. Never had he been so far from his dream of finally winning a tournament on clay and never had a 'nobody' outclassed the world number two so completely. However, just as people were getting ready for an early prize-giving it began to rain and the players had a break of more than an hour. When they came back, Becker reached 6-6 in the third set and only lost the tie break 8-10. Perhaps he might have managed to turn the whole match round if he had won that third set. But there is no perhaps in tennis.

It was also a grotesque situation for Juan Aguilera. He wasn't a 'nobody' in Hamburg at all - he had *won* there in 1984, when he was ranked seventh in the world. But then came the setbacks - his father died, he was continually injured and he plummeted to around number 300 in the rankings. The life of a professional tennis player, which so many people dream about, is not always easy. In 1984 the world was Aguilera's oyster: he was young, and rising up the rankings to be among the best in the world seemed quite natural to him. Today he is mature and knows that nothing should be taken for granted.

It wasn't only Juan Aguilera who had changed over this period. The home of the German Open had also altered. The old Club an der Alster is now one of the most renowned tournament venues in Europe. The new centre court has expanded a bit each year. There is almost no more room for spectators - the last days of the tournament are always completely sold out months before. Above the clubhouse there is now a restaurant from which you can watch the matches. They have even installed a loudspeaker system which enables you to hear the sound of the racquets, balls, players and umpires as clearly as if you were sitting beside the court: tennis in stereo. The club is now the headquarters of the German Tennis Federation. There is a new building which houses all the Federation's administration since it moved from Hanover, its home for the past 30 years.

There is no comparison between the image of a modern organisation which is starting the 1990s with more than 2 million registered members, and the sleepy club where the German international championships used to be played. The last relic of that time, the clubhouse, has now also disappeared. This was a reminder of the times when players like the 'Tennis-Baron' Gottfried von Cramm were playing, when Wilhelm Bungert won, and when the word 'money' was almost an obscenity. Then, 25 or 30 years ago, the press centre was in the cellar and consisted of one room with a telephone, a table and a few chairs.

A bird's eye view of the newly re-modelled Club an der Alster, one of the best venues in Europe.

The advantage of this location was that the changing rooms were just next door and if one needed a quick interview, one could go into the shower and ask the new or old champion what he though of his opponent's service. These were romantic tennis times indeed - ask Rod Laver, Manuel Santana or John Newcombe, who met his wife here. Times when an amateur winner at Wimbledon had a discreet cheque passed to him; when the world rankings, compiled by Lance Tingay, appeared in the London *Daily Telegraph* and were accepted by everybody; and when no computers existed. It was what Germans call 'gemütlich' - completely cosy. But is was also less honest than today when the winner collects the cheque openly after the match or, to put it more explicitly, today players have to pay taxes.

Of course Juan Aguilera and Boris Becker know nothing about all of this, and if one tells them about it they look a little dubious. They have a strong organisation behind them and a strict schedule in front of them. A never-ending circus sorts out the best from the not quite so good.

US Men's Clay Court Championships

By Ken Burger

Kiawah Island, 7-13 May
Tournament Director: Michael J. Burns

Although clay court tennis has become the wandering gypsy of the American tour, it still serves well as a launching pad for future stars. And even a major hurricane couldn't keep it down. For the 1990 US Men's Clay Court Championships were just one of the things tossed around when Hurricane Hugo ripped the South Carolina coastline in the fall of 1989. Among the hardest hit was Wild Dunes Resort on the Isle of Palms near Charleston which took the full force of the 135-mile-per-hour winds. In the aftermath, the small barrier island and the resort were laid waste. Wild Dunes, which had proudly hosted the Clay Courts for the previous years would take at least a year to recover. And the fate of its tennis tournament was unknown, lost somewhere in the debris and destruction of the storm. But the South Carolina Lowcountry is not a place that gives up easily. People were determined to clean up and get on with life as quickly as possible. And part of that resolve meant keeping things that belonged to them before the storm.

Enter Kiawah Island Resort, another beautiful island resort just 20 miles south-west of Wild Dunes that had been spared the brunt of the hurricane's killer winds. In an unprecedented move among business competitors, Kiawah offered to take the tournament until Wild Dunes could recover and reclaim it. There was scepticism about the motives, but one would have to live through something like Hugo to know the kind of co-operation it takes to survive. In only a few months, the arrangements were made to hold the Clay Courts at Kiawah. It took a massive corporate commitment and the combined forces of untold numbers of volunteers from both resort communities to make it happen. But it happened, less than eight months after the storm, while millions of South Carolinians were still struggling to rebuild their lives, the Clay Courts came off without a hitch.

Although the Clay Courts had only been part of the Lowcountry sports scene for two years, it had already earned the reputation as a launching pad for new stars in the game. In 1988 it catapulted Andre Agassi into the stratosphere of the tennis world. In 1989, Jay Berger emerged as its champion and moved steadily upwards into the game's top ten. As the 1990 Clay Courts began, the tournament was sprinkled with many names most people didn't recognise. But the beauty of this tournament is the short distance between anonymity and stardom. And those who follow the game know this is where the stars are born. And they have learned to pay little heed to rankings and seedings. For this is a tournament where reputation is almost an invitation to disaster. In the first few days,

In only his second full professional year on the circuit, the promising young talent David Wheaton won his first career title at Kiawah Island.

top seeds fall like overripe fruit. That's because measuring talent at this level is not an exact science and because clay is a great equaliser. The results, therefore, can be both surprising and exciting.

The 1990 Clay Courts would be no different. After a week of preliminary matches and amazing upsets, the only seeded player left standing at Kiawah was David Wheaton, a tall, lanky stroker from Lake Minnetonka, Minn., ranked 48th in the world at the time. His opponent in the Sunday finals was equally unexpected - Mark Kaplan, a 22-year-old South African who came in ranked 168th in the world, but had eliminated two seeded players (Dan Goldie and Malivai Washington) as well as Tim Wilkinson and David Pate to gain the finals. In typical clay court fashion, it was the first ATP Tour final for both men. On that hot, muggy day in May, the 20-year-old Wheaton proved the better of the two as he took the title with a 6-4, 6-4 win. But it was not easy. Wheaton, who later would make a strong showing in the US Open, learned something that day. He learned to win. With victory within his grasp, up 5-2 in the second set, Wheaton double faulted at this crucial juncture and gave new life to his opponent. Although he eventually sealed the victory, he found out that championship points come harder than others. 'I was nervous because of the whole situation,' Wheaton said of his mistakes. 'I was serving for the match, for my first tour win.' Kaplan narrowed the gap by winning the next two games, but Wheaton overcame his nerves to close him out and claim the $28,370 winner's cheque.

With that, America had crowned another star on the rise. But, more importantly, it was a victory for thousands who had overcome the worst disaster of a century and pulled through it together.

XLVII Campionati Internazionali d'Italia

By Bud Collins

Rome, 14-20 May
Tournament Director: Franco Bartoni

The English may have invented tennis but the Italians humanised it. That thought infiltrated my neural mush shortly after I walked into Il Foro Italico, in 1973, and it hasn't departed. Maybe the Italian Open isn't as outrageous or uproarious as it used to be - 'no robberies any more,' says the star Italian telecaster, Rino Tommasi - but I still wouldn't miss it. As the world's No. 5 tournament (I suppose I'll get some arguments on that score), the Italian has an edge on the Grand Slams in setting, weather and spirit. The only thing they've done wrong, lately, was to install floodlights. Copying Flushing Meadow on anything is a mistake. Anyhow, nights in Rome are meant for romantic dinners - not tennis, no matter how good.

Yes, those robberies mentioned by Rino Tommasi have vanished now that officiating and supervision have been standardised worldwide. But, you must remember, the startling local thefts were made only in the name of patriotism. If you weren't playing against an Italian, you had no worries.

One of the beneficiaries, of course, was the noblest Roman of them all (at least of the open era), Adriano Panatta, champion in 1976, finalist, to Bjorn Borg, in 1978, and contender several years. Panatta, now the Italian Davis Cup captain, was sleek, brilliant, exciting, a volleyer of such range that he was known as the Goaltender. He didn't need much help ... ah, but a point here and there from the line judges didn't hurt. But the most aid and comfort came from the adoring crowds, who chanted AD-RIANO...AD-RIANO... punctuated by handclaps. Constantly they screamed, 'Dai! Dai!' (come on) urging him forward. Often they danced in the aisles as an offertory to the god Adriano. The customers were also naughty on his behalf, pelting his foes with coins and insults, causing two tough ones - Harold Solomon in '76 and Jose Higueras in '79 - to walk out, so enraged that they defaulted.

Until the next Panatta comes along - soon, I hope - the demonstrations for a homeland hero, or heroine, will be more subdued. And they can forget the coins, please. 'Romans,' chides Gianni Clerici, Tommasi's TV sidekick, 'are cheap. Why don't they make spitballs out of 1000 lire notes and throw them instead of low denomination metal?'

Occasionally the cops have been called when the 'tifosi' - fans - got overly boisterous. But nobody ever was hurt, and, if I may be subjective, the clamorous scenes made for good stories. Even as the centre of turmoil while he was winning the 1973 title, Ilie Nastase retained a sense

Andrei Chesnokov, who defeated Thomas Muster in the final of Monte Carlo, found the positions reversed in Rome.

of humour. The Pasta Kid, Paolo Bertolucci, and his countrymen were giving Nastase a hard time in the semis. Somewhat carried away by nationalism, a customer pitched a mineral water bottle in Nastase's direction. Picking it from the court Ilie muttered disdainfully, 'Water! Why doesn't the cretino have enough taste to throw champagne?' Australian John Newcombe, the champion of 1969, loved the Roman congregations that have rattled innumerable other foreigners such as Ivan Lendl. Newc knew how to handle them, with big moustachioed grin regardless of the situations - and they loved him back.

Should you wonder if the dictator, Benito Mussolini, who plunged Italy disastrously into World War II, ever did anything worthwhile, the answer is yes. An enthusiastic hacker, Mussolini had a hand in designing the Foro's handsome tennis playpen, to which his country's international championships shifted from Milan in 1936. Sometimes you can see the aged coach, Mario Belardinelli, in a good seat. Belardinelli was Mussolini's private instructor, and remembers being under orders to hit balls only to the boss's forehand. Even an absolute dictator couldn't appropriate a backhand for himself.

Laid out at the foot of the verdant hill, Monte Mario, close to the River Tiber, the sunken, salmon-tinted clay courts are hemmed in by magnificent landscaping and stunning architecture and statuary. Guarded by huge figures of athletes and soldiers, the principal court, Campo Centrale, has lost some of its original grandeur through the increased popularity of the game. Auxiliary stands rise above Mussolini's marble amphitheatre, blocking some of the statues, but raising capacity to about 11,000.

Tall hedges, sandwiching the backstops, separate the outer courts which are crowned by a green halo of Respighian pines of Rome. Roses entwine many of the trunks, vying in beauty with an extraordinary number of ever-present and stylish signorinas. Seasoned observers find spots at the crest of the terraced seats where they can watch four matches simultaneously.

Not long ago, I despaired as the Italian Open, snagging on an organisational crisis, seemed to be falling apart. The leading men were avoiding Rome. Imagine that? Skipping the Eternal City? But they did. Some days the place was so quiet you could hear the birds sing. The female pros had been, unwisely, evicted, and were forced to stage their Open in the hinterlands. I kept attending. It was still Rome, still the Foro, still so jovial, if no longer as consequential. Fortunately a marketing man named Cino Marchese was able to move into collaboration with the Italian Federation to work a revival. 'Rome has been down many times over the centuries,' said the scholarly Marchese, 'but if we could survive the barbarians, the wars, and much more, we would overcome the tennis slump.'

Sagely he brought the women back so that his city would have a tennis fortnight, like the Slams. Women first week, men second. Both did better than ever. Soon enough the crowds and enthusiasm returned to the Foro, along with the names. Ivan Lendl won in 1986 and 1988, Mats Wilander in 1987. Courts were added, and a new stadium planned.

In May sunshine those rising young Europeans, Monica Seles and Thomas Muster, made it a 1990 fortnight for masterful 'mancini' (left-handers). Yugoslav Seles beat Martina Navratilova, 6-1, 6-1, and the 10th seeded Austrian Muster struck down the 8th seeded Russian, Andrei Chesnokov, 6-1, 6-3, 6-1.

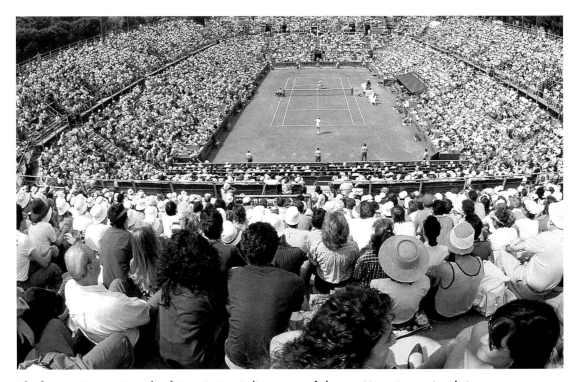

The famous Campo Centrale of Rome's Foro Italico, scene of Thomas Muster's emotional victory.

Thomas Muster came to Rome last year on crutches and vowed to win the tournament in 1990. He did exactly that.

By the third round, the unprecedented Nos. 1-2 seeds - that is, Americans - Brad Gilbert and Aaron Krickstein were gone, done in by defending champ Alberto Mancini and Guy Forget respectively. Chesnokov eroded Mancini in the quarters, 7-6, 6-0, and Emilio Sanchez by a matter of two points, 6-7, 6-4, 7-6. Meanwhile Muster had to run a gauntlet of his kind, lefties Forget in the quarters, 6-2, 3-6, 6-3, and Andres Gomez (holder of two match points) in the semis, 5-7, 6-4, 7-6. Only once before, in 1966, had southpaws swept: Briton Ann Haydon-Jones and Aussie Tony Roche.

Another lefty, Rod Laver, showed in 1962 that it was possible not only to win the French and Wimbledon in the same year, but, for foreplay, the Italian too. Laver was alone among the five Grand Slammers in tacking Rome onto the other four.

For some followers of the game, the ideal would be a personal Grand Slam, taking in Melbourne, Paris, Wimbledon and New York. Very nice. But if I had to choose, it would be the Old World Triple: Rome, Paris and the Big W. And always - Arrivederci, Roma.

93

Yugoslav Open

By Caroline Hutton

Umag, 14-20 May
Tournament Director: Slavko Rasberger

The Yugoslav Open, a new tournament on the 1990 ATP Tour, firmly established both the host country and its players on the world tennis map. Umag, south-west of Trieste on the Adriatic coast, hosted the event in the brand new Stella Maris Tennis Centre, which had been finished just weeks prior to the 14 May start. The facility, designed by local architect Marjan Videc, received universal approval from players and fans alike. Tournament director Slavko Rasberger ensured that the week ran smoothly and that the only dramas were to be on court.

The 32-strong field was headed by the then number one Yugoslav, Goran Prpic, who had been awarded the 1989 'Comeback Player of the Year' by the ATP Tour after recovering from the severe leg injury which had kept him off the courts for two years. Although still forced to wear a leg brace, by the end of 1989 he had climbed nearly 200 places back up the ATP Tour rankings. Prpic's promising namesake, Ivanisevic, was seeded number two. Prpic struggled in his first round match against Eduardo Masso but eased past Diego Perez and Roberto Azar for a place in the final four, setting up a semi-final clash with the unseeded Horacio De La Pena, an Argentinian clay court specialist In the other half of the draw Andrei Cherkasov, the fifth seed, had advanced to the

semis without dropping a set. But standing between the young Soviet and the final was the 18-year-old Ivanisevic. The second seed had faced three clay court experts on his route into the semi-finals, Nicolas Pereira, Fernando Luna and Tarik Benhabiles, but all had been swept aside by the power of the Ivanisevic serve, which allows him to play a fast serve-and-volley game even on slow red clay. Cherkasov, a baseliner, was to come up against the same barrage. After facing 18 Ivanisevic aces, the shell-shocked teenager, beaten in three sets, left the court and commented 'I've played against Becker before but I've never been aced like that in my life'. In the other semi-final Prpic held his nerve in a tight match with the wiry De La Pena to secure a 7-6, 7-6 win and an all Yugoslav final.

It was a tough and emotional battle, both players fighting for the honour of winning in this, the first major tennis tournament held in their own country. Rain delays had forced Ivanisevic to play three matches the previous day and even for an athlete in prime condition the strain on his mind and body showed during the final. Prpic quickly used this to his advantage, taking the first set 6-3. Ivanisevic retaliated and, with his devastating serve warmed up, levelled the match taking the second set 6-4. In the decider the more experienced Prpic let his younger opponent make the mistakes. His consistency earned him the break of serve he needed to triumph 6-3, 4-6, 6-4. 'I played a steadier game,' admitted the Yugoslav Open champion, 'I tried to stay calm on the big points.'

The Czechoslovakian duo, Vojtech Flegl and Daniel Vacek, having qualified for their place in the doubles draw, stormed into the finals where they defeated the Soviet team of Cherkasov and Andrei Olhovisky 6-4, 6-4. It was the first time they'd ever played on the ATP Tour.

The Yugoslav Open was an important new event on the ATP Tour that helped shape the future of many of the participating players. The following week, in Dusseldorf, the two protagonists of Umag, Prpic and Ivanisevic, helped take Yugoslavia to a surprise victory in the World Team Cup, while the doubles champions repeated their success at Prague and San Marino later in the year. Without doubt the confidence gained at the 1990 Yugoslav Open played a large part in these successes and in many more that were to be claimed by those who first excelled in Umag.

Goran Prpic, 1989 'Comeback Player of the Year', proved just how far he had come back in winning his first career title at the Yugoslav Open in Umag.

Peugeot ATP World Team Cup

By Meg Donovan

Düsseldorf, 21-27 May
Tournament Director: Horst Klosterkemper

Each year the Düsseldorf Rochusclub, situated on a nature reserve at Grafenberg Woods, plays exceptional host to a week-long 'Open Air' Festival when the Peugeot World Team Cup comes to town. The annual competition, the only team event on the ATP Tour calendar, is traditionally a showcase for some of the premier tennis talent in the world. The year 1990 proved no exception, as nine of the world's top 25 players led their national squads into battle on the red clay of the Rochusclub, where Horst Klosterkemper, a stalwart supporter of the ATP Tour since the early days, runs one of the best organised and best supported events of the year.

The 1990 line-up featured a good mix of old and new including former champions Spain, Argentina, the United States, Sweden and Germany. Joining them in the race for the title were three newcomers to World Team Cup competition - Yugoslavia, Austria and the USSR. The veteran of the group was the Spanish team, composed of Jordi Arrese, Sergi Bruguera and Tomas Carbonell, which had competed in all but one of the previous 13 World Team Cup competitions. The United States, led by squad member Brad Gilbert, Jim Courier, Ken Flach and Robert Seguso, entered the tournament with more Düsseldorf wins than any other participant, having come away as

champion in 1982, 1984 and 1985, and runner-up in 1987 and 1988. The German team consisting of Boris Becker, Carl-Uwe Steeb, Eric Jelen and Michael Stich, were the local favourites after winning their first-ever World Team Cup title just one year ago. Sweden, a winner here in 1988 and runner-up two years before, was ably represented by team members Stefan Edberg, Jonas Svensson and Magnus Gustafsson. Clay-court specialists Argentina, led by Alberto Mancini, Martin Jaite, Javier Frana and Christian Miniussi, had proved in their Buenos Aires Davis Cup win over Germany that they were always a force to be reckoned with, and were eager to repeat the feat of defeating the Germans in Germany itself. And finally, the 'novices' in this year's competition - Yugoslavia (Goran Prpic, Goran Ivanisevic and Slobodan Zivojinovic), Austria (Thomas Muster, Horst Skoff, Thomas Buckmayer and Oliver Fuchs) and the USSR (Andrei Cherkasov, Alexander Volkov, Andrei Olhovskiy and Vladimir Gabrichidze) which rounded out the field.

In the end, before a capacity crowd of 7800 on stadium court, it was one of the newcomers, the first-year squad from Yugoslavia, which emerged victorious. Led by the striking performance of 26-year-old Goran Prpic, they defeated the US by a margin of 2-1 to earn their first-ever World

Team Cup title. Prpic, who only one week earlier in Umag had earned the first championship title of his tennis career, was outstanding in leading the relative unknowns to victory over more highly rated teams. The Zagreb native completed the tournament with an unblemished 4-0 mark in singles and threw in two doubles victories for good measure. Prpic, the ATP's 'Comeback Player of the Year' in 1989, polished off No. 13 Martin Jaite, No. 53 Alex Antonitsch, the world's No. 2 player Stefan Edberg and No. 4 Brad Gilbert en route to Yugoslavia's historic win. Only a final round doubles loss with partner Slobodan Zivojinovic to the American pair Ken Flach and Robert Seguso marred an otherwise perfect record.

Yugoslavia advanced to the finals by virtue of its top standing in the tournament's Blue Group thanks to wins over Argentina, Sweden and Austria. The United States knocked off Spain, the USSR and Germany in similar fashion to set up the final confrontation. Prpic made short work of US Team Captain Gilbert to set the stage for teammate Goran Ivanisevic's 3-6, 7-5, 6-1 upset win over Jim Courier in three sets to clinch the title for Yugoslavia. It was the only loss of the week for Courier. Ivanisevic, then ranked 53 in the world, but destined to rise to No. 9 by years end, enjoyed the team cammarderie. 'I'm very happy,' noted the giant 18-year-old from Split. 'No one expected us to win here as first-time qualifiers.'

Goran Prpic, Goran Ivanisevic and Slobodan Zivojinovic with their hands full after taking Yugoslavia to victory in the Peugeot World Team Cup.

Murrati-Time Internazionali di Tennis '90

By George Rubenstein

Bologna, 21-27 May
Tournament Director: Franco Bartoni

Normally this charming Northern Italian city gets more plaudits for its culinary and cultural masterpieces than athletic excellence, but during the week of 21 May the courts of orange clay were taken over by the artisans of tennis. After the excitement of Foro Italico, it's difficult to sustain the same level of tennis over an additional week. But with the allure of the French Open as the light to seek, many players were trying to get their games together before the trek to Paris. They got a peek at some of the young stars in development, as Richard Fromberg emerged victorious to earn his first ATP Tour title, when he defeated another young thoroughbred on the circuit, Marc Rosset in a third-set tie-breaker to earn his best career mark at 27 on the ATP Tour computer. Fromberg exclaimed 'It's unbelievable. It's the happiest time in my life. Bologna will always have a special meaning for me. It will have a warm place in my heart. The win will definitely help me for the rest of the year.'

Sports abounded as there were the Italian basketball league finals, the Maratona di Bologna (a 42 km race through the historic city), Giro d'Italia (cycling tour of Italy), pre-World Cup hype in calcio (European football), as Bologna was to be one of the venues for the month-long tournament. There was even a visit from Alpine skiing World Champion Alberto Tomba at the courts. It seemed unreal that everything was able to occur simultaneously, but the quality of the tennis was able to stand up against everything else in store for the Italian public.

Education is one of the strong points of the city, as the university is the oldest in Europe, and Fromberg indeed learned a bit during the week of his first win. He emerged as the highest ranked Australian, something that really didn't faze or unnerve him during his quest for the crown in Bologna. 'It's something that I'm not really worried or give much attention to,' the tall right-hander said. 'I play my tennis, and I hope for the best results.'

Celebrations were also in store for some of the major contributors to Italian tennis. Matchball Magazine celebrated its twentieth anniversary: Rino Tommasi was given the Best Writer award, Angelo Tonelli received an award for Best Tennis Photographer and Adriano Panatta was chosen as Best Italian Tennis Player over the two decade period.

In doubles play Argentinian Gustavo Luza and German Udo Riglewski joined as a unit for the first time and they were rewarded with the title, defeating France's Jerome Potier and USA's Jim

Australia's great hope for the future, Richard Fromberg, came out of the tournament as his country's No. 1 player.

Pugh. Riglewski commented, 'Our styles work well together. Luza fights all the time and carried us in the second set. He really helped bring my game back.' Luza elaborated, 'It's nice to play with a talented partner. I'm proud of this victory.' The duo won all five tie-breakers during the week, including one during the final.

Now about that grand voyage to Paris: lower your expectations. Due to a general airport strike in Bologna on Sunday night and an air traffic controller's strike in Paris on Monday morning, there was no way that the singles and doubles finalists could arrive in Paris on Monday morning -

unless they drove. Jerome and Sophie Potier had Fromberg stretch out his full 6-foot, 5-inch frame in their back seat. It took ten hours or so, but Ms. Potier was destined for a family reunion. He sister, Nathalie, plays an integral role for the French Federation during Roland Garros in the player services area. In fact, Nathalie had been providing her brethren in Bologna with the qualifying results from Paris over the weekend. Jim Pugh, meanwhile, purchased six pizzas from a restaurant around the corner from the Grand Hotel in Bologna and munched his way through them to keep himself awake during the journey to the French captial.

The taxi drivers apart, there are worse places than Paris to spend a fortnight in early summer. As you stroll along the Bois de Boulogne, all seems right with the world: the horse chestnuts are in bloom, oysters are in season, the Beaujolais is served chilled, and the chocolate mousse still comes up in a great earthenware tub at *Au Clocher du Village* in the nearby rue Verderet. When the Olympian gods play tennis, they surely do it at Roland Garros, sliding around the terracotta clay under azure skies with the tip of the Eiffel Tower just visible above the woods.

Torben Ulrich, the bearded, pony-tailed Dane who played clarinet in a St-Germain jazz club by night and teasing drop-shots by day, would arrive at the front gates in the Sixties on a ramshackle bike, racquets tied to his back with string. Today's players arrive at the French Open in chauffeured limos, but little else has been allowed to change.

If the abiding image of Wimbledon is that of virginia creeper, umbrellas and the smell of wet barathea, Roland Garros is fashion, fun and glamour. If Flushing Meadow is Hawaiian

Jonas Svensson, another elegant Swede, reached his second semi-final in three years at Roland Garros.

shirts and Bermuda shorts, Roland Garros is Saint-Laurent and Versace. Jacques Chirac is a regular, as are Belmondo and Montand. Celebrity-spotting is de rigueur. Every day a lengthy castlist of famous faces is sighted amidst the crowd. On the first Monday this year Princess Stephanie was rumoured to be here, or was it simply another beautiful Parisian shop girl? On Wednesday it was Mickey Rourke, or perhaps he has a twin? On Friday it was Madonna, or maybe Maradona. Trouble is, at Roland Garros *everyone* looks as though he or she should be famous. At every table a pouting Bardot, all plunging neckline and rising hemline, is to be found gazing raptly across a Kir Royale at a Michael Jackson lookalike. The French schoolchildren have long since solved the dilemma; the trick is to collect everyone's photograph or autograph before sorting the celebrities from the nonentities later.

It can prove a humbling experience for anyone but the bona fide star. During one typical mad scramble around la Porte Suzanne Lenglan on the first morning, a moderately well-known American player found himself autographing a 20-franc note thrust under his nose. Less than an hour later, he discovered the same banknote amongst his change after buying an ice-cream. French history, it seems, is littered with fallen heroes; Robespierre went to the guillotine, Napoleon went into exile, and Michael Chang, who became the youngest man ever to win a Grand Slam title when he triumphed in Paris in 1989, surrendered his Roland Garros crown when he bowed before Davis Cup team-mate Andre Agassi.

Dubbed A'Ghastly by sniffy haute couture traditionalists, Agassi wore his graffiti-inspired ensemble all the way to the final where, pleasingly if somewhat unexpectedly, he met Ecuador's greatest sporting personality, Andres Gomez. This surely was the classic example of the generation gap. Gomez belongs to a bygone age. A huge, kindly bear,

The longer you wait, the sweeter the triumph.
The veteran Gomez from Ecuador, gives the cup a kiss.

the Ecuadorian is blessed with a touch as fine as gossamer; a delicate brushstroke here, a gentle dab there, another dab of colour in the corner, he takes a delight in covering the whole canvas in subtle tones. If Gomez is a graduate of the academy for the performing arts, Agassi is a brash high-school kid who attends classes in grey denim. Gomez's palette comprises only pastel shades. Agassi works in spray paint: shocking pink, fluorescent orange, fire-engine red. The exaggeration of his shots a perfect accompaniment to his garish outfits.

To the delight of all France (except, perhaps, the teenage division which regards Agassi as a heroically rebellious figure) Gomez won the 60th French championships at the age of 30. Gomez smiled fit to burst, wife Anna-Maria tearfully hugged 24-month-old Juan Andres Jnr., and the Guayquil ambassador to France jumped up and down in the front row while waving the biggest Ecuadorian flag in all Paris ... (well, everyone assumed that that was what it was). But, as ever, the last word goes to Ilie Nastase who, noting the return of the mini-skirt, summed up Paris 1990 thus: 'If you don't like what you see at Roland Garros, you're too old to be looking.'

The Stella Artois Grass Court Championship

By Ron Atkin

London, 11-17 June
Tournament Director: Clive Bernstein

On the face of it, the Stella Artois Championships at Queen's Club, London, were a vindication of Ivan Lendl's meticulous preparations for his most determined challenge yet to lift the Wimbledon title. He won the Stella crown for the second successive year, beating his grass court nemesis Boris Becker for the first time on turf, and did not drop a set all week.

Yet, less than three weeks later after crashing out of Wimbledon to Stefan Edberg at the semi-final stage, Lendl would say that he left his best tennis on the lawns of Queen's Club. In other words, he had peaked too soon in his unending pursuit of the one Grand Slam crown which continues to elude him. Once he had polished off Becker 6-3, 6-2 in the 73-minute final, Lendl termed it 'easily the best week I've had on grass for putting five matches together like that'. He was in fine form, as John McEnroe agreed after his 6-2, 6-4 defeat by Lendl in the semi-finals. 'He gets an A plus for preparation,' said McEnroe. 'I get about a D.' It was McEnroe's first ATP Tour event since Philadelphia in February and the man who had won the Queen's title four times was comprehensively outplayed, his lack of preparation for Wimbledon was exposed and the price he paid the following week was a first-round defeat.

A famous old club house, now with a re-modelled forecourt, all dressed up in its Stella Artois colours.

Her Royal Highness The Duchess of Gloucester, flanked by tournament director Clive Bernstein, hands over the giant trophy to Ivan Lendl, while Boris Becker seems suddenly allergic to grass.

The semi-finals - Lendl vs McEnroe and Becker vs Edberg - were as close to a dream tournament as you could wish. Tournament director Clive Bernstein, who has suffered some traumatic moments in previous years trying to assemble a high-quality field for his high-quality event which comes immediately after the French Open, was a happy man this year. The weather stayed dry, if not particularly bright, and the crowds rolled in. The week's attendance was a record 46,000, testimony to the organisers' ability to present a field containing Lendl and four previous Wimbledon champions.

One of them, Pat Cash, crashed out in the first round to Paul Chamberlin but the others - Becker, Edberg and McEnroe - came safely through to the semi-finals, even though McEnroe's progress was shaky in the extreme. He dropped a set to Ramesh Krishnan, came within two points of defeat against Veli Paloheimo (who was himself foot-faulted at match point), and was a break point away from trailing 5-3 in the third set against Richard Fromberg. Pete Sampras, who would go on to win in Manchester the following week, was knocked out by Fromberg in the third round, losing a tight third set 10-8.

Lendl's win over Becker in the final was his first over the German since 1987 and his first-ever in their four meetings on grass. Becker had his chance early on when he missed five break points in the second game. After that he was closed out by Lendl who yielded only ten more points on serve in the match, four of them on double faults as he pressed to keep Becker on the defensive with deep serving. The victory left Lendl praising the perfect state of the Queen's Club centre court and sent him into Wimbledon in a dangerously confident mood.

Since its inception more than a century ago as the London Grass Court championships, this event has grown steadily in importance as a testing ground for Wimbledon. The names of some of its winners are as historic as Queen's Club itself - people like Jean Borotra and Fred Perry, great players who went on to leave their imprint at Wimbledon. The event's huge trophy has been lifted by such as Lew Hoad and other Australians who dominated in the post-war years and Lendl was only the latest in a line of world number ones to add his name to the list of one of the greatest of that diminishing genre - grass court championships.

The Continental Grass Court Championships

By Bertold Palthe

Rosmalen, 11-17 June
Tournament Director: Wim Buitendijk

It takes some courage to organise a grass-court tournament in Holland the same week that Queen's opens its doors to the best grass-court players in the world. Queen's, the famous English grass-court tournament that takes place immediately before Wimbledon, with its tradition - not to mention the amount of prize money it has to offer - was sure of a strong field of players. But Rosmalen's tournament director Wim Buitendijk has guts, and, with far less financial backing than the organisers of the Queen's tournament, was able to attract players of the calibre of Yannick Noah, Miloslav Mecir, Jakob Hlasek, Jim Grabb, Alexander Volkov, Paul Haarhuis and Amos Mansdorf. It is no exaggeration to state that the courts at Rosmalen, a tiny village in The Netherlands, some 70 miles from Amsterdam, are now the setting for the most important grass-court tournament on the European mainland: The Continental Grass Court Championships. As a warm-up for Wimbledon it was an undoubted success. Both Rosmalen's finalists played fine tennis on Wimbledon's grass courts - Mandsdorf being the only player to take Edberg to five sets before the Swede faced Becker in the final there.

> *Yannick Noah was one of the first stars to declare his interest in playing at Rosmalen*

Signs direct spectators to the Car Museum, called Autotron, which is hidden in the woods. Buitendijk chose the grounds of this open-air museum, where the old Model-T Fords contrast with a super high-tech house of the future, as the setting for the first Continental Grass Court Championships. There Miloslav Mecir could indulge his passion for fishing, and other players were able to visit the museum between matches if they wanted to. Spare-time activities abounded for the players - boredom was banished. The whole atmosphere was relaxed; no stressed journalists trailing players to find out about the latest lines in rackets and shoes. Instead, they sat in the sun, chatting with players or linesmen and, of course, watching the matches.

Five years after the first exhibition matches were fought on the continental grass, Rosmalen became part of the official circuit when it joined the ATP Tour as a World Series event in 1990. Yannick Noah was one of the first star names to declare his interest in playing at Rosmalen in order to prepare himself for Wimbledon. But, with players coming from the slow European clay court events,

Head Wimbledon groundsman Jim Thorn flew over to Rosmalen to inspect a continental phenomenon - tennis courts made of grass! His expert opinion was much appreciated.

the first-round matches had some some surprising results in store for the crowds. Noah, for instance, who had done quite well in the French Open, surprised everybody by losing to Milan Srejber. Miloslav Mecir was also ousted from the tournament after his first match, as was the Dutch favourite Paul Haarhuis.

But there were positive surprises too. Volkov and Mansdorf, in particular, seemed to find their natural footing on the Dutch grass.
The tournament saw an outsider performing well in Patrick McEnroe, famous as a doubles player and now trying to make a name for himself in singles. In the semi-final he lost to Alexander Volkov in an exciting three-set match. Overall victory in the championship went to Amos Mansdorf from Israel - who was unstinting in his praise for the organisation of the event. He beat Volkov in straight sets in the final.

Another surprise came when top seeds Patrick McEnroe and Jim Grabb were defeated by Jakob Hlasek and Michael Stich in doubles. Although Hlasek and Stich had never played together before, their reputation and respective rankings put them as the No. 2 seeds. Hlasek said he played one of the best doubles matches in his life thanks to the great time he had enjoyed that week. The 22,000 spectators who showed up during the week all admired the courts. Groundsman Tijn Walraven proudly showed them to anybody who expressed the slightest sign of interest: 'It's beautiful here, so the courts have to be top class.' And they were, as players like Patrick McEnroe, Jakob Hlasek, Alexander Volkov and tournament's winner Amos Mansdorf all stressed. Even Wimbledon groundsman Jim Thorn came over to have a closer look at Walraven's work. And he too had to admit that Walraven had done something special.

105

Torneo Internazionale Città di Firenze

By Ubaldo Scanagatta

Florence, 11-17 June
Tournament Director: Sergio Palmieri

One of my favourite pastimes at the US Open is joking with USTA Publisher Harold Ziman about Rino Tommasi's predictions on 'Morning Line', the daily programme edited by Ziman, or 'Big Zee' as we call him. Harold threatens laughingly to fire Rino, and I - also laughing - volunteer for the job. Big Zee ends up saying, 'I should really think about it!' Well, I should most definitely have been fired if I had not been editing my own, similar, programme for the eighteenth year (Open Era) of the Florence tournament. This is the tournament that has been held at the aristocratic *Circolo Tennis Firenze* deep inside the gorgeous Cascine Park since 1898.

If anyone had thought to ask the famous Las Vegas bookmaker Jimmy the Greek what the odds were of a Florence Open final between Lawson Duncan (ranked 138) and Magnus Larsson (ranked 124), he would almost certainly have offered something in the order of 200 to 1. Never in seventeen years had none of the top eight seeds of a 32-player draw failed to reach the semi-finals. Two of the favourites withdrew at the very last minute: Andrei Chesnokov had a swollen hand thanks to a motorbike accident in Paris - he couldn't even sign autographs. Goran Ivanisevic, after defeating Boris Becker at Roland Garros, suddenly decided that he would prefer to practice on grass for Wimbledon. None the less, many clay-court specialists featured in the main draw. Sergio Palmieri (who took over from me as Tournament Director recently) was pleased to have Perez-Roldan, Skoff, Mancini, Davin, J. Sanchez, Agenor, Bruguera and Mattar among the top seeds, a very good field indeed for a $250,000 event. In the end, it was Magnus Larsson, class of 1970, who captured the singles title after coming through the qualifying rounds. The tall, blond Swede (with a two-handed backhand) defeated, in succession, Dennhardt, Ostoja, Jabali, Mattar, Koevermans, Perez-Roldan, Rahunen (who had knocked out Mancini and Javier Sanchez) before beating Duncan 6-7, 7-5, 6-0.

So, my simple advice to all those wishing to attend the Cassa Risparmio Open next year is: 'Play the qualifying competition even if you are able to enter the main draw!' Last June, I worked out that out of about 1400 Grand Prix (now ATP Tour) tournaments since 1970, only fourteen had gone to qualifiers - and of these, four were played in Florence. The smell of the lime trees at the Cascine must play funny tricks! It was in Florence in 1978 that Jose Luis Clerc earned the first title ever as a qualifier. History repeated itself in 1985 with Sergio Casal winning the title, and again in 1989 with Horacio de la Pena. Now Magnus Larsson has joined them in pulling of the same trick.

Magnus Larsson was the only qualifier in 1990 to win a tournament. The clay court of his victory is reflected in his trophy.

Four of the eight seeds were out after the first round: Skoff (2) lost to Camporese, Bruguera (7) to Luna (unbelievable for a player who had defeated Edberg at Roland Garros only 15 days before). Two more fell out in the next rounds: Mancini (3) to Rahunen, Agenor (6) to Carbonell. The remaining favourites were out in the quarter finals: Perez-Roldan (1) lost to Larsson, J. Sanchez (5) to Rahunen, nicknamed 'the Finnish Chang', because of his skinny figure, good temper, and his smooth, 'hit on the rise' two-handed backhand. Of the four semi-finalists, Larsson (124) and Rahunen (78) were in the top half of the draw, while Duncan (138) and Camporese (77) were in the bottom half. Camporese was the highest ranked player, and the only Italian remaining in the main draw after Pistolesi lost in the early rounds. The organisers, already facing competition for publicity from the events of the Soccer World Cup, desperately hoped to see the Bologna-born player reach the final. But the boy from Asheville, North Carolina, made it through thanks to fresh reserves and greater experience of the courts at Florence - this being his third straight semi-final in the Fine Arts capital of the world. Only Paolo Bertolucci (do you remember 'Pasta Kid' as Bud Collins used to call him?) had done better than Duncan by reaching five consecutive semi-finals, while 'Speedy Gonzales' Raul Ramirez had done as well by making it to three semi-finals. Duncan knocked out Camporese 6-2, 6-3, and Larsson beat Rahunen 6-4, 6-4 in an 'all Nordic' semi-final.

Before the final match, I wrote that there was a definite probability of a three-set win by Duncan because of his 0-5 W-L record in final rounds, while Larsson was a first-time finalist. I also added: 'The future, however, is for Larsson.' In the event, Duncan won the first set, stretched out to reach Larsson at five games all in the second, then collapsed, not winning a single game, stunned by the Swede's cannonball serves and punishing forehand winners. I now imagine Big Zee and Rino smiling at me. But no matter - the worst that could happen would be to see Duncan break into the top ten and Larsson crash down past the 500th spot.

IP Cup

By Anna Legnani

Genoa, 18-24 June
Tournament Director: Sergio Palmieri

Genoa was back with a place on the world tennis scene this year when it staged the IP Cup, the first major tournament there in almost a decade. At the beginning of this century, the Ligurian capital was one of the poles of world tennis activity, but since then it has slowly lost its supremacy, with international tournaments and exhibitions played there only periodically at long intervals in time. The recovery of Genoa in the international tennis circuit began in 1987, when the city hosted a Satellite which developed into a Challenger over the next two years, and finally matured into an ATP Tour event in 1990 with $225,000 prize money on offer.

Some of the world's top clay courters gathered in the Valletta Cambiaso club, set among luxuriant vegetation in a residential area of the city. A week of intense matches saw Frenchman Tarik Benhabiles and Haitian Ronald Agenor promoted to the championship round. Both players had once ranked as high as 22 in the world lists, but had subsequently slipped back in the rankings. With two such fighters the final could only be a showdown, and Agenor finally prevailed 3-6, 6-4, 6-3. For the second time in his career, Agenor, son of a Haitian diplomat, had the pleasure of unfolding the national flag he always carries in his luggage and seeing it flying on the pennant during the victory ceremony.

Clear blue skies over the centre court of Agenor's triumph.

Thomas Carbonell and Udo Riglewski took the doubles title with a 7-6, 7-6 win over the surprising young Italians Cristiano Caratti and Federico Mordegan. Riglewski had started his singles competition here in Genoa by serving top seed Martin Jaite off the court, but was eliminated in the quarters by Cedric Pioline, who had also taken out his doubles partner in the first round. Genoa was one of the cities hosting the Football World Cup, and the tournament suffered a little competition with the from other great sports event. Cases of the 'football fever' ravaging Italy were manifest even at the IP Cup as players crowded in front of the TV set in the lounge to watch the World Cup matches. For fans who could afford to spare a little time in their intense sporting week, Genoa proved a mine of cultural activities and offered an ideal base for excursions to the myriad charming seaside villages and towns on the Italian Riviera.

Ronald Agenor powered his way to the title in Genoa showing an improvement in form that was carried through later in the year when he won the Berlin Open.

Direct Line Insurance Manchester Open

By Reginald Brace

Manchester, 18-23 June
Tournament Director: John Feaver

A week which began in the time honoured Manchester tradition of duckboards, sopping grass and glowering clouds ended with a sell-out finals day and Pete Sampras emphasising his status as one of the game's rising talents. Eighteen minutes play on the first day of the Direct Line Insurance Manchester Open was a glum way to celebrate the debut of the Northern Club on the ATP tour or indeed on any major circuit. But in the end the week became a marvellous tournament for its hard working hosts.

The World Series event, which cost £350,000 to stage, did not materialise without herculean efforts by the club's committee: they had no sooner announced the event in January than an arsonist started a fire which destroyed the clubhouse. A gutted pavilion was replaced by temporary accommodation as the club refused to let the blaze interfere with restoring pride and prestige to its courts in the Manchester suburb of Didsbury. 'It all amounts to a new dawn for the Northern,' said Jim Cochrane, club president. 'We see it as a return of top quality tennis to the North of England. This is an old club and we have had great players here, from Sedgman and Hoad to Connors, McEnroe and Edberg. But we have never achieved the standing which the ATP Tour gives us.' Although the rain gave way to equally frustrating winds, nothing could diminish the series of workmanlike performances

by the unflappable Sampras. Weather delays meant the young Californian had to win his quarter final and semi-final on one breezy day. After beating Kelly Evernden 6-3, 7-6 he accounted for Eric Jelen with a good deal more difficulty 6-7, 6-4, 6-4.

Eric Jelen of Germany plays well in England; last year he won in Bristol and here he stretches himself into the semi-finals.

The USA flag waves Pete Sampras onto his second ATP Tour title of the year at Manchester.

Meanwhile the Israeli left-hander Gilad Bloom was reaching the final by a similarly demanding route, defeating the Kelly Jones 3-6, 7-5, 6-1 and Britain's huskily competitive Nick Brown 6-4, 7-6. Bloom produced the quote of the week: 'I was so bad in practice when I arrived here I was ready to go home and never see grass again. Suddenly I'm in the final and a grass court specialist!' Bloom - who had been match point down to Jim Pugh in a first round contest which represented his first appearance on grass for two years - put up a nimble and combative challenge before losing 7-6, 7-6 to Sampras after missing set points in both sets. He was impressed by his conqueror: 'There wasn't too much between us but he concentrated better on the big points. He gets a high percentage of first serves in, is quick at the net and has fast hands. He could beat anybody on a fast court.'

Sampras accepts compliments like that, not only from Bloom but people like Fred Perry and Charlie Pasarell, with a pleasing mixture of modesty and confidence. 'It's nice to hear these things but I don't want to dwell on them and start thinking I'm great. The main thing is to take one match at a time, just go out and try to win. And keep enjoying it. Yes, I really do enjoy playing tennis.'

Manchester applauded the technical purity of his style and the inbuilt virtue of calmness under pressure which no coaching manual can impart. Predictions that Sampras would make an impact at Wimbledon foundered when he lost to Christo van Rensburg in the opening round. But the glory of the US Open was not far away, confirming that the Northern had been watching an emerging star.

111

Wimbledon

By John Parsons

London, 25 June-8 July
Tournament Director: Richard Grier

Lunch in a fashionable restaurant in Paris laid the foundations for Stefan Edberg, the 1988 champion, to regain the most coveted Wimbledon men's singles crown 25 days later. The tete-a-tete between Edberg and his coach, Tony Pickard, was no cosy chat during a relaxing break from Roland Garros - but an inquest on the Swede's crushing first-round defeat in the French Open by the wily clay court Spaniard, Sergi Bruguera. Pickard, in the role of coroner, not only bluntly analysed the cause of the previous day's disaster but laid down regulations to try to prevent something similar happening at Wimbledon. For all that, as Edberg received the gleaming Wimbledon trophy for his 6-2, 6-2, 3-6, 3-6, 6-4 victory, it also encompassed one of the great match mysteries of the year.

Just how much Edberg's triumph on that sunny, slightly gusty Sunday afternoon in London SW19 was due to the firm resolve he demonstrated under acute pressure in the closing stages of the final - and how much was due to the two reckless volleys which Boris Becker delivered when poised to take what would surely have been a title-winning 4-1 lead in the final set - will never be known for sure.

All one can say is that it was a final full of twists and turns, as Edberg took the first two sets but then seemed all but beaten before the German offered him a lifeline. This he grabbed with style, to provide a thrilling climax to the Championships fortnight.

Determination and concentration took the unseeded Ivanisevic into his first Grand Slam semi-final.

112

It is doubtful whether even Agatha Christie could have dreamed up so tantalising and devious a plot as the one which unfolded in that final set. Serving at 1-2, Edberg reached 40-15 uneventfully enough but worrying double faults had been creeping in, and there were more to come. In fact, at break point down, Edberg struck a second serve which flew at least six feet over the top of the net and landed just inside the baseline. It left Becker to serve at 3-1 but he not only promptly started what was to be the most crazily decisive game of the final with another double fault, but at 30-30 missed two of the sort of volleys - netting one and hitting wide off the other - which one normally expects him to kill with his eyes closed. Suddenly Edberg was back in the match and he capitalised on the German's unintentional generosity four games later by breaking him again to lead 5-4 with a devastating lob. He dropped to his knees with a rare display of public emotion. The despair he must have been feeling a few games earlier had been replaced by elation and renewed excitement. There would be no further hiccups. He confidently struck a service winner on his second match point to take a title worth far more in stature than the $400,000 prize.

Partly because of England's summer success in the World Cup, which kept people glued to their television sets and partly because of crowd safety restrictions (since eased) that limited the number of matches one could wander round and see, the overall attendance at Wimbledon dropped by 55,000 to 350,000. Not that there was any lack of action and surprises in the first week, with only nine of the original 16 seeds surviving to the second round. Among those who departed so prematurely were Pete Sampras, tipped by Don Budge and Fred Perry as a future Wimbledon champion, and John McEnroe.

Sampras went down 7-6, 7-5, 7-6 to Christo Van Rensburg ... McEnroe to fellow American, Derrick Rostagno, 7-5, 6-4, 6-4. 'Ten years ago I dreamed about beating

Wimbledon's champion, Stefan Edberg with a winning smile and tennis' most coveted trophy.

McEnroe on the Centre Court at Wimbledon but never really believed it would happen,' said Rostagno, whose good looks and often classical groundstrokes make him welcome wherever he plays.

The only unseeded semi-finalist was Goran Ivanisevic, whose 26 aces more than compensated for his 12 double faults during his rapid-fire quarter-final against Kevin Curren. Becker, after being lucky not to fall two sets behind against the Yugoslav teenager said he had just beaten 'a possible future Wimbledon winner'. 'He has the hardest and best serve of anyone I've ever played, reminding me of a 17-year-old who played like that five years ago,' added the German, fondly and impishly recalling his first Wimbledon triumph in 1985.

Rick Leach and Jim Pugh described their triumph in the men's doubles as 'a child-hood dream come true for both of us'. A remarkable feature of their success was that in both the quarter finals and then the final against Piet Aldrich and Danie Visser they won eventually on tie-breakers.

Rado Swiss Open

By Jurg Vogel

Gstaad, 9-15 July
Tournament Director: Jacques H. Hermenjat

As the champagne in the glasses threatened to boil and the snow on the nearby glaciers melted, the result was 'Caramba! Martin Jaite'. In the best of five final of one of the toughest clay court tournaments of the ATP Tour (cut-off No. 61), played under a merciless sun, the Argentinian snatched away the title from Spanish talent Sergi Bruguera. 'My legs were tired,' said the Spaniard after reaching his first ever final. Twenty-five-year-old Jaite was already a happy man when he arrived in Gstaad; the week of the Rado Swiss Open he had moved into the top ten for the first time in his career. Jaite's victory was the latest episode in the 'Argentinian Connection' with Switzerland, Guillermo Vilas having won this title in 1974 and 1978 and Jose-Luis Clerc in 1982.

The population of the chalet village of Gstaad (2400 inhabitants) increased seventeen-fold for a week of world-class tennis. The 40,811 tennis fans produced a new spectator record for the sixth year running. On five days the centre court in Gstaad, close to the language border between German- and French-speaking Switzerland, was completely sold out. Two of the seven members of the Swiss Federal Council were present. In addition there were 66 hours of television coverage shown throughout Europe in 30 different countries in seven languages. Top-seeded Andres

Gomez, winner of the French Open, was less successful against his adversaries than Roger Moore, English actor and Gstaad Tennis Supporter, used to be in the role of James Bond. Gomez, the left-

Martin Jaite clocked up his eleventh career title with a win over Sergi Bruguera in the final at Gstaad.

Mountain greenery surrounds the idyllic seeting of the Rado Swiss Open's centre court.

hander was eliminated in the second round by Ronald Agenor after giving away five match points. On the other hand, the Ecuardorian thus found time to take a helicopter trip to the magnificent Diablerets Glacier at an altitude of 3100 metres.

Marc Rosset, the new Swiss sledgehammer, found the diet of 'Spanish paella' only partly to his taste - victory over Emilio Sanchez after saving two match points - then defeat by Sergi Bruguera in the semi-final at his first appearance in Gstaad. 'The sky is the limit,' wrote Heinz Gunthardt, Switzerland's long-time tennis ambassador, in an article about the highly talented play of banker's son Rosset.

The quality of the competitors in Gstaad gave rise to another premiere: it was the only event with a draw of 32 on the 1990 ATP Tour in which all eight seeds reached the second round. The depth of talent at the tournament was also underlined by the fact that none of the four qualifiers (Ostoja, Pescosolido, de la Pena and Suk) managed to advance to the second round. Two new faces in Gstaad, Andrei Chesnokov and

Jim Courier, in spite of stumbling in the quarter finals, were enthusiastic about being able to play aggressive tennis on a fast court at an altitude of 1052 metres. In his duel with Jaite, Courier had a chance to serve for the match at 5-4 in the second set - but the South American broke back and succeeded in turning the match around for a 3-6, 7-6 6-4 win.

For the second time since 1986, the doubles title went to the top seeded Spanish pair, Emilio Sanchez and Sergio Casal, who defeated Omar Camporese and Javier Sanchez 6-3, 3-6, 7-5 for their 26th career title. 'They're eager to play every time they step out onto the court,' said their long time coach Pato Alvarez.

Sanchez, who has played in Gstaad regularly since 1986, is extremely popular in the Bernese Oberland. After lightly 'caressing' a Porsche 911 with the official car placed at his disposal by tournament director 'Kobi' Hermenjat, Sanchez left a note with his apologies and phone number under the windscreen wiper - fair play on and off the court.

Swedish Open

By Bjorn Hellberg

Bastad, 9-15 July
Tournament Director: Thomas Karlberg

Lanky Australian Richard Fromberg, 20, deservedly took the first prize of $32,400 in the Swedish Open at Bastad, but it was Mats Wilander who stole much of the attention. Wilander, a three-time winner of the Swedish Open, made his comeback after an absence of more than four months. And, considering the long 'holiday' from tennis, Wilander's return was impressive. After winning his first test, 6-0, 6-3, over Johan Anderson (the young Australian born in Sweden), Wilander then lost a thriller to Uruguayan Marcelo Filippini, who won the title in 1988. 'After losing at Indian Wells in the beginning of March, I didn't touch a racquet for several weeks,' admitted Wilander. 'I started to practise shortly before the Swedish Open, and now I think it's fun to play again,' he added.

Surprisingly, Wilander's neighbour from Vaxjo, Magnus Larsson, already a winner this year in Florence in June, played with great confidence all week with one exception: the first 20 minutes of the final against Fromberg. Larsson lost the first five games and later admitted, 'I was a bit nervous stepping on the court with 4500 spectators, but when I won my first game, I started to play much better.' Fromberg and Larsson, both with strong serves and powerful forehands, lifted their level of play in the second set. Larsson even held set point on his

opponent at 5-3 in the second set. Fromberg survived the scare and later won the match 6-2, 7-6 when he thundered an untouchable forehand in the middle of the court on his second match point. Fromberg, with the win, is now the highest ranking Australian on the ATP Tour computer, as he jumped to number 27 in singles. 'I will remember this victory for the rest of my life,' said Fromberg. 'I like it here at Bastad since it reminds me of my home in Tasmania, and I certainly hope to be back next year.'

In the doubles Ronnie Bathman and Rikard Bergh won their first title of 1990, defeating fellow Swede Jan Gunnarsson and West German Udo Riglewski 6-1, 6-4.

Tennis has been played at Båstad on the Swedish west coast since the 1880s. And immediately after the First World War regular competition started in this picturesque seaside village. The King, Gustaf V, had a great influence on the tennis in Sweden in general and at Bastad in particular. In fact, he played a lot of tournaments himself (in doubles) and became the reason for a change of surface. Once, during a match, the grand monarch fell on the hardcourt and scratched his knuckles. Soon afterwards, Båstad switched to clay courts - and that surface is still in use today.

In 1948, the tournament at Bastad gained the status of International Championships of Sweden. The first Champions to be celebrated on the centre court were Eric Sturgoss of South Africa and the German-born Hilde Krahwinkel-Sperling of Denmark. Twenty-two years later, the name of the event changed to the Swedish Open. With Australian Dick Crealy as a surprise winner, this was the fourth oldest Grand Prix tournament (only the British Hardcourt at Bournemouth, the French Open at Paris and Wimbledon were on the Grand Prix circuit earlier). Tournament director, Thomas Karlberg, has big ideas for the future: 'We intend to increase the tournament, but to be able to achieve that goal, we need a more international flavour in the stadium and its surroundings. And that we will get!'

Volvo Tennis/Hall of Fame Championships

By George Rubenstein

Newport, RI, 9-15 July
Tournament Director: Mark L. Stenning

Newport, Rhode Island, a sea-faring town, is the headquarters of the International Tennis Hall of Fame, a lovingly kept storage house for some of the game's historic treasures. The America's Cup has been a fixture in the community for nearly 100 years as challenge after challenge has been waged off these shores, primarily by the United States, Britain and Australia, duelling to be the fastest at sea.

The Hall of Fame, as an institution, does not go back as far as that although the game's history does, of course, and every year new pages are added as famous names join the honour roll. This year there were two inductees, Jan Kodes of Czechoslovakia, a powerful champion at Stade Roland Garros in 1970 and 1971 and now tournament director in Prague and Joseph Cullman III, the former chairman of the board of Philip Morris and the man whose foresight enabled the Virginia Slims sponsorship to launch an independent women's tour back in the early Seventies. Kodes and Cullman took the number of Hall of Famers to 151.

It was also a monumental week for Pieter Aldrich, known more for his doubles prowess as member of the world's premier tandem with Danie Visser. This was his 40th career singles participation, his first final, and then, his first title. He became the first unseeded player to win the tournament

since Vijay Amritraj, ATP Tour Board President, pulled the trick in 1984. Aldrich explained the emotions and situation behind his 7-6, 1-6, 6-1 triumph over Darren Cahill. 'I feel great inside. I hardly missed any first serves, even though I had a little trouble with my arm, and I played with a really loose racquet. I just tried to take one match at a time. The first set was the key (tie-break won

Doubles specialist Pieter Aldrich proved to be a serious threat in singles too when he won in Newport.

Australian Darren Cahill enjoyed his finest singles performance for two years as runner-up to Aldrich.

by Aldrich 12-10), and the longer the tie-break went on, the more of a mental advantage it would be to be the winner. That may be where I've made my biggest adjustment - in my mental game. I love the setting here, and I was really able to relax.'

Aldrich was returning from Wimbledon, where he and Visser had a tremendous run, losing in three tie-break sets to Rick Leach and Jim Pugh. However, neither team in Newport was treated with the fanfare and patronage normally bestowed on great champions. They were bounced

in third set tie-breakers. Aldrich-Visser were defeated by the eventual champions, Cahill and Mark Kratzmann, in the semi-finals, and Leach-Pugh were edged in the second round by the young South African duo of Wayne Ferreira-Piet Norval. Cahill-Kratzmann won their second title of the year, Kratzmann his sixth of 1990, having achieved this with four different partners. Kratzmann felt they were on a mission to show they were for real. 'We didn't do well at the French or Wimbledon, and we were out to prove something to ourselves. We feel we're the best Australian doubles team.'

Mercedes Cup

By Judith Elian

Stuttgart, 16-22 July
Tournament Director: Bernard Nusch

I can win the tournament,' predicted Goran Ivanisevic at the beginning of the Mercedes Cup in Stuttgart. 'If I continue to serve well on this clay, which seems rather quick, there is no reason for me to lose. Anyway, I don't fear anybody.'

The tournament took place - let us not forget - just over a week after the Wimbledon championships, where the young Yugoslav - then under 19 years old - had gone through to the semi-finals. There he was leading by two sets before losing in five to Boris Becker, who considers this match as the best he has played during the whole season. Nevertheless, Ivanisevic confirmed his confident prediction by the end of the week in Stuttgart.

> *'In two years time, I'll be number one,' declared the 19-year-old Yugoslav after his first career title.*

After the withdrawal at the last moment of Ivan Lendl (injured), the eight seeds of the 48-man draw were led by the 30-year-old French Open champion Andres Gomez; Thomas Muster took the second seeding while Emilio Sanchez, Martin Jaite, Andrei Chesnokov, Jim Courier, Juan Aguilera and Guy Forget followed hot on their heels.

Gomez, still 'recovering' from the emotions of winning at Roland Garros, lost - after leading 4-2 in the final set - to Horst Skoff, in the round of 16. Skoff's fellow countryman Muster, the No. 2 seed, was forced to retire in the same round, in the third set of his match against Germany's Eric Jelen because of the injury to his right arm which he sustained the week before at the Austrian National Championships. Among the main contenders, Martin Jaite went out early, beaten by the big server Karel Novacek; Chesnokov could not do much against a very sharp Henri Leconte; Courier was eliminated by the evergreen clay court player Marcello Filippini; and Aguilera could not prevent an eager Masur from advancing to the round of 16.

During a perfect cloudless summer week on the beautiful green hill where the Weissenhof Club is situated, two of the most spectacular (and, incidentally, left-handed) players on the circuit - Leconte and Ivanisevic - advanced to the semi-finals. Leconte, eager to prove himself after disappearing in the second round at Wimbledon, quickly became the public's favourite, with his

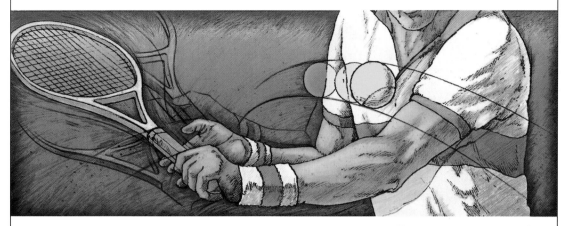

74. Internationales
Weissenhof-Turnier

Mercedes-Cup

14.–22. 7. 1990

1.000.000 US $
Championship-
ATP Tour TURNIER

Tennisclub Weissenhof e.V.
Parlerstr. 102–110, 7000 Stuttgart 1

antics and sportsmanlike behaviour. The 8000 spectators who filled the Centre Court every day were effectively rooting for the Frenchman more than his own public in Paris.

Leconte played two good matches to beat - one after the other - the Russians Chesnokov and Andrei Cherkasov. Unfortunately for him, the Frenchman did not have enough stamina to defeat the solid Argentine Guillermo Perez-Roldan in the semis. With temperatures of up to 50 degrees Celsius, Perez-Roldan won - after two hours and 10 minutes of a very even match - by seven points to five in the tie-break of the last set. Earlier, at 5-4, 40-15 on his serve in that same set, Leconte had

had two match points. He missed one backhand volley on the first, and Perez-Roldan hit a stunning forehand passing shot along the line to save the second. Sportsmanlike, Leconte applauded the shot. The match went down to almost nothing,' commented the Argentinian player afterwards. 'My passing shot could have been in or out. If it had been out, Leconte would have been in the finals rather than me ...'

Goran Ivanisevic, the other spectacular player, went all the way. After beating Javier Sanchez, Wally Masur (with great difficulty) and Eric Jelen, the young Yugoslav defeated Emilio Sanchez - without much effort in the semis.

Jumping for joy. Goran Ivanisevic wins his first career title in Stuttgart.

The second of four doubles titles on the 1990 ATP Tour for South Africans Danie Visser and Pieter Aldrich pictured here with tournament director Bernard Nusch.

On a hot and sunny Sunday afternoon, the young Yugoslav had to fight for three hours and 2 minutes to win beat Perez-Roldan and so win his first ever career title on the ATP Tour. The accurate passing shots of the Argentinian forced Ivanisevic to stay back and fight for each point from the baseline. With the exception of the second set, in which he lost only two points on his serve, Goran was in danger throughout the whole encounter. He won the tie-break, however, clinching his 16th ace of the match. 'I was terribly nervous throughout the match,' confessed the winner. 'Perez-Roldan returned so well, and his passing shots forced me to stay back. I did not play well. But I won. Isn't that the most important thing?

In the week of the Mercedes Cup, during which the players enjoyed many parties - one of them in a castle in the countryside - Goran Ivanisevic had demonstrated once again his potential to become one of the best players in the world. 'In two years' time, I'll be number one,' declared the Yugoslav, adding 'Already I see myself as one of the four best players in the world.' He may well be right ...

The top-seeded doubles team of Pieter Aldrich and Danie Visser won their second title together this year, defeating the Swedish combination of Nicklas Utgren and Per Henricsson 6-3, 6-4. The title was worth $54,780 and marked their seventh win as a pair. 'This was our first win on red clay,' said Aldrich, who won his first singles title a week earlier at Newport. Visser added, 'This is a great tournament and we had a lot of fun here.'

Aldrich was not the first player to voice such sentiments about this tournament which has always been popular with the players even before it acquired official status on the Tour. The allure of a visit to the factory of leading men's fashion designer Hugo Boss, located just outside Stuttgart, where players pick up designer clothers for a fraction of the shop price is just one of the many incentives that the Mercedes Cup has to offer! More importantly, the energetic Ranold Mjornell ensures that the ambitious sponsors, Mercedes, know how to look after the players and if they did not actually offer a 500 SL as a bonus then an awful lot of players have decided that a Mercedes is the car for them.

Sovran Bank Classic

By Josh Young

Washington, 16-22 July
Tournament Director: Josh Ripple

The 20th chapter of the Sovran Bank Classic was billed as the most exciting ever, with the 20-year-old Andre Agassi as the featured player. For the 17 years the tournament was staged on clay, promoters struggled to sell it to the public. Heat and humidity were bad enough, but watching long rallies from non-American players was never suited to those who followed tennis in the nation's capital. The heat, which has eliminated more players over the years than any one other player, claimed defending champion Tim Mayotte in the third round in 1990. Todd Witsken survived a 97-degree day and beat Mayotte 2-6, 6-4, 7-5 in two hours and 38 minutes of sheer perspiration. Fans learned to battle the heat to watch Ivan Lendl, Boris Becker and Jimmy Connors in 1988. In 1989, the humidity reached maximum proportions and brought rain for the final weekend. Late on Sunday night before about 50 spectators, Mayotte claimed the 1989 title. This year, heat and humidity were back at the National Tennis Center, and so was steam with Agassi and John McEnroe sending advance ticket sales soaring.

It was the first chance since 1978 for the fans to see McEnroe. Since then, McEnroe became the best player in the world and the most hated player in the world by many, got married and became the most liked player in the world by many. Several aborted comebacks have highlighted McEnroe's

John McEnroe, who in the first round of Wimbledon lost to Derrick Rostagno, suffered the same ordeal in the round of 16 at Washington.

Jim Grabb, runner-up to Agassi, demonstrates his forehand at the obligatory post-match press conference.

recent years, and this year was no exception. Coming into DC, McEnroe had been defaulted from the Australian Open, skipped the French Open and lost in the first round at Wimbledon to Derrick Rostagno. McEnroe played his way to the third round for a re-match with Rostagno and announced, 'I see no reason not to kick his butt.' Rostagno won 6-3, 1-6, 6-1, but DC fans got what they wanted: McEnroe. A few weeks later, McEnroe got what he wanted when he reached the semi-finals of the US Open.

The other attraction for the tennis fans was the new love him or love to hate him man of tennis, Andre Agassi. Possessed with talent beyond his years and behaviour often behind them - much like the McEnroe DC saw in 1978, Agassi coasted through the tournament. He spent much of the time deflecting criticism in the press and fighting off teenagers looking for something to do with their summer vacation. One girl and her father travelled from Baltimore to watch the tennis. When she discovered that Agassi was not playing that day, she had her father drive her to Agassi's hotel so she could stake out the lobby for a photograph.

As sure as the Baltimore teenager got her photo, Agassi barrelled through the week without the loss of a set. Richey Reneberg, the gentleman American with a serve-and-volley game that suggests he could be in the top ten soon, pushed Agassi to a tie-break in the first set of their quarter-final contest. No one came close the rest of the week. Certainly not Michael Chang, who ran all over Washington chasing Agassi's angled groundstrokes in his 6-3, 6-1 semi-final loss.

After No.3 seed McEnroe was dispatched in the bottom half of the draw, No. 2 seed Brad Gilbert looked like the only hope to derail Agassi in the final - until a doubles specialist named Jim Grabb eliminated him in the best match of the tournament, 7-5, 0-6, 6-4 in the semi-finals. Outside a few aces and a half dozen service winners, Grabb could do nothing that worked against Agassi in the final. A full house of DC tennis fans watched the 20-year-old from Las Vegas win the 20th Sovran Bank Classic 6-1, 6-4 over Grabb. 'It was a lot quicker than the finals we watched on clay, and we had two Americans,' one fan said. In fact, seven of eight quarter finalists were Americans. 'It's great,' Agassi said. 'This is our capital city.'

Players Ltd International Canadian Open

By Tom Mayenknecht

Toronto, 23-29 July
Tournament Director: John Beddington

American Michael Chang used the $1.2 million Player's Ltd. International Canadian Open to complete a comeback from the untimely hip injury which temporarily derailed his promising career in December 1989. And he completed the comeback by, well, coming back ... again, again and again!

After receiving a first-round bye and dismissing qualifier Brad Dyke 6-2, 6-3 and ninth-seeded David Wheaton 6-0, 6-3, Chang scored three consecutive come-from-behind victories to win his first ATP Tour tournament title. Playing in temperatures that were 'thirtysomething' on the Celsius scale - hovering over 100 degrees Fahrenheit - throughout the Canadian Open event, the 18-year-old displayed much of the courage and determination that made him the 1989 French Open champion in erasing one-set deficits against top-seeded Andre Agassi, fifth-seeded Pete Sampras and fourth-seeded Jay Berger. Against Berger, Chang needed two hours and 50 minutes to carve out a 4-6, 6-3,7-6 victory in the longest final in Player's Ltd. International history. That was after a two hour and 40 minute semi-final against Sampras, 3-6,7-6,7-5, and a 130-minute quarter-

> 'It feels good to be back in the winner's circle,' says Chang, the youngest player to win the title.

final in which he outlasted Agassi, 4-6, 7-5, 7-5. In all three cases, Chang dropped the first set. In all three cases, Chang trailed in the third and final set before rallying at the finish. The results: $155,000 first prize and a notch above the million-dollar mark in career earnings. More important, Chang was back, winning his first tournament in his first final since fracturing his left hip while practising in Florida for the year-end Masters in 1989 in New York. 'It's definitely a confidence booster for me,' said Chang, the youngest player to win the Player's Ltd. International. 'It lets me know that I'm back on the way up to where I was. It feels good to be back in the winner's circle.' Chang followed the likes of Ivan Lendl (a six-time winner, 1980,1981,1983 1987,1988,1989), John McEnroe (1984 and 1985), Boris Becker (1986) and Bjorn Borg (1979) into the Canadian Open record books, but not until he went the full distance in his last three matches.

It wasn't until the dramatic third-set tie-breaker in the final against Berger that Chang sensed victory was within his reach. 'I wasn't confident that I would win the match,' said Chang. 'I was

Michael Chang and the Canadian Open trophy - a welcome return to form after injury for the youngest-ever French Open champion.

kind of drained. But I was lucky to hang in there and stay with him. Jay was hitting some unbelievable shots.' The final set was a marathon in which the two Americans exchanged six service breaks in the first eight games. But neither player was willing to fold in the stretch run. In the tie-breaker, Chang jumped into a 3-1 lead when Berger double-faulted. He won four of the next six points to close out his biggest payday since Roland-Garros in 1989. 'It feels good but my first priority in tennis is not to make money, but to be the best in the world or be the best that I can be,' Chang said moments after the match. Chang succeeded where several top-notch players ranked ahead of him did not. Berger, on the other hand, admitted that the lengthy match was wearing him down. 'The heat just got to me at the end. I was struggling and I didn't concentrate well,' he said.

Among those to fall in Toronto were second-seeded Brad Gilbert, a 7-5, 4-6, 6-2 loser in the second round against Todd Witsken, third-seeded John McEnroe and seventh-seeded Tim Mayotte. Mayotte bowed out to Berger in the quarter finals, 7-6,6-4, while McEnroe was ousted by the New Kid on the Block, Pete Sampras, 7-6, 4-6,6-3.

The Sampras-Chang semi-final gave Toronto tennis enthusiasts another look at the eventual 1990 U.S. Open champion, but Sampras had already made believers out of many with his victory over McEnroe and a 4-6, 6-3, 6-2 comeback against Canadian Davis Cup team member Andrew Sznajder in the third round. Sampras appeared headed for the final after taking a 3-0 lead over Chang in the third set of their semi-final. But the

The Centre Court in Toronto - dressed and presented in typically elegant style by John Beddington.

talented serve-and-volleyer began to crumble when he blew what should have been a bread-and-butter shot. With Sampras serving at 3-1, Chang made a desperate lob which appeared to be on its way out wide. An over-anxious Sampras volleyed the ball out of the doubles court wide, opening the door for Chang to break serve and begin another of his patented comeback efforts. 'That 3-1 game took the air out of me,' admitted Sampras. 'I didn't know where I was on the court on that lob. If I had let the ball go, I would not have had any chance to hit it. I played a stupid cross-court backhand and blew it.'

Chang won six of the last eight games, repeating the gutsy performance he turned in against Agassi in the quarter final, when he survived a severe bout of leg cramps in the third set to knock out the No. 1 seed. 'I'm playing real good tennis right now,' said Chang after his first win in six tries against Agassi. Agassi was forced to three sets in his second-round match against Michael Stich of West Germany before posting a 6-3, 6-7, 6-3 win. He also beat Australian Darren Cahill 6-2, 6-4, before running into a rejuvenated Chang, who was making his first-ever appearance in the

Canadian Open. It was, however, a triumphant return to Toronto for Chang, a member of the United States under-16 national team which won its zonal qualifying matches in the World Youth Cup at the nearby Donalda Club back in the summer of 1986, three years before the then 14-year-old would make underhand service the rage at Roland Garros.

In doubles, Paul Annacone and Wheaton never looked like a team that had been paired up at the last moment. They beat Dyke and Peter Lundgren, 6-1, 7-6 in the championship final after eliminating Peter Doohan and Laurie Warder 6-3, 7-6 in the semi-finals. Annacone and Wheaton began their impressive run with a 3-6, 6-1, 6-3 win over Canadians Martin Laurendeau and Brian Gyetko and a solid 6-4, 6-3 upset win over eighth-seeded Neil Broad and Kelly Jones. The top-seeded Canadians, Grant Connell and Glenn Michibata, won a pair of tough three-set matches but dropped a third; their 6-2, 4-6, 6-2 semi-final against Dyke and Lundgren. Earlier in the week, Connell and Michibata rallied for a 4-6, 7-5, 7-5 win over John McEnroe and Mark Woodforde and a 6-7, 7-5, 7-6 marathon over Todd Nelson and David Shelton.

In the Player's Ltd. Festival of Tennis Legends event, over 25 former greats graced the National Tennis Centre at York University as part of Tennis Canada's 100th Anniversary celebrations.

Rod Laver and Fred Perry were on hand as guests of honour while the courts featured the likes of Pancho Gonzales, Pancho Segura, Vic Seixas, Ilie Nastase, Vitas Gerulaitis, Eddie Dibbs, Harold Soloman, Dick Stockton, Cliff Richey, Manuel Orantes and Alex Metreveli. It marked the second straight year that such a Legends event was orchestrated by Tournament Director John Beddington and it attested to the appeal of nostalgia in the world of tennis.

Pink thigh-huggers and a double-fisted backhand - all part of the Andre Agassi persona.

International Championships of The Netherlands

By Bertold Palthe

Hilversum, 23-29 July
Tournament Director: Peter Van Eijsden

Way back - when tennis only existed in the wildest dreams of English noblemen - tradesmen and farmers found a little tollhouse in Hilversum on their trips to the major trading centre of Amsterdam, just 15 miles west of it. The weary men stopped at the tollhouse to clear their throats from dust with milk. Nowadays 'The Little Milkhouse' still welcomes thirsty people from the dusty red clay courts. But that's the only thing which reminds players of the old tollhouse. Diet Coke and beer have replaced the milk, and big cars drive them from the courts to their luxurious hotel and back. For 33 years now, The Little Milkhouse has been the scene of a unique tournament. The best clay court specialists are eager to come to the Dutch Open Championships, which are held here and bear the name of the old tollhouse. In the past it attracted such big names as Rod Laver, who won back in 1962, Tom Okker and Guillermo Vilas.

But one of the most impressive performances was made by Balazs Taroczy. Six times the talented Hungarian emerged as the winner of the tournament and it is no secret that some people

The bigger smile wins it! Francisco Clavet festooned with flowers, side by side with the man he beat in the Hilversum final, Eduardo Masso.

The cover of the Hilversum programme, announcing the International Tennis Championships of the Netherlands.

sighed that they would like him to have a bad day. Not out of dislike, for they really loved the man, but just for the excitement. Taroczy now coaches Goran Ivanisevic and maybe one day he will win the Little Milkhouse again through the skillful hands of his pupil.

For the 1990 event from 21-29 July, most people put their money on Emilio Sanchez, who had won the tournament back in 1988 and who was beaten in the 1989 final. In fact his chances improved day by day as the other favourites had to bite the red clay dust and shake hands with a less famous name than themselves. Juan Aguilera, Mark Rosset, Guillermo Perez-Roldan, Alberto Mancini and Martin Jaite, the No. 2 seed, all bowed out.

Finally a Belgian player, who proved to be an Argentinian with Belgian nationality, Eduardo Masso, faced Francisco Clavet, a Spanish youngster who impressed many people with his play against Yannick Noah in the first round at the French Open. Masso, a qualifier exuding Latin-American charm, was the public's favourite. He had the week of his life, or so he told everyone he encountered in his broken English. He played very attractive tennis, but had to acknowledge Clavet, a lucky loser, as the better player in a four-set final. Never in the history of the ATP had a qualifier and a lucky loser both reached the final of a tour event. Clavet had no problem with this curiosity. 'I had a wonderful week. I like it here,' he said. He should have done, because most of the players spoke Spanish and had the temperament that goes with it.

San Remo Open

By Anna Legnani

San Remo, 30 July-5 August
Tournament Director: Sergio Palmieri

San Remo, 'City of flowers', on the Italian Riviera, is not only a renowned beach resort, but boasts an international sporting tradition. Milano-San Remo is one of the most famous cycling classics and the Giraglia Regatta is well-known to all sailing fans. World-class tennis was back in the front of the scene this season in one of the oldest tennis clubs in the Peninsula, founded by British residents at the turn of the century. The forty-seventh leg of the 1990 ATP Tour was staged in the club which had hosted some of the finest tennis events up to the sixties, where Rod Laver, John Newcombe and Manuel Santana had basked in the sunshine during the traditional New Year's tournament, and Pierre Darmon, now Director of ATP Tour in Europe, had enjoyed the shade of olive and eucalyptus trees after his Davis Cup matches.

The Italian Riviera spoke Spanish for one week as two Spaniards and two South Americans battled to the semi-finals in the San Remo Open. With Jordi Arrese defeating Marcelo Filippini and Juan Aguilera's success over Roberto Azar, the final was a Catalan affair as the two players from Barcelona advanced to the championship round. Arrese and Aguilera had only met in one official match before, yet they knew each other's game by heart. Born in the same town and having trained and travelled together for five years when both where trained by Luis Bruguera, they are close friends off court. In San Remo, as in most other tournaments, whenever one of them played, the other was in the stands for moral support.

Jordi Arrese of Spain on his way to a first career title after eight years on the pro tour

Ballboys and officials line up for Aguilera and Arrese on the charming centre court of San Remo's tennis club.

The pair had only dropped one set each on their way to the finals, and Arrese had boosted his confidence by eliminating top-seeded Argentinian Guillermo Perez Roldan in the quarters. 'I had the feeling then that I could win the tournament,' said Jordi after defeating his more titled opponent with his solid baseline game. 'I saw that Juan wasn't at his best, so I kept to the baseline and tried to make as few mistakes as possible. If Aguilera had played his usual game I would have had to attack more.'

His 6-2, 6-2 victory gave Jordi Arrese his first career title and made him the fourth Spaniard after Emilio Sanchez, Juan Aguilera and Francisco Clavet to win an ATP Tour singles event this season. The victory also confirmed his excellent performance in the World Team Cup in Dusseldorf in May and put an end to a series of poor results following the French Open. Jordi's fiancée Maria was even happier, because in San Remo the Spaniard put an end to another negative streak; he had not won a single match before with his girlfriend present!

Most of the other players had also brought their families along to enjoy a week in this beautiful holiday resort. The beaches, shopping and the Casino were among favourite activities, and those wishing to prove their sporting ability had the opportunity to take part in the ladies tennis tournament or in the highly contended mini-football matched that opposed an Italian organising staff team to a 'rest of the world' side, in which the Italian girls were, like their World Cup compatriots, defeated on penalty shots.

The Eastern European team of Minhea-Lon Nastase and Goran Prpic defeated Swedes Ola Jonsson and Frederik Nilsson 3-6, 7-5, 6-3 in an exciting doubles final. All four contenders had reached their first championship round here in the Riviera, and the San Remo Open was the Romanian's first event on the ATP Tour. Ilie Nastase's nephew, a doubles specialist with a powerful serve, and Yugoslavian Prpic, '1989 Comeback Player of the Year', had only played together once before, when they made the juniors final in the 1982 US Open.

Philips Austrian Open/Head Cup

By Caroline Hutton

Kitzbuhel, 30 July-5 August
Tournament Director: Hellmuth Kuchenmeister

Kitzbuhel is one of the venues on the ATP Tour that lifts the spirits and clears the cobwebs. Like Gstaad, Kitzbuhel is a fashionable ski resort during the winter months but in summer the mountains come alive with wild flowers and during the week of 30 July-5 August the sound of tennis balls echoes through the hills into the crisp fresh air.

A fairy-tale setting produced a happy ending for Argentinian Horacio de la Pena. Not only did he celebrate his 24th birthday during the week, but at the end of it he'd won the prestigious title with a 6-4, 2-6, 6-2 defeat of Czechoslovakia's Karel Novacek.

The victory was sweet for de la Pena for, as he noted, 'It was the first time in over a year that my knee didn't bother me'. After his title in Florence last year he suffered bouts of patellar tendonitis and bursitis and this year had been forced to play qualification rounds in an attempt to secure a place in the main draw of tournaments. But after his surprise victory at Kitzbuhel (he was the only unseeded player in the final eight), and with precious bonus points gained from wins including over No. 2 seed Brad Gilbert, No. 8 Sergi Bruguera and in the semis the defending champion and No. 3 see Emilio Sanchez, de la Pena shot up the rankings from 191 to 86. De la Pena gave much of the credit for his remarkable performance to the help he received from his father-in-law, Roy Emerson, the man who has won more grand slam titles in singles and doubles (28) than anyone in history. They had worked hard together for two weeks in Gstaad before coming to Kitzbuhel. Their style is different to be sure, as Emerson notes, 'Horacio uses excessive topspin and hardly ever comes to the net, while I don't use excessive topspin and spend all my time at the net!' But it is exactly these differences that enable Emerson to improve his son-in-law's serve and volley technique. 'It helped me a lot to work with Roy before coming to Kitzbuhel,' said de la Pena, 'because now I'm able to do some things that the other players don't expect.'

While de la Pena had used his 'unexpected' improvements to dismiss Gilbert in straight sets, Novacek had caused an even greater sensation in the quarters by doing exactly the same thing to the No. 1 seed: none other than Boris Becker. Becker has never won a clay court title and Novacek was in no mood to allow the German to get any closer to changing that. Continually frustrating Becker's attempts to serve and volley, the Czech displayed an impressive set of nerves to win a tidy 6-3, 6-3. 'It was,' Novacek said, 'the best I've ever played.'

An ecstatic Horacio de la Pena with the cup: his comeback trail after injury reached its peak in Kitzbuhel.

As far as the Austrian spectators were concerned the nail-biting match of the week was the quarter final between the two arch rivals of Austrian tennis, Horst Skoff and Thomas Muster. Not only did Skoff tie up the victory 6-4, 6-2, but later the same day found himself opposite Muster once again in the doubles quarter final. Skoff was teamed with Francisco Clavet, the singles winner a week before in Hilversum, while Muster was partnered by Becker.

Perhaps Skoff's earlier win gave him extra confidence for he and Clavet won that match and later reached the finals together where they were beaten 7-6, 6-2 by Javier Sanchez and Eric Winogradsky. While Javier's elder brother Emilio had been unable to retain his 1989 singles title, at least Javier had kept the famous Sanchez name on the honours roll at Kitzbuhel.

Tournament director Hellmuth Kuchenmeister had built a brand new 6000-seater centre court for the 1990 Philips Austrian Open/Head Cup. The perfect summer weather helped attract a record-breaking 70,000 fans over the seven days. Such was the enthusiasm of the autograph-hunters that players had to be bustled straight off the centre court into a waiting mini-bus, to be driven back to the locker rooms, as they were unable to walk the distance without severe risk of being crushed.

Volvo Tennis, Los Angeles

By Thomas Bonk

Los Angeles, 30 July-5 August
Tournament Director: Robert Kramer

Stefan Edberg's victory in the Volvo/Los Angeles tournament had a twist to it. Edberg defeated Michael Chang in a third-set tie breaker, thereby establishing his margin of victory. Edberg won by a foot, or more precisely, by an ankle - the one he twisted in the second set against Chang only to undergo a startling transformation as a baseliner and record an improbable 7-6, 2-6, 7-6 victory. As the match ended, Edberg smiled wryly and looked to the sky. The message? 'It was very hard to believe that I won,' Edberg explained. Few could have expected such an outcome after Edberg had twisted his ankle as he moved along the baseline to retrieve a shot. But the sell-out crowds at the Los Angeles Tennis Center on the campus of UCLA have grown accustomed to witnessing important victories by Edberg. If there is one player who leads a charmed life on the green asphalt courts, with box seat regular Johnny Carson as close as a commercial, then it is Edberg.

Edberg was only a highly touted 18-year-old policeman's son from Vastervik, Sweden, when he captured the gold medal for tennis, a demonstration sport, at the 1984 Olympic Games on the very same court. Edberg returned to play the Volvo/Los Angeles tournament the next three years and reached the finals each time before losing. He remained, however, one of the more popular figures in the long and rich history of the tournament, which for many years was known as the Pacific Southwest and features such great champions as Bill Tilden, Ellsworth Vienes, Don Budge, Jack Kramer and Pancho Gonzales. To reach the finals, Edberg needed to defeat a player who within a few short weeks would become a worldwide figure at the US Open - Pete Sampras. Still an 18-year-old, from the nearby South Bay and Rancho Palos Verdes, Sampras won the second set of his semi-final with Edberg in a tie breaker, but fell behind, 0-5, in the third set and went out quietly, giving only a few hints of what was soon to come by cracking serves that reached 115 miles an hour. Dutifully impressed, Edberg offered his prophetic assessment of Sampras: 'He plays unbelievably at times ... he's just got to give himself a little bit of time.'

There seemed to be more than the usual number of happenings during the week, including defending champion Aaron Krickstein's first-round defeat. But there was more. Edberg was pleased he wouldn't play his quarter final match under the lights - 'I'll get my suntan back,' he said. Gary Muller lost to Chang in the semi-finals, understandably distracted when a spectator fell out of a tree beyond the grandstands. Said Muller: 'I had a spare ticket, if anyone needed it.'

Michael Chang was kept on the run by Stefan Edberg in the final. *Below:* Doubles specialist Gary Muller revealed his singles prowess at the UCLA Tennis Complex by reaching the semi-finals.

Finally, this was where Sampras came through with his now-famous rejoinder to Fred Perry, who had claimed during Wimbledon that the All-England Championships surely would be captured one day soon by Sampras. Sampras shook his head sadly and said 'You're out of control, Fred'.

Well, soon Fred didn't appear so reckless, not with Sampras' stunning Grand Slam victory at the US Open. As for Edberg, he reached another high point the next week at Cincinnati when he achieved the No. 1 ranking for the first time. And, after all, Los Angeles was Edberg's first tournament since he won Wimbledon. So for both Sampras and Edberg, this was one tournament that seemed to push them along in the right direction. In the doubles, Scott Davis and David Pate captured their third title of the year by defeating Peter Lundgren and Paul Wekesa.

Thriftway ATP Championship

By Phillip S. Smith and Susan Schott

Cincinnati, 6-12 August
Tournament Director: Paul Flory

Swedes have always had a special fondness for the Thriftway ATP Championships which has blossomed year by year at Kings Island just outside the river-boat city of Cincinnati. But this year was special. Stefan Edberg not only won the tournament for the second time to become the sixth Swedish winner in 12 years but, by beating Michael Chang in the quarter final, took over from Ivan Lendl as the No. 1 player in the world. That made the 24-year-old from Vastervik the member of one of sport's most exclusive clubs. Since the inception of the ATP computer in 1973 only seven other players have made it to the top - Ilie Nastase, John Newcombe, Jimmy Connors, Bjorn Borg, John McEnroe, Ivan Lendl and Mats Wilander. 'It has become more and more important throughout the years to be No 1 because of how hard it is to get there,' Edberg said, 'So I'm going to remember this week. It's always going to be very special to me.'

'It has become more important to be No 1 because of how hard it is to get there.'

Edberg could not have celebrated his elevation more emphatically. It took him just 51 minutes to crush Brad Gilbert 6-1, 6-1 in a dramatic reversal of the previous year's final when the Californian had defeated Edberg to extend a winning streak to 17 straight matches. Ironically, by beating Gilbert, it was now Edberg's turn to stretch his unbeaten run to 17.

Due to an ankle he twisted while winning Los Angeles, Edberg started slowly but then gathered steam as the week progressed. After surviving a tough first round against Milan Srejber and a three setter against Chang, the reigning Wimbledon champion took out French Open champion Andres Gomez 7-5, 6-3. Gilbert's path to the final was cleared considerably thanks to 15th seeded Australian Richard Fromberg who surprised second seeded Andre Agassi in a third round battle while Scott Davis accounted for John McEnroe, seeded eighth, in a nerve-wracking duel that went to 6-4 in the fourth set.

Along with McEnroe, two former top ten players continued their struggles in 1990. Tim Mayotte, working on technical changes in his game, and Mats Wilander, playing in only his third tournament after a four-month layoff, were both

Stefan Edberg at full stretch, continuing the Swedish tradition at King's Island where Swedes have won the singles title six times over the past twelve years.

beaten by Darren Cahill back-to-back. Mayotte fell in an opening round three-setter, while Wilander, a four-time winner in Cincinnati, was defeated 6-3, 6-2, in the following round. Cahill, however, could not build on two of the best victories he had secured since reaching the semi-finals of the US Open in 1988 and went down to Gomez, 7-6, 6-3 in the round of 16.

Neverthless in the doubles Cahill went all the way. Teamed with his regular partner Mark Kratzmann, the seventh seeded Aussie pair gained revenge for the defeat they suffered at the hands of Neil Broad and Gary Muller in the quarter-final of the Australian Open when they defeated the Anglo-South African pair 7-6, 6-2 to take the Thriftway doubles title. For Kratzmann it was his seventh doubles title of the year and the victory did much to ensure that he and Cahill would secure a berth in the ATP Tour World Doubles Championship at Sanctuary Cove.

As usual, Paul Flory's tournament offered visitors a varied array of entertainment. Both players and fans take advantage of the nearby Kings Island Amusement Park, one of the largest of its kind in America while on site, the foodcourt, located under a giant tent allows patrons to gorge themselves on lobster salad and fettuccine Alfredo while listening to a classical pianist in black tie and tails. Not far away the mood changes. Strollers through the gardens blooming with flowers and exotic plants find themselves toe-tapping to a Dixieland band.

The tournament site is also part of the Jack Nicklaus Sports Center which players may use freely. The Center boasts a Championship golf course which hosts a Seniors Professional Golfers Association tournament each year. The huge success of the ATP Championships, which has been associated with the players' association for many years, is not however simply about people having a good time. The tournament is played for the benefit of Cinicinnati's Children's Hospital Medical Center, one of the world's leading pediatric centres. More than $1.8 million has been donated to the charity since 1974 andevery year

children enjoy visits at their bedsides by players. This year Jim Courier, Jonas Svensson, Miguel Nido, Jay Siegel and the ATP's Benjy Robins spent time with youngsters suffering from cancer and other debilitating diseases.

Miguel Nido befriended a Puerto Rican girl by talking to her in Spanish. "She was in need of a liver transplant and it was frustrating to listen to her talk about what she wanted to do with her life knowing that, unless she found a donor, it was unlikely she would be able to do those things," said Nido.

The players also conduct clinics on public courts for healthy children of the various Cincinnati and Dayton neighbourhoods. Every year hundreds of children benefit from personal tennis lessons given by some of the sport's biggest stars.

With Indianapolis, Cincinnati forms the heart of tennis in the mid-west and with a roster of past champions that includes three former No. 1's in McEnroe, Lendl and Wilander, it is not surprising that Paul Flory can claim with a happy smile, "We break attendance records every year!"

Above: The magnificent Stadium Court packed to capacity at the Jack Nicklaus Sports Center.
Left: Brad Gilbert gets the ball dead centre but still got killed by Edberg in the final.

Czechoslovak Open Tennis Championships

By Caroline Hutton

Prague, 6-12 August
Tournament Director: Jan Kodes

The winds of change that have swept through Eastern Europe climaxed for Czechoslovakia in November 1989 when, after more than 40 years, the country finally broke from the chains of Soviet domination. A new democratic Czechoslovakia raised its bruised and weary head as a free land at last. Prague, 'The Golden City' and a jewel of old Europe, is the venue for the Czechoslovak Open Tennis Championships and, in its fourth year as a professional event, proved to be one of the most controversial tournaments on the ATP Tour.

Austria's Thomas Muster, the number 1 seed, retired from his first round match against Claudio Pistolesi after three minutes on court. Muster was later fined $25,000 and suspended from the Tour for ten weeks for, amongst other violations, 'Conduct contrary to the integrity of the game'. Muster was to appeal the decision and the penalty was subsequently reduced by an independent arbitration panel to $15,000 and a three-week suspension.

There was more: Christian Saceanu of Germany pulled out of the tournament, after securing a berth in the quarters, to play for his club in Bundesliga. Fined $15,000 and suspended for ten weeks Saceanu did not appeal the decision of the ATP Tour. Once committed to play an ATP Tour event players are not allowed to 'hedge their bets' and enter themselves into two tournaments in the same week. 'No-one enjoys fining or suspending players, but the integrity of the Tour has to be our prime concern', said Mark Miles, CEO of the ATP Tour. 'The public must not be short changed'. Meanwhile the rest of the 32 draw were getting on with the object of tennis; trying hard to win their matches.

Jan Kodes, tournament director and former great pro who won French Open titles in 1970 and 71 and Wimbledon in 1973, drew consolation from the fine efforts of his 18-year-old-son, Jan Kodes Jnr. Given a wildcard by his father, the former No.3 junior in the world delighted the crowds by winning his first ever match on the ATP Tour in the first round over Cedric Pioline. In the second round he took the first set off clay court expert and eventual champion, Jordi Arrese of Spain. It was the sole set during the week that Arrese was to concede. Kodes Jnr joked, 'I'm too thin at the moment. I need to take up body building before I'm ready to tackle the pro tour'.

It was another teenager who was to confront Arrese in the final, 19-year-old Niclas Kulti of Sweden who had moved quietly and steadily through the draw. Alexander Mronz, defending

Flowers for the runner-up in Prague. Niclas Kulti, one of the rising young Swedes, will not have to wait long for the silver.

champion Marcelo Filippini, Franco Davin and Horacio de la Pena were outplayed by some fine serving and superb passing shots as Kulti enjoyed the best week of his young career.

But in the final Kulti admitted he had 'choked at the vital moments'. He held three set points in the first set and two in the second but could not prevent them slipping through his grasp. Arrese was confident - the week before he had won the title in San Remo. Although it took the 26-year-old Spaniard 2 hours and 34 minutes to finally clinch the match 7-6, 7-6, it was a well deserved victory. Under blazing sunshine and tired from a fortnights continuous play, Arrese kept his nerve and concentration.

Having being beaten by Czechoslovakia's Petr Korda in his two previous visits to Prague, Arrese had done his homework before coming again. 'I asked Petr if he was playing here again and when he said he wasn't I decided to try my luck once more'.

The doubles competion was won by the homeboys, Daniel Flegl and Vojtech Vacek. The increasingly mature partnership defeated the veterans George Cosac and Florin Segarceanu, 5-7, 6-4, 6-3. It was Flegl and Vacek's second victory of the year following Umag three months before. The friendly pair, who started the year without a team ranking, were to finish the season as the 34th best doubles pair in the world.

143

GTE/US Men's Hardcourt Championships

By David B. Noland

Indianapolis, 13-19 August
Tournament Director: Stephen Devoe

It's really amazing,' said Fred Stolle as he looked out over the busy new players' lounge. 'I've been to a few tournaments in the last 30 years, and players spend more off-court time together at Indianapolis than at any other tournament on the Tour. The folks at the GTE Championships have come with a special mix of activities and hospitality that makes the players want to stick around and spend time together. I think that's great for the players. Their attitude is reflected on the court and that makes it great for the fans also.'

The player support in Indianapolis does seem almost endless. A festive atmosphere pervades a week full of activities. This year was highlighted by a new Players Lounge complete with ping-pong and pool tables, video games and a Monte Carlo race simulator. Robert Seguso (low gross) and Danie Visser (low net) won the Championship Players' Golf Tournament. Players participated in a mock 'Super Stars Contest' throughout the week, while the annual softball tournament, complete with umpires, announcers, cheerleaders and uniforms, once again brought out players, ATP Tour staff and 'Catfish' Stolle in friendly competition. Tournament director Steve Devoe is pleased that Indianapolis is known as a 'players tournament', but is quick to point out other key factors in the success that made the 1990 GTE

Championships record-setting. 'On the court the new ATP Tour gave the tournament its strongest field ever. Boris Becker, John McEnroe, Andre Agassi and Yannick Noah were joined in Indy by

Peter Lundgren handles his guitar as lovingly as his racquet; he was runner-up in Indy.
Opposite: Boris Becker reaches for the stars as he clinches his third title of 1990.

After the final of the GTE/US Hardcourt Championships Becker annd Lundgren received their just rewards.

some of the Tour's best young players ... Pete Sampras, Mark Kratzmann, Jim Courier, and Richey Reneberg. Off the court, our title sponsor, GTE, along with presenting sponsors Bank One and Eli Lilly and Company, more than doubled the purse to $1 million. That kind of leadership is significant and made this year's tournament exciting and successful, as verified, in part, by our record attendance.'

The players, for one, have acknowledged the 'GTE' success. For the last two years they have voted the GTE Championships their Tournament of the Year, an unprecedented stamp

of approval. The players also see Indianapolis as a key warm-up for the US Open. That was reaffirmed by the fact that the final four at the US Open - Boris Becker, Andre Agassi, John McEnroe and Pete Sampras - all played at Indianapolis just two weeks earlier.

World-class tennis began coming to Indianapolis over 60 years ago. Past winners of major tournaments there read like a Hall of Fame roster: from Bill Tilden to Chris Evert. To the surprise of many, Indianapolis is a hot bed of tennis activity and is known as a 'tennis town'. The site of the GTE Championships, the Indianapolis

'We feel the GTE Championships has a distinct advantage - its tennis tradition, and the Indianapolis commitment to host and produce sporting events of national and international significance. It is an exciting new era for professional tennis.'

On the court, defending champion, John McEnroe, and 1988 winner Boris Becker headed the powerful line-up of players. Becker became a two-time GTE Championships title-holder, topping unseeded Peter Lundgren of Sweden 6-3, 6-4 in the finals. The Indianapolis win was Becker's third of the year, having won previously at Brussels and Stuttgart, and the win broke a three-final losing streak (Hamburg, Queen's and Wimbledon). The points he amassed here enabled him to claim the No. 2 spot on the ATP Tour rankings.

Lundgren, who had not appeared in a final since Newport last year, was the surprise of the week, defeating No. 2 seed Andre Agassi easily in the quarter finals on his way to the final. The long-haired Swede also had big wins over No. 7 seed Martin Jaite and No. 14 seed Richey Reneberg. With his big serve as a weapon, Lundgren closed out his matches with Agassi and Reneberg with aces. Lundgren earned $72,380 and moved from No. 153 to No. 72 on the ATP computer. When asked about the four service breaks he held and then lost against Becker, Lundgren stated, 'I couldn't find my toss. I just couldn't find a rhythm in my serve. But I got to play a lot of matches. I thought I played pretty well.'

Only the No. 8 seed, Jim Courier, stretched Becker to three sets this week, but unfortun-ately was forced to retire at 3-1 in the third set. Richey Reneberg outlasted Pete Sampras in an exciting three-set match.

In a hotly contested doubles final, the No. 4 seeded American duo, Scott Davis and David Pate, defeated the Canadian pair of Grant Connell and Glenn Michibata, the No. 2 seeds, 7-6, 7-6. Davis and Pate picked up their fourth title this year and a cheque for $55,000.

Sports Center, is also one of only four USTA Regional Training Centers helping to develop future world-class tennis players. At yet another level, national recognition comes in junior programmes such as Indianapolis' model National Junior Tennis League chapter which provides tennis instruction for 2000 inner-city children each year. It was, therefore, no surprise to 'Hoosiers' when the Association of Tennis Professionals turned to Indianapolis and chose its brilliant young tournament director, Mark Miles, as their new chief executive officer. 'We are excited to have a native son and capable leader like Mark leading the new ATP Tour into the '90s,' said Paul T. Nolan, President, GTE North Incorporated.

Volvo International Tennis Tournament

By Richard Finn

New Haven, 13-19 August
Tournament Director: Jim Westhall

Tennis went to a seat of higher learning on 13-20 August when innovative promoter Jim Westhall took his perennial summer tour favourite, the Volvo International, to the prestigious Ivy League campus of Yale University. For countless years, the Volvo has been tucked away in the picturesque New England mountain countryside - first in New Hampshire and then in Vermont. With its scenic charm and down-home tournament hospitality, it had gained a legion of loyal fans and players.

When he needed to have a permanent tennis stadium in order to stay on the Championship Series schedule - a criterion of the first year of the ATP Tour - Westhall found that the smart people at Yale were ready to accommodate the tournament and to get in on the world tennis map by building a state-of-the-art tennis facility next to the ivy-covered walls of the Yale Bowl football stadium. Ground-breaking of the stadium was started in September-October and the spanking new stadium is set to be ready in time for the 1991 Volvo.

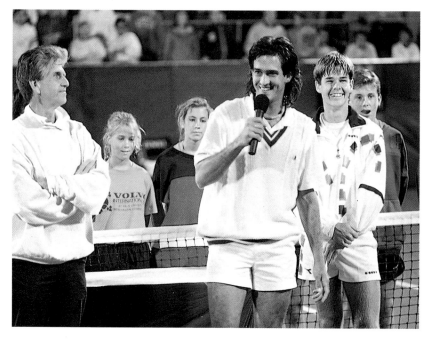

Todd Woodbridge (left), the runner-up, sportingly laughs at the jokes of the champion, Derek Rostagno, while tournament director Jim Westhall looks on.

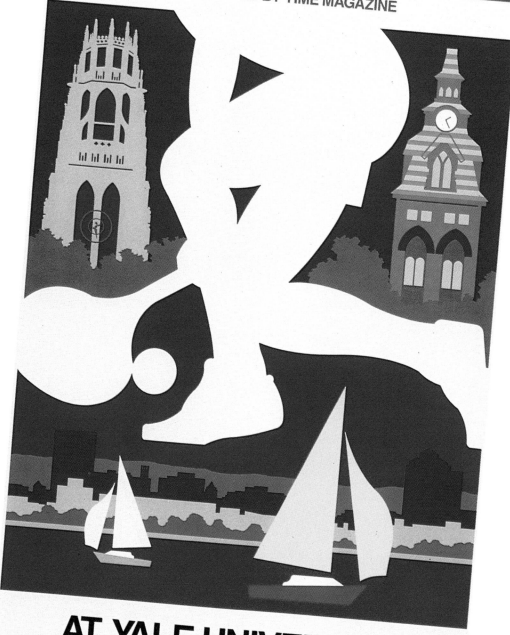

So, off to New Haven went Westhall with a blueprint of his tennis stadium in his pocket, with the fans from New England still following their tennis pied-piper as well as a host of the world's finest players (Australian Open champion Ivan Lendl, defending champion Brad Gilbert, French Open winner Andres Gomez, former French Open champion Michael Chang, former No. 1 Mats Wilander, former Wimbledon winner Pat Cash, the wildly entertaining Goran Ivanisevic and the up-and-coming American David Wheaton) to battle it out in the hot summer sun for a share of the $825,000 purse.

While students in the nearby classrooms have always found matters to go in textbook fashion, subjects were not so orderly on the courts during a topsy-turvy week of exciting tennis which mirrored the entire ATP Tour year of welcoming new faces to the forefront of the game.

Gone within the first two rounds were a volume of seeded stars - Lendl, Gilbert, Chang, Ivanisevic, Tim Mayotte, Richard Fromberg, Petr Korda, Wilander and Wheaton. By the third round Gomez was excused from the tournament. But, staying around and getting high marks for their court skills was a stack of fresh, quick learners such as Malivai Washington, Cristiano Carratti, Todd Woodbridge and Derrick Rostagno. The hard-serving former University of Michigan standout Washington bounced out Lendl while the Italian Carratti ousted Gilbert and Paul Chamberlin subdued the serving prowess of Ivanisevic. Just two years after they had waged a classic Australian Open final, Cash beat Wilander in a first-round royal battle. Woodbridge sent Chang packing and went on to his first career final. Getting the highest marks, however, was Rostagno, the nomadic free-spirited Californian, who had gained much of his previous tennis notoriety by living out of a camper as he travelled from tournament site to site. In a summer during which his racquets had begun to make the news (refer to first-round upset of McEnroe at Wimbledon), Rostagno claimed his biggest pro title by outlasting the rain and the young Australian Woodbridge in the championship match.

Located on the calendar just two weeks before the start of the US Open - about three hours down the highway at Flushing Meadow - many of the players were using this week as a grooming time for their games. With the wave of upsets flooding the draw sheet, the obvious question was whether this was a sign of things to come at the Open.

Obviously it makes for a more open Open,' said South African Christo van Rensburg who had been responisble for knocking out Gomez. 'It is not like there has been just one guy

Petr Korda (centre), tucking in at the players party. Goran Ivanisevic is pretty in pink.

winning all the tournaments this year. It's good for tennis,' said Woodbridge 'It's a little bit of a changing of the guard.' Three weeks later, at 19 years and one month, Pete Sampras became the youngest US Open champion when he beat fellow American Andre Agassi in straight sets in the final.

If the singles tournament wasn't testimony enough to 'the changing of the guard' then the doubles proved the point equally well. Qualifiers Jeff Brown and Scott Melville knocked off No. 2 seeds Goran Ivanisevic and Petr Korda 2-6, 7-5, 6-0 to win theirfirst ATP Tour doubles title which, due to rain, was played on the Monday. They were the second qualifying team of the year to go on and take the trophy after the Czechoslovak pair Vojtech Flegl and Daniel Vacek won at Umag in May. It was a sterling week of play for the young team, for en route to the final they had to defeat such established teams as Jim Grabb and Patrick McEnroe and the top seeds Rick Leach and Jim Pugh. End of tennis lesson.

Norstar Bank Hamlet Challenge Cup

By Doug Smith

Long Island, 20-26 August
Tournament Director: Wendy Parr

For nine years, the Norstar Bank Hamlet Challenge Cup was merely a US Open warm-up exhibition, a chance for a few top pros to calm their nerves and sharpen their strokes before jumping into the two-week pressure cooker of grand slam competition. The Challenge Cup lost its exhibition status last year when it became one of the 77 stops on the inaugural ATP Tour. The status change didn't stop several top pros, including Stefan Edberg and John McEnroe, from being a part of Long Island's only major pro event. The Hamlet Golf and Country Club is the new home for the $250,000 event which included a 28-player singles draw and a 16-team doubles draw.

Appropriately, Edberg, No. 1 in the world, became the first pro to grab the biggest cash prize at a bank-sponsored tournament. He knocked off Goran Ivanisevic 7-6, 6-3 in the final. Edberg received $32,800 and Ivanisevic got $19,400 at the rain-hampered tourney, which raised more than $100,000 for Long Island's Child Life Program.

The Swede struggled a bit in the first set, then had no trouble brushing aside the lanky 18-year-old from Yugoslavia. No. 5 Ivanisevic had advanced to the final by defeating No. 4 Pete Sampras 7-6, 6-3 in the quarter finals and Guy Forget 6-2, 1-6, 6-3 in the semis. Edberg beat

compatriot Jonas Svensson 6-4, 6-2 on Saturday in a rain delayed quarter final match, and then overpowered McEnroe 6-1, 6-4 several hours later in the other semi-final. Said McEnroe: 'Edberg is playing the best he's ever played with the most confidence.' Forget upset No. 2 Andres Gomez 6-7, 6-0, 7-5 and No. 6 McEnroe eliminated No. 3 Brad Gilbert 6-3, 6-2 in quarter final matches.

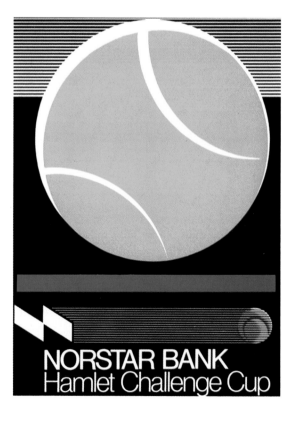

With his triumph in Long Island Edberg took his match winning streak to 21 which tied with Lendl as the longest consecutive number of wins of the year.

The victory gave Edberg his fourth consecutive title and stretched his match-win streak to 21. 'This has been a great week,' said Edberg. 'I played four good matches, I feel I'm in excellent shape, and it's actually good to play a match like this before the Open.'

Edberg had dislodged Ivan Lendl from No. 1 on the rankings three weeks earlier after his win over Brad Gilbert in the final at Cincinnati. He notched up his most satisfying victory in July at Wimbledon where he claimed his second title on the grass courts of London SW19, defeating Boris Becker in the final. 'I don't know how Becker is playing now, but Edberg is playing very well,' said Ivanisevic. 'His backhand volleys were unbelievable. I played good but he played better.'

Tony Pickard, Edberg's coach, believes the quiet Swede made a firm commitment to be No. 1 after winning Wimbledon. 'Your focus goes a bit when you win a big title like Wimbledon,' Pickard said. 'But this time, we sat down and discussed what I thought he could achieve. Now that he's No. 1, he's got to work three times as hard to stay there.'

Forget and Jakob Hlasek captured the Norstar Bank Hamlet Challenge Cup doubles title on Sunday, winning successive three set victories. Forget and Hlasek kept their nerve when they saved four match points before defeating Jeff Brown and Scott Melville 6-4, 2-6, 7-6 in the semi-finals, then sacked Udo Riglewski and Michael Stich 2-6, 6-3, 6-4 in the final.

OTB International Tennis Open

By Nick Kennerley

Schenectady, 20-26 August
Tournament Director: Nitty Singh

Schenectady is 'an unprepossessing town' according to a New York State guide book. It's the sort of place where nothing ever really happens. Some years ago GEC shut down the town's major factory and it seems that Schenectady has never really recovered. Horse racing is the major pastime in this area with the famous course of Saratoga nearby, and in August the renowned Travers Stakes takes place. So why does sleepy Schenectady host a major tennis tournament? And why, nine years on, do top players on both the men's and women's tours keep coming back?

The answer is Nitty Singh, a small Indian lady, who is the tournament director. What she lacks in height, she makes up for in sheer dynamism. She makes everything happen, and everyone adores her. Nitty is a lady whom everyone would love to have on their team, because she runs around drawing on the enthusiasm of sponsors, participants and the public to make the tournament the biggest event of its kind in Schenectady. The fireworks display alone attracts some 30,000 people.

This is a real community event,'says Nitty Singh. 'It has a carnival atmosphere.' What she has organised is a celebration, something more than just a tennis competition for some of the world's top players. The week is packed with activites including canoe racing, parachuting, picnics, aerobics contests, barbeques, fireworks and even an art exhibition - and they are for everybody, not just the tennis elite. What's more, apart from the food, they are all absolutely free, including the tennis.

Free Admission

$225,000 OTB TENNIS OPEN

International Tennis Players

Featured in 1990:
Martin Jaite *(Top Ten in the World)*
Amos Mansdorf
Wally Masur
Jaime Yzaga *(Tournament Winner '87)*
Alberto Mancini
Laura Gildemeister *(1989 Winner)*
Raffaella Reggi
Larisa Savchenko

August 20-26, 1990

Central Park Tennis Complex
Schenectady, NY

Sponsored By
Capital District Regional Off-Track Betting Corporation

Presented By
New York Telephone

IBM · Corporate Graphics Resource Inc. · capital OTB · A‸A · KRAFT GENERAL FOODS · ATP Tour

For information call Nitty Singh (518) 370-5151

From left to right: tournament director Nitty Singh, singles champion Ramesh Krishnan, President of OTB Davis Etkin, Sr., Vice President Fred Denefrio and runner-up Kelly Evernden.

What is so unusual is that it all takes place in the public park, in the beautiful and tranquil setting of the Central Park tennis courts. You can walk the dog, and stop to watch a few games from a Martin Jaite/Ramesh Krishnan match, and then wander on to catch the ladies semi-final. It's so informal, a far cry from the hustle and bustle of the regimented US Open, less than a week away. The tournament started nine years ago with a purse of $3,400. Now it boasts $225,000 in prize money - not bad for an event held in the park. The community orientated programme is organised by Capital District Regional Off-Track Betting Corporation (OTB) and is presented by the New York Telephone Company. It is one of the few events on the ATP Tour calendar that runs concurrently with the Kraft General Foods World Tour for the women.

The 1990 OTB International Tennis Open should have been reduced to a damp also-ran because of the atrocious weather, but somehow with the help of some indoor tennis and Schenectady's special atmosphere, sponsors, players and the public persevered, and with a collective will brought out the sunshine for finals day to see Ramesh Krishnan capture his eighth title with a 6-1, 6-1 win over New Zealand's Kelly Evernden before a capacity crowd at the Central Park courts. In the semi-finals Krishnan put out top seed Martin Jaite, and Evernden defeated No. 2 seed Amos Mansdorf.

The doubles competition was won by Australia's Richard Fromberg and America's Brad Pearce, who beat Brian Garrow and Sven Saluma in a tough three-setter 6-2, 3-6, 7-6. For Pearce it was a third doubles title and for Fromberg his first. It was an exciting match with some great tennis. It's a pity that American television frowns so much on doubles. Having spent a fortune in installing a large outside broadcast to cover a singles final that lasted just over an hour, would it not have made sense for the local CBS affiliate to have shown the doubles as well? As often happens it turned out to be the more exciting of the two matches.

Arthur Ashe, the first Presidnet of the ATP and holder of 33 career titles, was in Schenectady to explain the virtues of the '15-love' inner city tennis programme, whilst Billie Jean King headed up Domino's Team Tennis. There was a reminder that not only able-bodied people can play, with a display of wheelchair tennis organised by Everest & Jennings, and there was a pro-am tournament in aid of cystic fibrosis. A young girl's year was made as she became Court Queen, and a rabbit walked around giving everyone cake. Truly this was a Wonderland as the fireworks over Central Park flashed reminders of Nitty Singh's statement, 'This is the way tournaments used to be.' Forget the horse racing - as long as Nitty's in charge, come to Central New York State for the tennis.

155

Campionati Internazionali di Tennis di San Marino

By Anna Legnani

San Marino, 20-26 August
Tournament Director: Sergio Palmieri

Set in the heart of motor-crazy Emilia Romagna, the Republic of San Marino vibrates with enthusiasm every year for the Formula One Grand Prix in nearby Imola. Baseball and volleyball come next in the list of favourite sports, but tennis has been increasing in popularity, thanks very largely to the thrilling, if somewhat erratic, exploits of Paolo Cane and the steady progress of Omar Camporese, the best Italian players in recent years, both from nearby Bologna.

The two Bolognese were among players who appeared on the courts of the multi-sports complex that hosted the second year of the International Championships of San Marino. Cane, who was playing his first tournament since undergoing surgery for a discal hernia in May, was unable to get past the second round - in spite of enthusiastic support from the crowd, and in particular from skier Alberto Tomba, Olympic gold medallist in Slalom and Giant Slalom.

Camporese, on the other hand, made it to the first final of his career against the 20-year-old Argentinian Guillermo Perez-Roldan. Camporese had battled it out in three-set matches against Cedric Pioline, Franco Davin and the young Swede Niklas Kulti, who had eliminated second seed Horst Skoff in a very tense second round match.

In the top half of the draw, Perez-Roldan, meanwhile, had defeated three Italians, Massimo Cierro, Paolo Pambianco and Renzo Furlan before beating Uruguayan Marcel Filippini in three sets in the semi-final. Perez-Roldan and Camporese knew each other well, having played together when they were younger, but the Argentinian surprised his opponent by coming to the net with powerful accelerations from the baseline - he earned a 6-3, 6-3 victory. One of the most consistent clay courters this year, Perez-Roldan finally captured his first ATP Tour title this season after having made it to the finals in Casablanca, Barcelona, and Stuttgart.

In the doubles, the Czechoslovak team of Vojtech Flegl and Daniel Vacek earned their third crown in four appearances in ATP Tour events; before San Marino they had won in Umag and Prague, their other success being a semi-final in Kitzbuhel. Such impressive results had earned them the No. 2 seeding in San Marino. Spaniards Jordi Burillo and Marco Aurelio Gorriz put up a hard fight, and only went down after three sets, 6-1, 4-6, 7-6. The pair had only played together once before - San Marino was the first ATP Tour event for Burillo, a big server with a powerful forehand return. They had not dropped a set before the final.

Argentinian clay-court expert Guillermo Perez-Roldan collects his trophy from the President of the San Marino Tennis Federation, Remo Raimondi.

The Internazionali di San Marino offered players and spectators the chance to visit the historic Rock, seat of the centuries-old Republic, and the fashionable Adriatic seaside resorts of Rimini and Riccione, just half-an-hour's drive away. For those who could not afford to leave the site, even for a couple of hours, Tournament Director Sergio Palmieri organised a track meeting in the adjoining athletics stadium. He staged 100 and 400 metres events, which starred players, officials, members of the organising staff and commentators from Italian and San Marino television.

The sprint between Referee Luigi Brambilla, IBM's Gianni Pontiggia and Omar Camporese's father was an unforgettable moment, as was Chair Umpire Romano Grillotti's boogie dancing at the player's party. Every night, the small but cosy hospitality village swung to the rhythms of Nevio Devide's brilliant guitar playing, and players and staff would join in the singing, while the most enthusiastic dancers had an ample choice of indoor and outdoor discotheques just a few miles away. The Italian love of life was in full evidence for the seven days the players enjoyed San Marino.

US Open

Flushing Meadow, 27 August-9 September
Tournament Director: Marshall Happer

It was well after midnight but Pete Sampras still couldn't sleep. Over and over again he saw Ivan Lendl's last lunging backhand lob floating towards him. He saw himself reach back, crush a final overhead and throw his arms into the air as 20,000 people shook the National Tennis Centre with their cheers. 'I sat up in bed and asked myself whether I was dreaming or whether I really had beaten one of the best players of all time on his favourite court that afternoon,' Sampras said the next morning as he ate a breakfast interrupted by people coming up to congratulate him. 'The whole thing still doesn't seem real to me. I keep thinking I'm going to wake up and find out it didn't happen.' Pete Sampras never did wake up from his dream during that remarkable week in New York. Not only did he beat three-time champion Lendl in the US Open quarter finals, he then beat four-time champion John McEnroe - also on *his* favourite court - in the semi-finals, and capped it all off by crushing American glamour boy Andre Agassi in the final. In five days Pete Sampras went from promising teenager to US Open champion. In doing so, he became the first American to win the Open since McEnroe won his last title in 1984. He ended Lendl's extraordinary skein of eight straight trips to the final. And he

proved once and for all that funny-looking clothes and an entourage aren't nearly as important in big tennis matches as a 120 mile-per-hour serve and nerves that don't snap under pressure. 'I got my butt kicked,' Agassi said simply and honestly after Sampras had won the final 6-4, 6-3, 6-2. 'When a guy is serving 120 and hitting the lines, there isn't much you can do.'

This tournament didn't start out as the Pete Sampras Show. Less than two weeks after turning 19, Sampras arrived in New York as the 12th seed after a solid summer. But he was little more than an intriguing dark horse when play began on an August Monday made miserable by heat, humidity and a monsoon-like thunderstorm. The favourites were the usual suspects: Stefan Edberg, the Wimbledon champion and recently crowned No. 1 player on the planet; defending champion Boris Becker and Lendl. Agassi was the fourth seed and, numerically at least, the best American hope. McEnroe arrived unseeded for the first time in 12 years after a miserable summer that had started with a first-round loss at Wimbledon and ended with a third round defeat in Indianapolis. At 31, many wondered if this would be his farewell. It turned out instead to be his redemption. The first 10 days of this tournament belonged to McEnroe. His play, and the crowd's response to him, over-shadowed everything, including Alexander Volkov's stunning straight-set defeat of Edberg in the first round. McEnroe grew up just a few miles from The National Tennis Centre and had always longed for the kind of affection showered on Jimmy Connors over the years by the New York crowd. As a teenager he was too brash and in his 20s he was too good to receive that kind of adoration. Now, as the old man and the underdog, he finally had it. In the third round, he whipped 10th-seeded Andrei Chesnokov in front of a frenzied Friday night crowd. But that was just a warm-up. On the middle Sunday, McEnroe and Emilio Sanchez staged an epic that will be talked about for as long as they play tennis here. Down two sets to one, with the crowd in complete hysterics, McEnroe clawed his way back, finally beating Sanchez after more than four hours of wonderful, gripping tennis. It was a match as emotional as any final McEnroe has played in, one that left the entire crowd drained and exhilarated all at once. That victory put McEnroe into the quarter-finals against young American David Wheaton who, like Sampras, has the potential to be a Grand Slam champion in the near future. The other quarter-finalists were Sampras-Lendl, Becker-Krickstein and Agassi-Cherkasov.

Only Lendl-Sampras was close. McEnroe, rolling now, whipped Wheaton in three sets. Wheaton did get some consolation when he and doubles partner Paul Annacone reached the final before losing to Pieter Aldrich and Denis Visser, the South Africans making up for their loss in the Wimbledon final with a straight-set victory. In the meantime Agassi, having survived an ugly profanity/spitting incident during his second round match against Petr Korda, easily beat Cherkasov - who had reached his second Slam quarter-final of the year by upsetting Michael Chang. Becker was sluggish in dropping the first set to Krickstein, but survived. Lendl-Sampras was worth remembering, the kid sprinting to a two-set

Power from Pete Sampras on his way to the Crown.

lead, blowing it, then steadying himself to win the fifth. Lendl, a one-time mentor of Sampras, didn't think his loss was any fluke. 'He's very talented,' Lendl said. 'I like his chances in the semis.' Lendl proved prescient. Even with the crowd going crazy, McEnroe had no answers for the California kid's bombs, losing in four tough sets. The other semi-final was a strange one. After Becker had won a superb first set from Agassi, he decided to spend the rest of the match two feet behind the baseline. Result: Agassi in four.

That sent Agassi into his second Grand Slam final of the year. He should have been the cool one, the nerveless one on Sunday. He had been there before. Instead, it was Sampras, breaking Agassi in the third game of the match and never looking back. No Pete, it wasn't a dream. It was, though, a dream come true.

Grand Prix Passing Shot

By Yannick Cochennel

Bordeaux, 10-16 September
Tournament Director: Jean-Pierre Derose

If there are some successes that one will never forget, then it will be Bordeaux 1990 that will always stay in Guy Forget's memory. He needed courage - a great amount of courage - to win the 12th Open Passing Shot de Bordeaux, for his father, Pierre, died in the middle of the week.

On the verge of withdrawing from the event after his second-round victory over the Spaniard Carlos Costa, Guy nonetheless battled on. 'My mother prompted me to go on in spite of sorrow, all the journeys back and forth to home and the nervous exhaustion I was suffering. I won

here thanks to her.' Strangely enough the tragedy gave him the power to play without the usual pressure. 'The worst thing that could happen here was to lose. Nothing disastrous in that.' Usually nervous, and especially so when he competes in France, Guy was able to play almost totally relaxed, performing at his highest level in the semi-finals against Ronald Agenor and then in the finals against Goran Ivanisevic. Against the Yugoslavian in the final, on the red clay at Villa Primose, Forget needed only 70 minutes to beat an opponent who was not in his best form. It was the first time since Yannick Noah's triumph in 1979 that a

Mansour Bahrami and Yannick Noah, two of the sport's great entertainers, crack the jokes but Thomas Carbonell and Libor Pimek have their hands on the silverware after the doubles final.

Frenchman has won in Bordeaux. Guy's victory was his third career title and strangely enough both the other two were also won in France: Toulouse in 1986 and Nancy in 1989. His efforts allowed him to rise up the rankings from 19th in the world to 15, his highest singles ranking ever at that time. It also strengthened his role as the new leader in French tennis. Over and above the $38,000 he received as the winner's purse, Guy had the privilege of taking home 1990 bottles of Bordeaux and was awarded a prize for his 'fair-play' throughout the tournament.

During the tournament, the public of Bordeaux, who came in great crowds this year, had the pleasure of seeing Goran Ivanisevic, one of the new stars of tennis. The Yugoslav had come close to defeat in the second round as he had to save two match points against the Spaniard Fernando Luna before recovering in order to defeat Fabrice Santoro (Noah's victor) in the quarter finals and Guillermo Perez-Roldan in the semis. Ivanisevic's game was missing its usual flair in the finals but we might excuse him a little for the youngster had celebrated his 19th birthday that week ....

A poignant moment for Guy Forget who won the title in the week his father died.

Barclay Open

By Rene Stauffer

Geneva, 10-16 September
Tournament Director: Daniel Iegenheer

It was one of the last warm and sunny Sundays of a Swiss Autumn and more than 3000 spectators found their way to the beautiful Parc des Eaux-Vives on the lake of Geneva to enjoy the final of the Barclay Open.

The only thing not quite perfect in the view of most of them was the line-up for the Championship match: Austrian Horst Skoff against Sergi Bruguera from Spain. Neither defending champion Marc Rosset, the hometown hero of Geneva, who had exploded into big-time tennis exactly one year ago with a sensational triumph over Guillermo Perez-Roldan, nor Henri Leconte, who adopted Geneva as his hometown, made their way through to the final. And Swiss No. 1 Jakob Hlasek had already disappeared after two rounds.

The No.1 seed Leconte took a wildcard into the tournament and reached the quarters before bowing out, weakned by a pain in his neck. 'This is my biggest ever win', admitted his conquerer Michael Tauson from Denmark, who was the last player to make it into the main draw. No. 4 seed Rosset didn't drop a set on his way to the semifinals, although he

Horst Skoff's aggressive attitude to his tennis paid off in Geneva where he won his first title in two years.

The Barclay Open takes place in Geneva's beautiful Parc des Eaux-Vives.

couldn't find the superb form of a year ago. After winning the first set against Horst Skoff, his first serve let him down and he lost 4-6, 6-3, 6-2. The tall Swiss later complained about Skoff's behaviour, which disturbed his concentration; 'He insulted and provoked me in a way I have never seen before'.

Nineteen-year-old Bruguera had a much easier ride to the final than Skoff, losing a mere 16 games against his first four opponents, blowing away Horacio de la Pena in the quarters 6-0, 6-2 and Tauson in the semis 6-1, 6-2. The Spaniard had already reached the final of the Swiss Open earlier in July, but as in Gstaad, where he lost against Martin Jaite, he couldn't manage to win the last and vital match in Geneva.

With the final on its way, the crowd soon forgot that Rosset and Leconte were missing. Bruguera seemed in control at first, leading 3-1, but he was unable to avoid a tie-break. Down 2-6, the Spaniard won the next five points - only to lose the first set after 83 minutes with the tie-break score of 10-8. 'Horst's forehand was too strong for me today - he really played great', Bruguera later said. The No. 6 seed kept his fighting spirit alive and forced another tie-break, but once again he had to leave the better end to his opponent. 'It was a great week for me and a great tournament', Skoff said after tying up the match 7-6,7-6 in two hours and 26 minutes. He celebrated his first title for two years and his third overall after Athens and Vienna, both won in 1988. 'In the end I was a little lucky. But during this year I have been short of luck when I lost close matches in tie-breaks'.

For a straight-set victory the match could hardly have been closer and some of the tennis, fast, powerful and inventive, offered prolonged glimpses of the clay court game at its best.

The victory, which earned him $32,400 and a Swiss watch, came at a very important moment: the following week Skoff was due to take on Andre Agassi and Michael Chang in the Davis Cup Tie in Vienna against the United States. 'That was the best preperation I could have had, and a tremendous boost for my confidence' said Skoff, the first Austrian winner of a major Swiss tournament.

Swiss Indoors

By Daniel Fricker

Basel, 24-30 September
Tournament Director: Roger Brennwald

The Swiss Indoors Championship in Basel marked John McEnroe's first appearance on the ATP Tour since his magnificent semi-final performance at the US Open. It was also his first official visit to Switzerland since he played the Basel tournament in 1978 when he lost in the final to Guillermo Vilas.

This time, McEnroe did better. He played a heart-stopping final against Goran Ivanisevic of Yugoslavia, surprising everyone by recovering from a two set to love defecit, down 2-5 in the third with a match point against him at 3-5. He took home his first Swiss title and a winner's cheque of $65,000. The score itself - 6-7 (4-7), 4-6, 7-6 (7-3), 6-3, 6-4, after four hours and 40 minutes - says much about the high quality of the final. It was the third final in the ATP Tour to be fought by two left-handers. It entertained 8100 enthusiastic fans and a worldwide TV audience. 'I can't remember having won a final in five sets, after being down match point. Now I know I am on the right path.' McEnroe was proud of a gutsy performance that gave him his first win in the ATP Tour, his 76th singles title and his first win for more than a year. Only once before in his long career had the 31-year-old American managed to recover after being two sets down - against Darren Cahill in the first round at Wimbledon in 1989.

Wild-card entry Ivanisevic was clearly disappointed at his defeat: 'I can't believe that I lost this match.' But the 19-year-old Yugoslavian added on a note of respect, 'McEnroe played a great match.' The surprising part of it all was this: on this occasion, it was neither McEnroe's skilful play nor his fabulous touch that brought about the unexpected overturn.

Instead, it was the American's indestructible will to win this tournament and his imperturbable aggressiveness. Two stupid netted forehands by Ivanisevic gave McEnroe all he needed: the re-break in the third set that destroyed his opponent's confidence. The rest - pure formality. Another problem for Ivanisevic was that he had no experience of the 20-minute break after three sets.

Throughout the week, McEnroe lived up to the high expectations of the new record attendance of 61,100 fans. Meanwhile, another hero of American tennis made a quick exit in the first round: Jimmy Connors, 38 - who was playing his first tournament since February, when he had problems with a wrist injury - lost in two sets to Michael Stich of West Germany. Connors' 24-year-old countryman Scott Melville, however, put in an impressive performance. The tall Californian accepted a wild card for the qualifying tournament

John McEnroe, who in 1990 at Basel became the first player to win titles spanning three decades, is flanked by tournament director Roger Brennwald and Goran Ivanisevic. Ivanisevic appears to be biting back his tongue in frustration at letting slip what appeared to be an assured victory.

- and made it all the way through the semis for the main draw, leaving behind Frank Dennhardt of West Germany, Jean-Philippe Fleurian (who had eliminated top seed Andrés Gomez in the first round) and Yannick Noah of France, all shaking their heads and pulling uncomprehending faces. Melville even gave McEnroe a tough run for the final berth, though he lost eventually in three sets. His week's efforts lifted him from No. 322 to a career high, No. 186 in the singles ranking.

Also happy with the first semi-final appearance of his career was Finland's Veli Paloheimo who outlasted two seeded players in a row, No. 4 Andrei Chesnokov and No. 6 Magnus Gustafsson. But he wore himself out and, in the end, was not up to giving Ivanisevic a hard fight. Nevertheless the talented 23-year-old gave Finland's tennis another welcome boost with his performance here and finished the year with an ATP ranking of 69.

Marc Rosset, the giant from Geneva, inevitably carried the hopes of the crowd with him but he shocked his fans by losing a close first round encounter to Mansour Bahrami the Paris based Iranian who had not won a single match in his previous six tournaments. Only those who have never seen this incredibly talented performer would query Roger Brenwald's decision to give the 679th ranked player in the world a wild card entry into the main draw. Bahrami's droll personality was so infectious that the crowd quickly forgave him for removing Rosset and he went on to dazzle over 8000 people with a brilliant performance against his good friend Yannick Noah. It was a match made in heaven for those who like large slices of comedy sandwiched in between their serious tennis and the pair produced some barely believable shots; throwing in the odd table tennis ball for fun and imitating Boris Becker, Ivan Lendl and John McEnroe.

38th International Championships of Sicily

By Richard Evans

Palermo, 24-30 September
Tournament Director: Cino Marchese

The Sicilian Open may have had more celebrated winners in the past - Bjorn Borg won here in 1979 and Mats Wilander in 1988 - but no one could suggest that Argentina's Franco Davin did not deserve the title he plucked with such care from Juan Aguilera's grasp in the final. Davin wrapped up his first singles title of the year, and only the second of his career, 6-1, 6-1 in just one hour and six minutes to earn himself $38,840. The brevity of the final was, of course, a disappointment to the fans who were expecting more of Aguilera. Indeed, the elegant Spaniard had promised more as he glided over the red clay of the Club Circolo del Tennis, removing Javier Sanchez in the second round, Claudio Pistolesi in the quarters and No. 2 seed Guillermo Perez-Roldan in the semis without the loss of a set.

In fact, prior to the final, only the 19-year-old Italian wild card Stefano Pescosolido managed to win a set from Aguilera who, for most of the week, looked very much like the clay-court maestro who had dominated Nice and Hamburg earlier in the year. But for artists like Aguilera, tennis is a soufflé that cannot be guaranteed to rise on demand. If the recipe is slightly off, everything can fall flat and the

The plucky Argentinian Franco Davin played a topspin baseline game to clinch his second career title.

Sanchez and Casal with an unusual trophy; Daniella Calandra who looks after the players in Palermo.

thin man from Barcelona looked like a chef who had lost his cookbook in the final. Nothing worked for Aguilera, and the harder he tried the less it looked as if he was trying. Miloslav Mecir would have understood the problem exactly. He, too, has been accused of not caring on days when the timing is awry and the concentration fluttering in the wind.

Although decisive in his victories over Paolo Cane and Martin Strelba, Davin had to battle hard to overcome the French Open quarter-finalist Thierry Champion who pushed him to 7-5 in the third. It was in that grittily fought duel that Davin earned his title and, in doing so, offered further evidence of the continuing strength of Argentine tennis. Two more players from the land of the gaucho, Horacio de la Pena and Carlos Costa made it through to the doubles final but this time Spain had the final word with Emilio Sanchez and his long-time partner Sergio Casal taking the title 6-3, 6-4.

This was the 39th edition of the Sicilian Open and the 12th under the expert stewardship of IMG's Cino Marchese who views the tournament as his pet project of the year. Cino, in his expansive style, enjoys staying at hotels where the fading tapestry on the walls hangs together better than the telephone service and taking guests to dinner at favourite trattorias in the dodgy end of town. Palermo, to a first-time visitor, is everything one had expected ... and so much more. The broad Via della Liberta matches anything one finds in Rome or Milan as a shopping street of style and opulence; while over at the beach area surrounding the Mondello Palace where the players stay, bars and restaurants light up the evening hours in true Sicilian style.

Making the most of their association with the big wide world of the ATP Tour, the city of Palermo decided to host a dinner at the ATP Tour World Championship in Frankfurt, a public relations gesture that may soon be imitated by other cities.

Commonwealth Bank Queensland Open

By Craig Gabriel

Brisbane, 24-30 September
Tournament Director: Graham Lovett

Picture a tennis court surrounded by tropical plants. Bright, sunny days leading into balmy nights, and all you can hear is the sound of tennis balls connecting with the strings of a racquet, or crickets chattering away in the bushes almost appearing to discuss whether the ball was in or out, or still better to some, the 'pop' of a champagne cork.

It could be some exotic location in the south seas, and in a way it is, as Brisbane, the sunshine capital of Australia, played host to the $250,000 Commonwealth Bank Queensland Open in late September.

Under the inspirational leadership of tournament director Graham Lovett, the Milton Tennis Centre underwent a makeover that would leave any artist gasping - indeed Zsa Zsa Gabor would have been proud. The example was set in 1989 when the stadium was left unrecognisable ... it had never looked so good. 1990 was even better. It took three weeks to go from the bare essentials to the full 'Raffles'-inspired theme, and corporate guests were forgiven for thinking that they were in Singapore, the island-city that still bears his legacy.

Mr. Consistency - Brad Gilbert consolidates his position in the world's top ten with a title Down Under.

Four semi -trailers of scaffolding arrived and, over a week and a half and some $120,000 later, the tower was constructed to accommodate the banks of lights surrounding the centre court so that those crickets could come out and watch the likes of Brad Gilbert and Aaron Krickstein and wildcard Mats Wilander play games. Another ten truck loads of tropical plants created the atmosphere that really is so typical of Queensland. The largest corporate entertainment marquee in Queensland was erected and decorated with lattice work, cane furniture and palm trees that swayed gently with the light breezes that flowed through.

The pace is just that bit slower and just that bit more relaxing in Brisbane as it hugs the river bearing its name. But that does not mean this city is missing the glitz and glamour of its more publicised sisters down south. The nightclubs and discos in 'Brissie', as the locals call it, are alive and rocking. Tennis is a way of life in Queensland, some of the country's all-time greats such as Rod Laver, Roy Emerson and champion doubles team Geoff Masters and Ross Case hail from there. And the locals most certainly know what the game is all about.

There was a strong international field, probably the best the event has enjoyed. Gilbert, Krickstein and Wilander (who fell to fourth seed Carl-Uwe Steeb in the first round) made their debuts at the tournament, although Gilbert had been to Brisbane four years before with not so pleasant memories of a Davis Cup tie. There was no doubt it was a success as almost 25,000 fans turned out to support the overseas players and the home-grown heroes such as John Fitzgerald, Todd Woodbridge and Mark Kratzmann. But Gilbert managed to rid himself of those Davis Cup memories and for the uninitiated a yell from the top of his lungs could have sounded like some sort of war cry as he stood on centre court following a backhand error from Krickstein that ended the final 6-3, 6-1. 'It was the first all Hebrew final of the year and it's the best match I have played all year,' said Gilbert after the 70-minute final in which he collected $32,400. 'It was my first win in Australia.'

In the doubles Todd Woodbridge and Jason Stoltenberg combined to win their first title, defeating the scratch pairing of Mark Woodforde and Brian Garrow 2-6, 6-4, 6-4.

Australian Indoor Tennis Championships

By Craig Gabriel

Sydney, 1-7 October
Tournament Director: Graham Lovett

Dare it be written with regard to a men's tennis tournament, but the women's circuit adopted a rather catchy slogan some time ago that was worded: 'You've Come A Long Way Baby'. Well the same could be said of the Australian Indoor Tennis Championships, for after a baptism with fire, the baby came of age in 1990, its eighteenth year. Indeed, the Australian Indoors, with its new title sponsor Uncle Tobys, has matured along with men's tennis as a whole.

Back in 1973 while on a trans-Pacific flight John Newcombe and Fred Stolle mulled over the idea of an indoor tournament for Sydney, Australia. They took the idea to senior executives at Slazenger, Australia, Graham Lovett, a quarter-finalist at the 1955 Australian championships, and Arthur Huxley and a partnership was formed.

Arrangements were made to stage the event in the Hordern Pavilion, generally known as 'the old barn', and with that the Australian Indoors was born. A title sponsor, Custom Credit Finance, was secured with total prize money of $50,000. In the first year the final was between the two Australian legends Rod Laver John Newcombe. Although Newc couldn't pull it off that year, he did so twelve months later by defeating Cliff Richey to win his 'own' event.

A grimacing Ivan Lendl, who was beaten in the semi-finals by Stefan Edberg, the man who had knocked him off the No. 1 position in the world seven weeks before.

In 1990 prize money hit the $US1 million mark and the tournament has become a veritable showpiece for Australian sport. One could not have imagined it would have got to this stage

The taste of success is sweet for Boris Becker who takes a shower in champagne after his victory.

when we started back in 1973,' said Lovett, the Tournament Director. 'We effectively introduced indoor tennis to Australia when sporting events were of an outdoor nature. Not only that, we also introduced the corporate box system of entertainment to sport and that was a concept that took hold very quickly. The Australian Indoors is a tennis tournament and a social event and that's the trend of international sport.'

So many of the greats of modern tennis, and even a couple from another era like Rosewall and Lew Hoad thrilled the gallery. Jimmy Connors won the title twice, Stan Smith and Arthur Ashe held the trophy, Roscoe Tanner was there as were Vitas Gerulaitis and Guillermo Vilas. It did not take a long time for the Hordern to start groaning at the seams because it was reaching spectator capacity. One year play was stopped because of

Above: Blue Supreme carpet on the centre court.
It is ideally suited to a fast serve and volley game
such as Becker's.
Left: Stefan Edberg, the most elegant of shotmakers,
reached his ninth final of the year in Sydney.

rain ... the roof was leaking. The 'old barn' had
seen its day. By the end of the tournament in 1982,
the Hordern had dished out all it could and it made
way for the plush new Sydney Entertainment
Centre and once that happened the tournament
started to realise its true potential.

Without doubt John McEnroe had the most
enviable record of all comers. He was the
only player to win at both sites. He never lost a
set and claimed the singles prize every year he
played from 1980 to 1983 and the doubles prize in
1980, '81 and '82. Incredibly, McEnroe only ever
lost one match in Sydney in four years and that
was the doubles final in 1983 when he partnered
Peter Rennart against Mark Edmondson and
Sherwood Stewart.

Enter Ivan Lendl, who has reached five finals
(more than any other player) for three wins,
Boris Becker and Pat Cash as they thrilled all with
their dazzling speed and power. The Australian
Indoors had certainly become a leading stop on the
Tour as Sydney turned on the charm like no other
city can do.

The Australian Indoors has provided its fair share of memorable anecdotes. Pat Cash revealing things that go bump in the night at his hotel, charity fund raising for the Variety Club, and then there was the rather 'full' waiter walking onto the centre court during a match and making a speech.

Now with a total of $1 million in prize money it has taken another step forward. It has developed 'elite' status on the ATP Tour. In 1990 the tournament played host to what was the greatest field in its history. It was a real who's who of tennis. Lendl, Becker, Edberg, Chang, Cash, Wilander, Gilbert, Krickstein and so on.

It marked the first time that the top three players had gathered at the same event since Edberg assumed the number one ranking in the world from Lendl in early August. It came down to that winning feeling for Becker as he defeated Edberg

in the championship match 7-6, 6-4, 6-4 and then proceeded to pour French champagne over himself. 'It feels very good,' said Becker. 'It feels very special to beat the number one player in the world. I wanted to beat him pretty badly ... that Wimbledon loss hurt and I wanted to win more than him.'

Earlier, in what was dubbed the finest match of the tournament's history, Edberg came back from a set and break down in the semi-finals to stop Lendl 3-6, 7-6, 6-3. For the Swede it was the first time since Wimbledon that he had faced Lendl and Becker back to back.

The doubles title went to Broderick Dyke and Peter Lundgren who defeated the scratch pairing of Lendl and Edberg 6-2, 6-4. The tournament ended with the world's top three players on the same court on the same day. A unique milestone.

With his grass court form still lacking the old Cash dash, Pat spent some extra time at the microphone in London during Wimbledon but his on-court form continued to show signs of improvement at the Sydney Indoors.

Grand Prix de Toulouse

By Bruno Cuaz

Toulouse, 1-7 October
Tournament Director: Christian Bimes

Everyone in Toulouse was hoping for it, but in the end the miracle didn't happen. Jonas Svensson dominated the French hope, Fabrice Santoro, 7-6 6-2 in one hour and 42 minutes, winning his fourth career title and his second one in France after his victory in Metz in 1988. Santoro didn't win but the 7,000 fans at the Palais des Sports de Toulouse honoured him with a standing ovation for his achievement throughout the week.

Aged 17 years and 10 months, this Frenchman Tahiti-born, who uses two hands for both his forehand and backhand shots, qualified for the first time in his career for a superb final, becoming the youngest finalist of the year on the ATP Tour and the first French player to achieve such an accolade. Yannick Noah, who until Toulouse had held that record amongst French players, reached his first final in Nice 1978 when he was 17 years and 11 months.

Fabrice, who was given a wild card by the tournament director, Christian Bimes, didn't have the easiest part of the draw for his first opponent was none other than the No.1 seed Andres Gomez. Taking advantage of the Ecuadorian

A roar of triumph for the normally quiet Swede, as Jonas Svensson claims the fourth singles title of his career.

174

At 17, Fabrice Santoro, who reached the final in Toulouse, is the new hope of French tennis.

player's weak form, Santoro took his victory in three sets, before dominating in succession Jaimie Yzaga, Christian Bergstrom and Ronald Agenor in straight sets. Agenor had put out the 1988 and 1989 winner, Jimmy Connors, in the first round.

But Fabrice was forced to give in against Jonas, the No. 3 seed, who was in top physical condition. Jonas Svensson, competing in his 7th Grand Prix de Toulouse, had been very unlucky at the same tournament the year before. In forgetting the sign-in deadline, he had to play the qualifying rounds and was defeated by Roger Smith. To earn the trophy and the magnificent gold pen, estimated to be worth 55,000 French francs (a record that has its place in the Guinness Book of Records), the Swede had to fight hard and eliminate Luiz Mattar, Veli Paloheimo, Magnus Larsson, Amos Mansdorf and then Santoro in the

Fabrice Santoro, the youngest finalist of the ATP Tour year, is defeated by Jonas Svensson.

final. Jonas, who hadn't won a tournament since 1988, rose up the rankings to 17th in the world, near to his career-best rank of 13 (July 1988). Jonas Svensson's victory - an early birthday present - and the accession of Santoro at the 9th Toulouse Grand Prix (which attracted 66,000 spectators) also produced a marvellous exhibition match between Yannick Noah and Mansour Bahrami which thrilled the public. Noah, who was due to play the No.2 seed Andrei Chesnokov, had a 'lucky win' when the Soviet player was forced to withdraw from the tournament owing to a bout of gastric flu. In order to give the public their money's worth, Yannick and Mansour stepped onto the court and put on a marvellous show, dressed up as each other and wearing make-up. It was too much for Ilie Nastase, sitting in his box, who couldn't resist taking part in the fun.

Athens Grand Prix

By Richard Evans

Athens, 1-7 October
Tournament Director: Dionyssis Gangas

One could hardly suggest that the arrival of the ATP Tour in Athens did anything to assuage the city's collective grief over the shattering and unexpected loss of the 1996 Olympic Games to Atlanta. But at least it offered tournament director Dionyssis Gangas a welcome distraction on his return from the IOC meeting in Tokyo just a few days before. Mr Gangas had been in charge of the Athens PR campaign there and was, naturally, more than a little disappointed at the result.

To his eternal credit, however, that did not allow him to offer his tennis-playing guests anything but the best in Greek hospitality at the charming Athens Tennis Club which might be a little cramped and old-fashioned for the modern professional tour but, lying as it does in the shadow of the Temple of Zeus, is not lacking in atmosphere. Certainly, it was ambience that seemed conducive to the Dutch players in the draw. Not only did Mark Koevermans win the first singles title of his career but two of his lesser known countrymen, Tom Kempers and Richard Krajicek, reached the final of the doubles after fighting their way through the qualifying rounds. They lost eventually

to Sergio Casal and Javier Sanchez - deputising for brother Emilio - but not before the Dutch newcomers had disposed of Uruguay's Diego Perez and Koevermans himself in the semis.

Taking the week off from doubles did not do Emilio Sanchez a lot of good as far as his singles was concerned. Like most of the other top seeds he found the slow clay courts something of a minefield and went out to a fellow Spaniard, Francisco Roig, who played the best match of his career to out-hit Sanchez from the back court and win 6-2, 7-6 in the first round. Top seed Thomas Muster only survived one round longer, going down 6-3 in the third to the Czech, Marian Vajda, while the No. 3 seed, Guillermo Perez-Roldan, was stunned by the ferocity of Franco Davin's attacking ground strokes when they met in the quarters and only won three games.

> *Koevermans was the first Dutchman to win a singles title since Tom Okker won in Tel Aviv in 1979.*

Davin, in fact, was still on the kind of form that had earned him the Palermo title the week before but the slightly built Argentine had to work hard to beat off Vajda's challenge in the semis before emerging a 7-6, 2-6, 6-3 winner and

176

Koevermans, not surprisingly, looked fresher in the final. The 22-year-old from Rotterdam, who had accounted for Roig and fourth seeded Jordi Arrese along the way, fought back grittily after losing the first set and eventually took control of a finely played final as Davin tired. Koevermans, who became the 13th first-time singles champion on the ATP Tour in 1990, was also the first Dutchman to win a singles title since Tom Okker won in Tel Aviv in 1979.

As Okker won 30 titles in his illustrious career and, in fact, stands 14th on the list of all-time title winners in the Open era (a list headed by Jimmy Connors with 109), Koevermans will need no reminding of just how far he has to go. But Koevermans has made a start and now, with the gods of ancient Greece in his corner, he can at least edge upwards on the ATP Tour's prosaic answer to Mount Olympus which we know as the computer ranking.

Diego Perez with his wife, Gabriela, framed by the ancient columns of the Temple of Zeus near the tennis club.

Seiko Super Tennis

By Craig Gabriel

Tokyo, 8-14 October
Tournament Director: Jun Kamiwazumi

It is the Land of the Rising Sun, where the Meiji Shrine and Buddhist Temples bring in a serenity from the outside world. It is where east truly meets west. It is the richest country in the world. And it is all controlled from one city where the night sky is made brilliant by billions of neon lights, as though emeralds, diamonds and rubies are being flashed around in a frenzy. This is the epitome of Tokyo, a metropolis of great extremes. Japan is also a sportsminded nation. It's one of those modern avenues the place has developed over the last three decades, in particular since 1964 when Tokyo was awarded the XVIII Olympiad - the first and, until Seoul in 1988, the only Asian city to host the Olympic Games. Japanese athletes have won marathon road races, they have performed well in swimming, hit out in baseball, taken to the rugby field, achieved great recognition in gymnastics and

Ivan Lendl walks on court with the photo-mad Japanese fans frantically clicking behind him.

Boris Becker (left) and doubles partner Eric Jelen are good friends on and off court.

made tremendous drives in golf. It should come as no surprise then that tennis is one of the leading participation and spectator sports among the 120 million people that inhabit the islands from Kyushu to Hokkaido.

The very first Seiko World Super Tennis (later to become the Seiko Super Tennis) was played in 1978. With a total prize money of $200,000, it was among the richest tournaments in the world. In its first two years it was staged at the Tokyo Metropolitan Gymnasium, built in 1964 for the Games, and the fledgling tournament was won both times by none other than Bjorn Borg. A year later it shifted to the Yoyogi National Stadium which was used in the 1964 Games as the site for swimming. This time, boards were laid over the swimming pool for the two tennis courts and different strokes were played.

In the first year of action Japan's leading player, Jun Kamiwazumi, had plenty to think about on court as he played the big Yugoslav Zeljko Franulovic. Kamiwazumi remembers the match in more humorous ways today, after all the score was

6-0, 6-0 to Zeljko. A lot of water has passed under the bridge since then. Franulovic has become the Vice President and Director of Marketing for ATP Tour Europe, while Kamiwazumi has matters to think about off court, as tournament director of the immensely successful Seiko Super Tennis.

In 1990 the Seiko Super Tennis has $1 million in prize money and once again it has changed venues. However, to steal the title from one of the most successful movies to be screened in Japan, its ... back to the future. The tournament returned to the Tokyo Metropolitan Gymnasium, now prefaced with the world 'New', a venue that was totally refurbished.

It became the only indoor tournament in the world with three match courts side by side, plus another two practice courts, all under the one roof. Then on the Thursday of the event the three match courts became one and Kamiwazumi was given the pleasurable task of passing out to everyone the 'oiribukuro', a traditional red and white envelope with a 100 yen coin that signifies it is 'house full'.

179

Australia's Todd Woodbridge with determination written across his face; unfortunately it still wasn't sufficient to beat Stefan Edberg in the second round.

For Ivan Lendl it was a different tournament. He had not defeated the world's number one player for five years, and it was pretty close to a decade since he accounted for the world's top two players back to back. Those statistics really should come as no surprise because for most of that time he has held down one of those places. The 30-year-old Czech played some blistering tennis to become the only player to win the event three times. He dismissed Stefan Edberg in the semi-finals 7-5, 6-3, and Boris Becker in the final 4-6, 6-3, 7-6 to win his 88th career title.

It's a success especially on this [very fast Supreme] surface,' said Lendl. 'I went into the match saying serve well and I was able to take the short ball.' Lendl collected $122,700 and claimed that this was his best performance since defeating Becker in the final of The Stella Artois Grass Court Championship in June. He trailed 1-5 in the first set and appeared to be playing right into Becker's hands as the German powered ground strokes and volleys away for winners. But the Czech admitted that he sensed Becker was 'becoming unglued,' and 'starting to weaken from 5-2 in the first set' as he clawed his way back into the final before clinching the title in the third-set tie-breaker.

He tried every shot,' said Becker who earned $66,000. 'He decided he was going to put it on the line and risk all. At the end it's one point and it depends a bit on luck. He was playing great tennis when it was the most important time and it was an extremely good match from both players.'

> *In '78 and '79 the fledgling tournament was won by none other than Bjorn Borg.*

In the doubles competition, No. 3 seeds Guy Forget and Jakob Hlasek claimed their third title of the year, winning 7-6, 7-5 over the Americans Scott Davis and David Pate. Following their win, Forget and Hlasek rose two places up the ATP Tour computer team-standing rankings to the No. 6 spot. As a result of their triumph at the Seiko Super Tennis their place in the ATP Tour Doubles Championship in Sanctuary Cove was secured.

An occupational hazard of life on the men's professional tennis tour: Scott Davis (left) and doubles partner David Pate hang around killing time in the players' locker rooms.

Berlin Open

By Richard Evans

Berlin, 8-14 October
Tournament Director: Jochen Grosse

The autumn leaves lay strewn along Jesse Owens Allee during Berlin's first week as a truly united city in forty-five years. Just down the street a new sporting complex had chosen a dramatic moment to open its doors to an international group of athletes as the ATP Tour arrived to contest the first major sports event to be staged in a city that was still trying to learn how to live without barriers or division or Checkpoint Charlie. So it was perhaps appropriate that the first Berlin Open should be won by a man who has embraced a multitude of languages and cultures, a man who, more than any other, epitomises the truly international make-up of the ATP Tour.

Ronald Agenor, who defeated Alexander Volkov of the Soviet Union in a tremendous final 4-6, 6-4, 7-6, was born in Morocco of Haitian parentage and now lives in Bordeaux where, presumably, he gets little chance to practise one of his languages which is Swahili. The excellence of the final was no more than Jochen Grosse deserved. It had not been easy implanting this new tournament in a strangely built building which stands in the shadow of the vast Olympic stadium where, in l936, that great black runner Jesse Owens infuriated Hitler by racing gloriously for gold. Grosse, one of the game's great enthusiasts, had been forced to move his event from Frankfurt

when it was decided to hold the ATP World Championship in that city and, as it turned out, neither the new facility nor the Berlin tennis community were quite ready for him. Grosse was unable to advertise for eight weeks during the summer because of a locally instigated lawsuit, and when the new US Open Champion Pete

Germany's Martin Sinner ousted top seed Goran Ivanisevic in the second round on his way to the semis.

Ronald Agenor claims his second ATP Tour title of the year in an undivided Berlin.

Sampras was forced to pull out with shin splints any chance of a distracted public being turned on to a tennis tournament at a new venue evaporated. Crowds were disappointing all week even though those who did turn up feasted happily on the buffet fare provided in the box holders hospitality area.

In between visits to what used to be East Berlin where players found a few remnants of wall to take a hack at, some excellent tennis was played, notably by Brazil's Luis Mattar who has rarely done well outside South America and the German newcomer Martin Sinner. Both reached the semi-finals and Sinner, ranked 151 going into the event, created the upset of the week by outplaying top seed Goran Ivanisevic 7-6, 6-4 in the second round. But well as the talented Volkov played throughout the week - a 6-3, 6-0 defeat of Jonas Svensson was indicative of his form - there was

no denying Agenor. Serving with ever greater authority and pummelling his ground strokes off both flanks in between darting sorties to the net, this small, wiry athlete out-hit Kevin Curren in the quarters, stopped Sinner in the semis and fought tooth and nail to parry Volkov's whiplash southpaw stroke play in a final that ranked amongst the best seen on the Tour in many weeks.

Despite a splendid victory over Ivanisevic and Petr Korda in the semi-final, the scratch team of Curren and Patrick Galbraith could not quite seal their new partnership with a title-winning performance in the doubles although it was a close-run thing. Despite the need to overcome the leading pair of the year, Pieter Aldrich and Danie Visser, Curren and Galbraith forced their opponents to win two tie-breakers before the South Africans could lay their hands on the $8,060 prize money.

Riklis Israel Tennis Classic

By Jonathan Marks

Tel Aviv, 8-14 October
Tournament Director: Ian Froman

They had to change the rules the day the ATP Tour came to Tel Aviv. Adults are usually forbidden to use the courts at Ramat Hasharon, one of the seven Israeli Tennis Centres. But the kids, whose sole preserve the 18 courts normally are, made an exception for the pros who turned up to contest the 1990 Riklis Open. And why not?

After all, two of the tournament's top seeds, Amos Mansdorf and Gilad Bloom, are themselves products of this unique system. Ian Froman, both head of the Israeli Tennis Centres and Riklis tournament director, attributes much of Israel's recent successes in tennis to foreign donations and support. But he still stresses the importance

Andrei Chesnokov was the first Soviet tennis star ever to play in Israel; winning the tournament and the hearts of the people in Tel Aviv by his decision to play despite the tense political situation.

of keeping the Centres for the young people: 'You can give a million dollars to a Tennis Centre here, but it still won't book you a court - they're just for the kids.'

On the courts where Mansdorf and Bloom had first learnt to play, and in front of a vociferous home crowd, both men progressed to the last four, though Bloom had to stage a miraculous recovery, saving four match points before seeing off Christo Van Rensburg in the quarter finals. Bloom's gutsy display earned him a match in the last four against top seed Andrei Chesnokov, who, ranked tenth in the world, needed computer points for his late push for a place in the end-of-year finals in Frankfurt. But Chesnokov's trip to Tel Aviv had historical significance also: in playing in the Riklis Open, the Muscovite became the first Soviet tennis player to compete in Israel. The Tel Aviv crowd took him to their hearts, even forgiving him for brushing aside Bloom in the semi-finals. And Chesnokov was not just enjoying himself on court. Renowned as one of the Tour's great socialites, Andrei did his reputation no harm at the player's party. Entering fully into the Middle Eastern spirit of the evening, he joined other guests in pinning money to a belly dancer. Just imagine the poor girl's frustration when she discovered that Andrei's currency was not 'hard', that the Soviet star had relieved himself of some of his spare Soviet bank notes.

No similar problems for Israeli No. 1 Amos Mansdorf, who made light work of Californian Jeff Tarango to join Chesnokov in the Saturday final. It was a result which set up the showdown that everyone had hoped for: the Soviet No. 1, who had won friends and admirers throughout the week, against Mansdorf, the homegrown local boy. A capacity crowd of 5000 turned out to witness the contest, cheering on Mansdorf to an early first-set lead. Indeed, it looked for a while as if, as sometimes happens,

In playing in the Riklis Open, Chesnokov became the first Soviet player to compete in Israel.

Chesnokov simply was not in the mood. Then the Soviet player found his rhythm and from that point there could be only one winner - Chesnokov in the end cruised home 6-4, 6-3. Chesnokov's victory deprived the locals of a Mansdorf victory. Even so, it was a popular win. In coming to play the Riklis Open, he had made an important gesture, the effects of which will be felt long after this year's tournament. The ATP Tour had allowed several players to pull out because of the situation with Iraq but Chesnokov had ignored the scare stories. As the champion left with his trophy and the crowds went home, things returned to normal at Ramat Hasharon. The kids regained possession of their courts inspired by what they had learnt during the week they let the pros play at their Tennis Centre.

CA Tennis Trophy

By Anna Legnani

Vienna, 15-21 October
Tournament Director: Leo-Gunther Huemer

Vienna, ancient capital of the Austro-Hungarian Empire, is a city unostentatiously proud of its glorious past. It guards its great tradition, yet it still finds time to look towards the future, especially since the recent political changes which have shifted Europe's centre of gravity towards the East. Anders Jarryd, the 29-year-old winner of the 1990 CA Tennis Trophy, could feel some affinity with this illustrious city. Ranked as high as No. 5 in July 1985, the soft-spoken Swede earned his seventh singles career title in the Wiener Stadthalle, his first singles victory since the WCT Dallas finals in 1986. Jarryd was still among the top performers in doubles in 1989, when he added the most precious jewel to his crown with his Wimbledon victory, and could thus boast winning all the Grand Slam doubles titles at least once.

An injury-plagued year has caused the Swede's ranking to drop vertiginously, well below the top thirty range where he had been placed constantly since 1983, and as low as 175 when he entered the tournament. 'One week ago I would

If he doesn't bite his tongue off, Anders Jarryd will put enough top-spin on this forehand to hit another winner.

Preparation for a little Strauss on the violin or a bit of racket juggling? Skoff worked hard to win over the fans.

not even have believed this victory possible,' commented Jarryd. 'I have had such problems with my shoulder and such a persistent cough that I have played very little this year. A fortnight ago I decided that I would try to train very hard to get my physical condition back, because I had the feeling sometimes that I was playing at a level that was too high for my body to take.'

Jarryd proved that his condition was back by aligning a string of two-set victories over Michael Stich, Patrick Kuhnen, John McEnroe and Alexander Volkov to defeat runner-up Horst Skoff 6-3, 6-3, 6-1 in the championship round. The Austrian, a winner in Vienna in 1988, had had a series of tough matches against compatriot Alex Antonitsch, the strong Russian qualifier Dimitri Poliakov and Lars Jonsson, leading to an inter-Austrian semi-final against Thomas Muster that had the Stadthalle vibrating. Tennis enthusiasm is growing rapidly in Austria with strong performances by the home players on the ATP Tour and in the Davis Cup. Vienna registered a capacity crowd for the first time in the tournament's history this year, with the Skoff-Antonitsch first-round match on the Tuesday,

and the Stadthalle was sold out for three days. For tournament director, Leo Huemer, years of dedication to the promotion of this tennis event was finally paying off.

In the doubles competition Udo Riglewski and Michael Stich won their third title together this season after Munich and Basle, with a 6-4, 6-4 victory over Jorge Lozano and Todd Witsken, direct contenders for one of the last spots in the ATP Tour Doubles Championship in Sanctuary Cove.

With such fascinating tennis action, a week seemed much too short a time to spend in Vienna - housed, as the players were, in the luxurious comfort of the new Plaza Hotel in the centre of the city. It proved difficult to choose between the beautiful State Opera House, where the season was in full swing, and a visit to the birthplaces and residences of the geniuses who had for centuries made Vienna the world's music capital. The Hofburg Palace and the Spanish Riding School ... or a quiet stroll around Saint Stephen's Cathedral, where some modern buildings and luxurious boutiques in no way detract from the old-world charm of the ancient alleys and palaces.

Grand Prix de Tennis de Lyon

By Bruno Cuaz

Lyon, 15-21 October
Tournament Director: Gilles Moretton

Du 15 au 21 octobre, Palais des Sports de Gerland.

'I came to Lyon to try out my new rackets'. Marc Rosset was the first person to be surprised by his success in the fourth Grand Prix de Lyon. After 10 days' holiday in Monaco where he is resident, the tall (1.98m) Swiss player started his training quite slowly. His ambitions for Lyon were limited, for until then he had never won a single match on carpet. During the US Open, after an epic loss to Pat Cash in the first round, he even considered limiting his play to clay court events. But on

Sunday 21st November, in the Palais des Sports de Gerland, it was he who was the first player to have the honour of lifting the 'Korloff Lion', a sculpture created by a Lyonnais jeweller this year. The figure is of a lion's head and the right eye is a gold tennis ball inlaid with hundreds of diamonds. The trophy is only kept by a player who wins the tournament three times in five years. At 20 years of age - he celebrated his birthday two weeks after the tournament - Marc Rosset is obviously a serious

The giant Swiss Marc Rosset kneels to take a firm grip of the spectacular Korloff trophy after beating Mats Wilander in Gilles Moretton's popular event.

candidate for success. He realised that he could play more aggressively than usual, thanks to his huge service. During the final, Mats Wilander salvaged 8 points off his opponent's service and two of these were double faults. Mats' popularity in France first began after his victory at The French Open in 1982. Nevertheless, his success in Lyon was something of a surprise as, like Marc, he'd had a few days of rest prior to Lyon. He was strongly motivated throughout the week. In the semi-finals Mats dominated the match against the German Alexander Mronz who had qualified for his place. Mronz only just made the sign-in for the qualifications - his flight from Dusseldorf Airport had been delayed 3 hours and, with only 2 minutes to spare, the German had managed to get his name on the list in order to play the qualifying rounds. Mronz won himself precious bonus points by eliminating the No.1 seed Aaron Krickstein in the quarter finals.

Despite late withdrawals from Connors and then Sampras, who phoned Florida for a long-distance press conference, the tournament was a great success. Fifty-five thousand people came to watch the matches in a town where tennis has been well-established since the start of the century. The tournament also rewarded tournament director, Gilles Moretton, with financial success. Moretton took over the organisation of the event immediately after his career as a tennis player had ended, and he took advantage of his relationship with Yannick Noah and John McEnroe, winners of the tournament in '87 and '89 respectively. Moretton's company now employs ten people and organises other events such as the Lyon Golf Open. Very involved in his town's economic life (Lyon is France's second most important town), where his father ran a textile company, Gilles Moretton is a fine example of how a tennis player can put his knowledge to good use in the business world.

Stockholm Open

By Richard Evans

Stockholm, 22-28 October
Tournament Director: Johan Flink

If the Globe, which sits like a giant golf ball on the edge of Stockholm, is futuristic in design, then Boris Becker's 21st century power game matched it when he demolished Stefan Edberg 6-4, 6-0, 6-3 in the final of the Stockholm Open. One remembered Ilie Nastase inflicting the same kind of embarrassment on a young Bjorn Borg in the Masters final when it was played at the Kunglihallen on the other side of town back in 1975. But Nastase was a master of the game's gentler skills and poor Borg was left befuddled and bemused rather than shot to pieces by cannon fire as Edberg was - in front of some 13,000 awe-struck Swedes.

The cosy little Kunglihallen was where it all began for this much-loved tournament, which was nurtured through its formative years by the late Hans-Acke Sturen. It was Sturen's dream to create a major indoor event that would be run the way the players would want a tournament to be run. 'You must tell us what we do wrong,' Hans-Acke would say. 'Give us your ideas.' So, from the moment Nikki Pilic won the first Stockholm Open in 1969, the tournament's stress on players' in-put and the caring nature of organisation, which is still very much in evidence today, have ensured the event's lasting popularity. Johan Flink, who succeeded Sturen as tournament director, has managed to transfer the homely atmosphere of the Kunglihallen to the very different surroundings provided by one of the world's most spectacular sporting arenas.

Saabs ferry the players back and forth to the Grand Hotel which remains an integral part of the Stockholm Open and, once inside the Globe, the players' area is still serviced by a seemingly unending line of attractive young ladies dispensing meals and snacks. One tries not to realise that some of them may be the daughters of those who used to pile spaghetti onto the plates of Fred Stolle, Arthur Ashe, Marty Riessen and Tom Okker all those years ago. With space to work with in its new home, the Stockholm Open has been able to march with the times and capitalise on the trend towards corporate hospitality. The result was one of the most imaginative sponsors' villages to be found on the Tour, decorated entirely in the manner of a 19th-century English sporting club, complete with the kind of art and artefacts that might have surrounded Joshua Pim or the Doherty brothers in the 1890s.

But, as I have said, the tennis out on court, was resonant of the future rather than the past. The new radar gun, which clocked the speed of serves, had Becker and Pete Sampras firing at 184

Boris Becker, in orbit after his space-age performance against Stefan Edberg, holds the globe aloft.

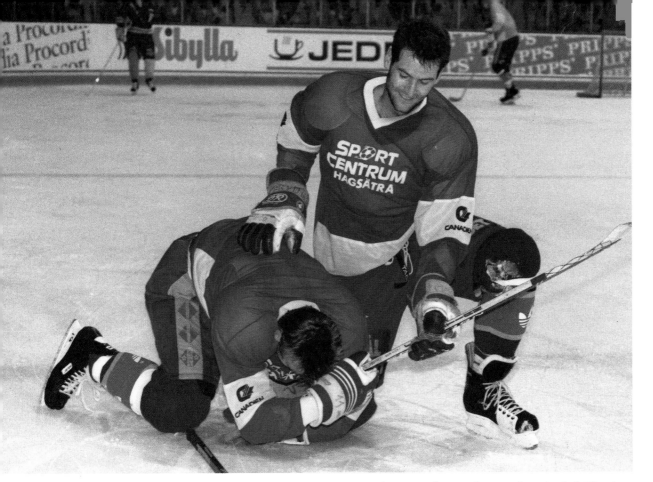

The Globe has an ice-rink, and the temptation was too much to resist for Karel Novacek and Jakob Hlasek.

kilometres per hour in the semi-final but it was Marc Rosset, the giant from Geneva, who touched the magic 200 kph mark during his titanic struggle with Jonas Svensson in the second round, which the Swiss finally won 6-7, 7-6, 7-6. Edberg was unimpressed by Rosset's blockbusters, however, and beat him 6-4, 6-4 in the next round. As Flink was quick to point out while praising the co-operation the tournament had received from the ATP Tour, the entry could hardly have been stronger. Only Ivan Lendl was voluntarily absent from the top 16 players in the world and, in such august company, it was good to see two of the game's most promising young stars, David Wheaton and Niklas Kulti upset seeds to fight their way into the quarter finals. Kulti, who had received a wild card into the event, had a dramatically successful week, disposing of Tim Mayotte, Andre Agassi and Guy Forget in successive rounds, which gave his bonus point

Boris Becker's power game shoots Edberg to pieces in front of 13,000 awe-struck Swedes.

column a serious boost on the ATP computer. Kulti was drained after all that, however, and Alexander Volkov defeated him easily in the quarter final.

Wheaton fought back from losing the first set tie-break to beat the French Open champion Andres Gomez before going on to remove Gomez's predecessor in Paris, Michael Chang before Sampras, making his first Tour appearance since his Flushing Meadow triumph, won another thrilling battle 7-6, 5-7, 6-4. Sampras was disappointed after losing 6-4, 6-4 to Becker in the semis which just shows how quickly one's expectations rise after the kind of success this 19-year-old enjoyed at the US Open. But the German's performance the following day must have mollified the young American somewhat because it became evident then that Becker was in devastating form.

Mr and Mrs Perez-Roldan and ATP Tour manager Vittorio Selmi help Guillermo cut the cake at a little birthday celebration for the Argentine star in Stockholm.

Boris thought it was one of the best matches he had ever played and, as veteran Swedish tennis writer Bjorn Hellberg noted, it was a 'fabulous exhibition of power tennis', verified by the fact that Edberg was only able to win six points off the ferocious Becker serve during the course of the entire match.

In the doubles Guy Forget and Jakob Hlasek confirmed their No. 1 seeding by defeating the former Wimbledon doubles champions, John Fitzgerald and Anders Jarryd, 6-4, 6-2. It was the fourth title of the year for the Franco-Swiss pair. Their victory guaranteed them a place in the ATP World Doubles Championships at Sanctuary Cove.

Philips Open

By Lauren Goldenberg

Sao Paulo, 22-28 October
Tournament Director: Ricardo Bernd

Concealed deep within the third largest city in the world, amongst the towering skyscrapers and twisting highways, lies a natural haven of open lawns and placid ponds known as Ibirapuera Park, where denizens seek refuge from the sprawling metropolis of Sao Paulo. A playground for families, friends and lovers, Ibirapuera Park also becomes a battleground for some of the world's best tennis players, when it hosts the $150,000 Philips Open each October. The 'paulistas', as the residents of Sao Paulo are called, are devoted sports aficionados who relish the opportunity to attend any professional sporting event, let alone a week of world-class tennis on the ATP Tour. Taking advantage of the free admission all week, over 15,000 spectators packed the grandstands of the four hardcourts in Ibirapuera Park. The stadium court bustled with activity as an emotional crowd delighted in the action of veteran stars and newcomers alike.

In the end though, the 1990 Philips Open proved to be a showcase for the new talent emerging on the ATP Tour, as unseeded American Robbie Weiss prevailed over an experienced international field.

Ibirapuera Park sees the emergence of some of the rising stars on the ATP tour

The 23-year-old from Wheeling, Illinois, who came into the event ranked 116, captured his first singles title with a 3-6, 7-6, 6-3 come-from- behind win over the fourth-seeded Peruvian, Jaime Yzaga.

The win in Sao Paulo moved Weiss into the top 100 for the first time to a career high of 85. Weiss, a former Pepperdine University standout, had been plagued by numerous injuries in his short professional career, but came into Sao Paulo healthy, eager and strong. He left with his first ATP Tour title and a new-found confidence in his ability to play with the Tour's best. Brazilian Danilo Marcelino and Dutchman Jacco Eltingh also proved to be rising stars reaching the semi-finals with gutsy wins over their fellow countrymen.

Marcelino, from Salvador in northern Brazil, defeated his country's best, Luiz Mattar, in a tough three-set match. Meanwhile, the previously unheralded Eltingh, who had only cracked the top 200 a month earlier, continued the biggest week of his career with a three-set victory of his own over Mark Koevermans in the second round. First-time winners also triumphed in the doubles competition. Former US Open mixed doubles champion, Shelby Cannon and Venezuelan Alfonso Mora defeated favourites Mark Koevermans and Luiz Mattar for the title.

In appreciation of the cultural and recreational benefits that the tournament and players brought to Sao Paulo, the city's mayor planted a pau tree in Ibirapuera Park in the name of all the participants in the Philips Open.

Greeting one of the biggest upsets of the year, Robbie Weiss from Wheeling, Illinois won the singles title at the Philips Open in Sao Paulo. Peru's more experienced Jaime Yzaga has to settle for the smaller plinth.

Open de la Ville de Paris

By Alan Page

Paris, 29 October-4 November
Tournament Director: Patrice Clerc

Whether you go by road or take the gentle, jam-free option of a Seine river-shuttle, the distance between Roland Garros on the chlorophyl-rich western edge of Paris and the Bercy Omnisport stadium over to the east, is only 16 kilometres. But the two sites are tennis worlds apart. It is not simply the difference between players making fast points on a Taraflex carpet rather than grafting on red clay in hot sun; the shift in style is created by the fans. Predominantly, the French Open crowd is made up of club players with a leavening of the 'beau monde', while the Paris Open welcomes the average sports fan in off the street. Roland Garros may provide vocal interludes but it remains a tennis Glyndebourne to Bercy's 'Last Night of the Proms'.

There are few events on the ATP Tour which have shown such steep growth as the Paris Open.

There are few events on the ATP Tour which have shown such steep growth as the Paris Open. The prize fund soared to a Tour-topping $1,650,000 this year when the field went from a 32-man draw to 48. A record 97,679 spectators - 8,500 more than last year - packed Bercy for the seven daily sessions. A 97% load factor made historical nonsense of Philippe Chatrier's initial reluctance to launch a major autumn tournament which he felt could saturate the Paris market. The commercial clout, box-office pull and player turnout (35 of the top 38 lined up), of the Paris Open, have proved those fears unfounded.

This year both Edberg and Becker played superbly up to their billing until the final. But no amount of contingency planning can heal a quadriceps tear in a champion's left thigh. No amount of enthusiastic support from the crowd can lift a player through fatigue-induced injury. The competitive crescendo to the ATP Tour season, orchestrated by the two men, was temporarily reduced to a single discordant note when the German hobbled sadly to the net and defaulted after 35 minutes playing time of Sunday's final. The score stood at 3 all.

After the fast-forward, late-season challenge launched by Becker with victories over Edberg to win Sydney and Stockholm and a losing final berth against Ivan Lendl in Tokyo, it was suddenly freeze-frame time. Had he won, Becker would have moved to number one a week later.

A dizzy shot of the futuristic Omnipalais at the Porte de Bercy under a Parisian sky.

Becker has often subjected himself to a punishing autumn schedule. Dominant though he then was, he finished the 1989 Paris final with a thigh strapped. This time, after a wearing semi-final win over Jonas Svensson by 4-6 7-6 (7-5) 6-1, Becker was limping and a subdued man.

Singles and doubles combined, his Paris final was Becker's 27th match in five weeks. 'I am not Superman,' the German reminded us. Both Becker's manager, Ion Tiriac and his Australian coach Bob Brett are aware of that. It is unlikely the same error will be made again.

Naturally enough, Edberg accepted the US$ 270,000 victory cheque and hoisted the trophy aloft with more than his usual show of modesty. In 1989 he had lost this final to Becker in circumstances beyond his control - the German had demolished him with a straight-set, no-nonsense 6-4, 6-3, 6-3 defeat. This year the Swede turned things around but without getting the chance to stamp the authority he had displayed all week in the final.

Edberg had complained of tiredness after Becker defeated him in Stockholm the previous week. His hold on the number one ranking seemed to be slackening. But there was no sign of physical fatigue or competitive apathy here. Dancingly swift, decisive, each component of his game oiled and meshing sweetly, Edberg spent only 4 hrs. 1 min. on court beating Andrei Cherkasov (6-2, 6-3), Aaron Krickstein (6-3, 6-2), Jakob Hlasek back to his impressive best (6-3, 6-4), and Sergi Bruguera (6-3, 6-3), before the truncated final brought him his seventh title of the year.

If the culmination to the tournament was anti-climactic, the buzz of upsets filled the air all week. Jonas Svensson almost provided two of them. At 24 Svensson's learning curve is far from flattening out under Tim Klein's off-beat tutelage. Svensson's thoughtful athleticism undid Ivan Lendl as it had at Roland Garros in 1988. The Swede took their round of 16 match 3-6, 6-4, 6-2. Had he not flinched on a smash at 6-4, 4-3 and 30-15 in his semi-final against Boris Becker, we could have seen the first all-Swedish final of the ATP Tour year.

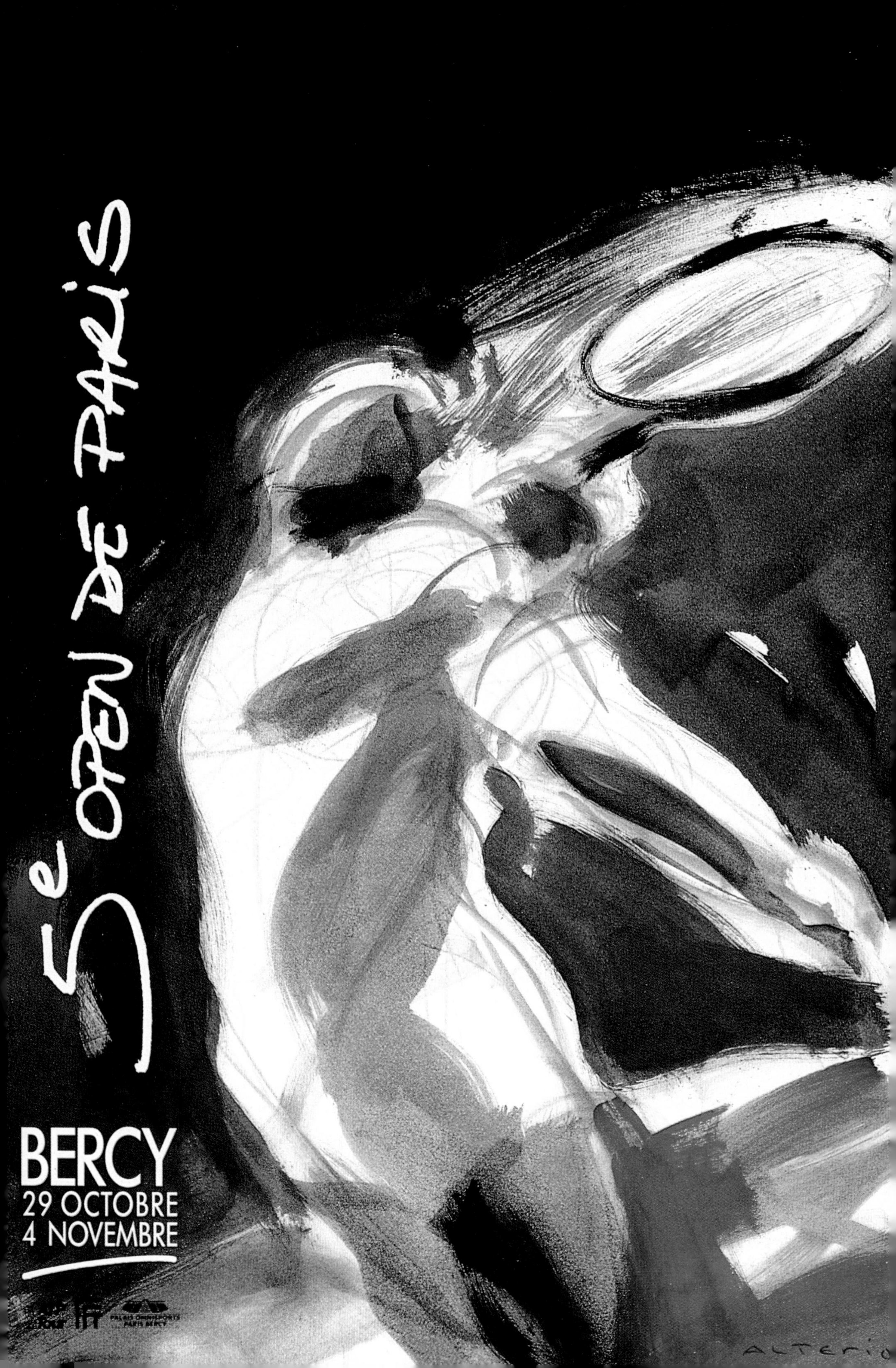
5e OPEN DE PARIS
BERCY
29 OCTOBRE
4 NOVEMBRE
ALTERIO

It was a reminder that the powerful Borg-generated wave that crested in the '80s is ebbing. Edberg, the only Swede with a natural attacking rythm, has been left high and dry by the receding tide. Paris confirmed the all-surface talent now needed to sustain ambition and survive in the higher echelons of the game.

Spain's Emilio Sanchez (a quarter finalist), that shambling joker with the clattering serve Marc Rosset from Switzerland, and now Sergi Bruguera have all digested the lesson. Bruguera, the tall, talented 19-year-old from Barcelona had a somewhat fortuitous run into the semi-final but one could sense him extending his talent throughout the week. He had after all, never won an indoor tournament match before. Bruguera and Svensson were not, however, alone in providing costly upsets at Bercy.

Still absorbing the celebrity status placed on his 19-year-old shoulders after becoming the youngest ever US Open champion, Pete Sampras had a tough three-set match against Carl-Uwe Steeb and then went bemusedly out 6-3, 3-6, 6-3 in the third round to French qualifier Guillaume Raoux. Raoux become a most unlikely local hero: the stocky bespectacled 20-year-old was ranked 134 on the ATP Tour computer rankings and held only the fourteenth best position in France.

But with his hit-or-miss power play he banged in his second serves with abandon, went for broke with his flat drives, and gave Sampras a through-the-looking-glass glimpse of treatment the American himself had meted out to others at Flushing Meadow. For Sampras the sequel came cruelly fast. Just two months before he had been in Wonderland.

The beginning of the end for Boris Becker. A thigh strapping on court could not prevent a default to Stefan Edberg a game later at 3 all in the first set - a sad end to a great week of tennis in the $2 million event.

Diet Pepsi Indoor Challenge

By Chris Martin

London, 5-11 November
Tournament Director: Michael Campbell

As Jakob Hlasek accepted the winner's cheque at the inaugural Diet-Pepsi Indoor Challenge he could have been forgiven if he had felt the urge to burst into song. With apologies to Frank Sinatra, the Swiss number one would have been justified in changing the words to one of Sinatra's big hits 'My Kind of Town' and inserted London instead of Chicago in the chorus. Hlasek's 7-6, 6-3 victory over defending champion Michael Chang was his third triumph at Wembley Arena in as many years. In 1988 he landed his first-ever pro singles title

there and, 12 months later, carried off the doubles crown in harness with John McEnroe. On that occasion, amazingly, it was McEnroe who had burst into song, leading the crowd in a rendition of 'Happy Birthday' for Jakob.

Now, the easy-going Swiss number one doesn't normally spend his spare time studying prospective opponents but when it came to the crunch in the final he found that an impromptu stint as a TV commentator had taught him an

It's not easy being the younger brother of tennis' most famous star, but Patrick McEnroe is making his own mark. A quarter-final berth in the singles and the doubles crown at the Diet Pepsi Indoor Challenge helped Patrick on his way.

invaluable lesson. Earlier in the week Hlasek had taken up an offer to supply 'colour' to the German service of European satellite TV broadcasters Eurosport. As luck would have it during his stint in the 'box' he had to cast his expert eye over Michael Chang's second-round dismissal of Jeremy Bates. 'Doing the TV was good for me because I had never played Michael before and I learned some things,' said Hlasek after beating the 1989 French Open champion.

Some of the 'things' included: 'Going for a lot of quick points on my first serve but if I had a second serve I knew I must never come in, he returns too well for that.' It was a strategy he certainly put into good effect leaving Chang suitably impressed: 'He was serving very well at the crucial moments and it was tough to break his rhythm,' said Chang.

But Hlasek very nearly didn't get the chance to try out the tricks he had learned. Chang, the tournament's defending champion, came close to losing in the semi-finals to Christian Bergstrom. Indeed, Chang only squeezed through by the narrowest of margins, 6-3, 3-6, 7-6, having trailed 0-4 in the final set. But Hlasek also had his share of good fortune when his third round opponent Goran Ivanisevic was struck down by 'flu. With Hlasek leading 4-1, Ivanisevic withdrew complaining that he could see 'three balls'. Most of the time he was on court, he was hitting the wrong one.

Chang and Hlasek apart, it was not a tournament that the seeded players will remember too fondly. Guy Forget (4), Aaron Krickstein (5) and Horst Skoff (6) all failed to make it past the second round, while top seed Pete Sampras fell victim to shin splints, an ailment that had bothered him since the US Open. Sampras was in such pain that he was unable to take to the court to play Bergstrom in the third round. But one player's bad tournament is always another's day to remember. Patrick McEnroe and Diego Nargiso are the perfect examples. Both came through qualifying; Nargiso survived to be beaten in the semis while McEnroe fell in the quarters to Bergstrom.

Jakob Hlasek recaptured the singles title at London's Wembley Arena that he first won in 1988.

But McEnroe at least had the consolation of keeping the London tournament's doubles title in the family when he partnered Jim Grabb to a 7-6, 4-6, 6-3 victory over Wimbledon champions Rick Leach and Jim Pugh. But Hlasek won the broadest smile of the week award as he celebrated his 26th birthday a day early.

Whether he will get the chance to throw another party for the fans in London in 1991 remains to be seen. Although Pro-Serv managed to rescue the event from extinction late in the day (following the decision of former sponsors, Silk Cut, to pull out earlier in the year) the crowd figures were disappointing and, as a result, the tournament may move to a new home at another English venue.

Bayer Kremlin Cup

By Eugene L. Scott

Moscow, 5-11 November
Tournament Director: Eugene L. Scott

Twenty-five years ago, an American battling a Russian in the final of the first-ever men's pro tournament in the USSR would have aroused suspicions of a 'fixed draw'. Twenty-five years ago, the suspicions of such a perfectly staged conclusion probably would have been correct. The fact that the Soviet Andrei Cherkasov won on his home turf over Tim Mayotte, who none the less enjoyed one of his best weeks of 1990, provided an ending that the poet Pushkin would have enjoyed. The inaugural Kremlin Cup was a ringing triumph for tennis in general and Soviet sport in particular, and the boggy swamp of bureaucracy that infests every aspect of existence in Moscow was, if not overcome,

at least neutralized for these championships. A number of historic firsts accompanied the event, including the three largest crowds ever to witness tennis in this part of the world - capped by sellouts of over 15,000 fans for the semis and finals.

The matches were played in the Olympic Stadium (site of the US-boycotted 1980 Olympics), and four tournament courts were prepared in the sprawling main arena, more than in any other ATP Tour indoor facility in the world. The apprehension of players, press, sponsors and officials about whether the Kremlin Cup could occur at all in these tumultuous times was palpable. Their worries

The Olympic stadium had record crowds entering its doors.

Gene Scott, pictured here with his finalists Andrei Cherkasov and Tim Mayotte, pulled off the coup of staging a pro event in Moscow.

were quickly quieted and replaced by curt nods of respect for what had been accomplished in so short a time. Both the singles and doubles qualifying were surprisingly over-subscribed. That John Fitzgerald, Thomas Hogstedt, Robert Van't Hof and Sergio Casal were prepared to fly so far for a shot at the hefty $3000 first-round fee is testament to how popular (and crowded) the new ATP Tour has become. The original cut-off for this World Series fixture was 62, an onerous standard for late in the year, and tougher than many Championship Series events.

A full-service player lounge for qualifiers and main-draw players provided lunch and dinner in comfortable, if not posh, surroundings. Daily sightseeing excursions were available to Red Square, the Kremlin and the Pushkin Museum. Cultural diversions were everywhere. Mayotte was seen at the Bolshoi watching the Nutcracker Ballet and David Wheaton negotiated a pass to the famed 'October Revolution' parade in Red Square.

A business symposium was organised for the multiple sponsors who dream of one day doing business in the Soviet Union and was presided over by Russian Prime Minister Ivan Silaev who was also chairman of the tournament's organizing committee. If the tennis sometimes took a back seat to the political and economic events swirling outside the arena, no one should be surprised. An obvious high-point of the occasion was Russian President Boris Yeltsin's appearance

for Chesnokov's quarter-final win over Emilio Sanchez. Cynical doubts exist of the USSR ever being able to move to its planned 'market economy'. But one disappointment to the tournament proved how far *Perestroika* has come.

The number one Soviet, Andrei Chesnokov, chose not to play in his country's first major championship because the press had ridiculed him severely. He was accused of being selfish in wanting to keep all of his prize money and not sharing his income with the Tennis Federation which had provided his early start. Perhaps no other event could so forcibly demonstrate the viability of a 'free market economy' than Chesnokov having the right *not* to play the Kremlin Cup.

The phenomenon of the first major professional sports spectacle, the offer of $330,000 in prize money, thousands more in officially sanctioned 'guarantees', and an opulent VIP village with French wines, Swiss chefs and fresh fruit flown in from Israel raised questions of 'appropriateness' in some quarters, considering the difficult conditions 285 million Soviets currently endure. The answer, that sport presents a proud front in the face of adversity, is forthright and credible. For example, no one ever suggested that the New York or London *Times* suspend their sports sections when the United States invaded Grenada, Panama, Vietnam and sent troops to the Middle East. Or did they?

Citibank Open

By Chiquinho Leite Moreira

Itaparica, 5-11 November
Tournament Director: Ricardo Bernd

The tropical island of Itaparica, outlined by thousands of palm trees, has recently been transformed into the most wonderful venue for the ATP Tour's unique tennis tournament, the Citibank Open. The island's natural beauty, however, was just one of the innumerable attractions of this $250,000-prize championship, which took place in a relaxed atmosphere - brimming with beautiful women, and featuring shows and parties every night.

Itaparica has already been elected as one of the best by many tennis professionals. It seemed the most perfect place to celebrate the return of the Swedish star, Mats Wilander, the former world No. 1, who mixed his sport with the pleasures of the good life: at night, he enjoyed playing the guitar with Juan Aguilera, Jonathan Canter and Ricardo Acioly; by day, he won matches with his racket. Happy and relaxed, and with his wife Sonya by his side, Wilander won his first championship after a two year drought. 'I enjoyed this week very much - the place, the shows - and it made me feel like playing tennis again,' he said. 'It was nice to win a tournament again and I would very much like to be in Itaparica next year,' he announced after receiving his trophy as the champion of the Citibank Open 1990. The first round in Itaparica, as usual, brought some surprises. Early in the opening matches, the Spanish Juan Aguilera,

the No. 1 seed, lost to the Brazilian Danilo Marcelino, and the Argentinian Martin Jaite, who was the champion in 1989, lost to the Netherlander Mark Koevermans. By the second round there were only two seeds left in the championship: Wilander and the Uruguayan Marcelo Filippini, the eventual finalist.

The ones who lost in the first round, however, didn't leave as usually happens in other tournaments. The players decided to stay on at the Club Méditerranée for a holiday. Some of them enjoyed themselves at the shows, as did Wilander and his band. The others got into the mood of the Club Méditerranée. The Frenchman Jean Fleurian and the Canadian Martin Laurendeau put themselves up as candidates for 'Miss Nivea', a beauty contest that was disputed by 25 girls. The more moderate preferred to watch the shows. The week began with a performance by the American singer Natalie Cole, which took place during a dinner right among the palms. Fireworks were set off to end the exciting night and to celebrate the beginning of the tournament. The plans for the week included the 'White Night', a typical evening's entertainment in Itaparica, with classical music played by the Orquestra Sinfonica de Sao Paulo, conducted by Diego Pacheco. In the Club's amphitheatre, the Brazilian singer Jane Duboc revived the

Above: Back on a pedestal at last, Mats Wilander won his first tournament since Palermo in September 1988 when he captured the Citibank Open.
Left: Long before Guy Forget and Jakob Hlasek shaved their heads for Sanctuary Cove, Roger Smith of the Bahamas had gone half way with this stylish trim.

greatest musical hits of the movies. On Friday the 'Red and White Night' brought to Itaparica the Brazilian singer and composer Djavan, whose romantic singing delighted Mats Wilander. With so many attractions outside the court, some players could hardly concentrate on the tournament. However, none of them seemed to care about that. And that makes Itaparica look like a prize for all the players, after such a hard season as 1990. It was also an important moment for Brazilian tennis. In the doubles, Mauro Menezes and Fernando Roese won the championship, as they beat the Spanish Thomas Carbonell and Marcos Aurelio Gorriz.

ATP Tour World Championship

By Roger M. Williams

Frankfurt, 12-18 November
Tournament Director: Zeljko Franulovic

When the ATP Tour decided to move the year-ending tournament, it made much more than a cosmetic change. The newly named ATP Tour World Championship left New York and, in recognition of Germany's lead role in the resurgence of European tennis, settled for at least three years in Frankfurt. The prize money more than trebled. And, for the first time, computer points were awarded.

The result, co-presented by the ATP Tour and Mark McCormack's IMG, was both an athletic and financial success. In an unusual race to the wire to see who would finish the year as number one, Stefan Edberg won a pressure match to solidify his place atop the rankings. But Andre Agassi beat Edberg to win the World Championships and showed in the process a strong serve-and-volley game that could make him an immediate threat to unseat the Swede.

Frankfurt's Festhalle holds a modest 9,000 spectators, but it was almost sold out the first evening and completely sold out each evening thereafter. Television carried the matches to some

70 countries, one-third of them via live transmission. Sponsors signed on in abundance, and the shops in the public part of the hospitality village - including a boutique selling the new ATP clothing line - did a brisk business.

Despite its 83 years of age, the Festhalle proved an excellent tournament venue. Municipal officials sand-blasted the outside of the venerable hall, refurbished the seating, and repainted the interior a pleasing combination of dark blue and cream. Combined with handsome wooden doors and subdued lighting in the spectator areas, the renovations created a softly elegant ambience that the builders of contemporary arenas would do well to study.

The ATP Tour stuck with the combination round-robin elimination format that was the mainstay of the old Masters event. The computer's top eight accepted invitations to play: in order, Edberg, Boris Becker, Ivan Lendl, Agassi, Pete Sampras, Andres Gomez, Thomas Muster, and Emilio Sanchez. The last three are primarily clay-court players, and, as always, they entered

A song for Andre as the confetti falls and Agassi savours his moment of glory in Frankfurt.

this indoor-carpet event at a disadvantage. It was magnified this time by the selection of hard and fast 'German Dunlop' balls, which made rallying difficult and had the backcourters serving and volleying far more than usual. The inevitable result was that the three slow-courters won only a single match - when one of them (Muster) played another (Gomez). Yet they all put up a spirited struggle: Sanchez edged past Edberg in the first set of their match; Gomez took a set from Becker; Muster forced Becker to 6-4, 7-5 before succumbing.

Attention inevitably focused on the final stage of the race for number one. Some of that drama had been defused two weeks earlier in Paris, when Becker's injury-caused default cost him a chance to overtake Edberg. Yet the German came into Frankfurt only 225 points behind; if he won the tournament, and Edberg failed to gain the semi-finals, he would finish the year as number one. But Becker was clearly not in prime form. He had to struggle to win his three round-robin matches, and in the semis he lost in straight sets to Agassi;

the American even outserved him, eight aces to five and 92 percent of first-serve points won compared to 73 percent. Lingering effects of the thigh injury seemed much less a problem for Becker than the monumental pressures he faces when playing before German crowds and German media. Normally amiable and cooperative, he refused to appear, after the loss to Agassi, at the mandatory post-match press conference.

On the surface, at least, the Festhalle crowds were both impartial and absorbed. They gave Becker rousing ovations and loud cheers but also did the same for others, notably Agassi. (The only unsportsmanlike notes: a few 'cuckoo' whistles directed at Lendl as he prepared to serve to Becker.) Indeed, the Frankfurters displayed no audible or visible distaste for Agassi's controversial scraggly look and day-glo clothing. They rooted for him in his round-robin meeting with Edberg, and Agassi nearly pulled off an upset. Belting service winners, passing shots, and swinging forehand volleys, he took the second set and led,

Boris Becker's intensively treated muscles are at full stretch here as he powers in another serve, but the thigh injury he had suffered in Paris just ten days before the tournament meant that German fans did not see their hero at his best.

four points to two, in the third-set tie break. Then, as he reached to hit a backhand approach shot into a half-open court, his lead foot skidded on the carpet, and he pushed the ball long. Edberg barreled into that slight breech to grab four of the next five points and the match.

Undaunted, Agassi as much as predicted that, if the two met in the finals, he would win: 'A year ago, I never would have been able to stay with Stefan on this surface ... But the next time I play him, I'd go to the casino and put money on myself.' Back in Las Vegas, Agassi's beloved hometown, the high-rollers were probably doing just that.

The rematch came three days later, after Agassi had dispatched Becker and Edberg had defeated first Sampras (the victory that assured him number one status) and then Lendl. Although the match was not as electrifying as the earlier one, it produced fine tennis, and it amply displayed both Agassi's new physical strength and his fast-developing service and volley. The kid who had meekly submitted to Sampras in the U.S. Open final was nowhere to be seen. In his place was a well-conditioned, confident young man who outrallied Edberg from the baseline, played him even on serve, and hit blistering service returns and passing shots.

Tournament officials including from left to right Horst Klosterkemper, German Tennis Federation President Claus Stauder, Zelkjo Franulovic, Richard Evans and George Rubenstein (with glasses) surround the finalists.

After a loosely played first set that saw five service breaks and a 7-5 decision for Edberg, Agassi took command. In the second set, at deuce in the llth game he twice served and volleyed for winners, then won an ensuing tie break. Edberg extended the third set to 5-7, but he was wilting under the strain of Agassi's hard and accurate hitting as well as his own heavy schedule during the previous several weeks. The last set went 6-2 for Agassi, who, with a grin as bright as his chartreuse shirt, proceeded to collect a check for $950,000 - more than 2 1/2 times as much as Edberg earned for winning Wimbledon. Agassi's addition of 400 ATP points was not enough to move him past Lendl into the No. 3 ranking, and Edberg increased his point margin over No. 2 Becker. In fact, the top eight rankings remained as they were when the week began. But the World Championship provided plenty of drama, computer and otherwise, as the finishing touch to the ATP Tour's first year in action.

The Frankfurt Festhalle, which dates back to 1907, packed to capacity for the inaugural ATP Tour World Championship.

ATP Tour Doubles Championship

By Bruce Matthews

Sanctuary Cove, 19-25 November
Tournament Director: Geoff Masters

Normally, doubles pair Guy Forget and Jakob Hlasek are easy to recognise. Forget *had* dark curls and Hlasek *was* a sweptback blond. Past tense became necessary to describe the French-Swiss combination prior to the last tour event of the year ... because both were completely bald! The pair shaved their heads in a weird pact to celebrate their place among the eight elite teams

playing the ATP Tour World Doubles Final at the spacious Sanctuary Cove Resort on the southern Queensland coast. Maybe the laughs were on Forget and Hlasek when they checked in to the palatial championship headquarters near Australia's popular Gold Coast tourist strip. But the Kojak kids certainly 'scalped' the opposition in the five days' competition. They remained the only

The Hyatt Regency Hotel at Sanctuary Cove was an idyllic home for the eight best doubles teams in the world.

'The Kojak kids',
Guy Forget (left)
and Jakob Hlasek
shaved their heads and
found that less hair
made for more speed
around the courts:
they emerged as the
triumphant pair at the
ATP Tour Doubles
Championship.

undefeated team after overpowering experienced Spaniards Sergio Casal and Emilio Sanchez in a tightly contested four set two hour and 52 minute final 6-4, 7-6, 5-7, 6-4.

In fact, the French-Swiss connection had to beat two rival teams on finals day to claim the rich title and leap to the position of second-ranked doubles team of 1990. Earlier, the duo survived a 'sudden-death' one-set shoot-out with Americans Scott Davis and David Pate, merely to earn the right to face another European pair in the final, 90 minutes later. Frankly, the sporting 'skinheads' clambered from a tennis grave to stay alive on the last official day of the ATP Tour calendar. Forget and Hlasek were down and nearly out in Saturday's semi-final. Somehow they managed to hang on to hope until bad light forced play to be suspended; the match resumed the following morning.

Davis and Pate must be still wondering how it came about that *they* were not the team squaring off against the Spaniards in the final. The Americans led the out-of-touch Forget and Hlasek by two sets to love, and then Pate served for the match at 5-4 in the fourth set. But the left/right-handed combination clinched a tie break in the gathering dusk to deadlock the match and send it into overtime the next day. A lone service break early in the fifth set allowed Forget and Hlasek to scramble out of the marathon struggle 3-6, 4-6, 6-4, 7-6, 6-4.

Casal and Sanchez had a rather more restful night on the eve of the championship match. They certainly needed it after an equally exhausting 6-4, 6-7, 6-4, 6-7, 6-3 five set marathon semi-final victory over brave Canadians Grant Connell and Glenn Michibata.

In retrospect, the one-set Sunday morning warm-up was the perfect pre-final preparation for Forget and Hlasek. 'We felt good and started off well in the final,' Hlasek explained. 'We felt quite confident during the whole match because we had a lot of chances to break them.' Sanchez double-faulted to surrender the opening set but, when Hlasek dropped serve early in the second set, the Spanish pair were poised to fight back in to the match. Casal, who had not lost service for two days, felt the pressure as he attempted to close out the second set at 5-4. The French-Swiss duo pounced and, when they grabbed the tie break 7-5, the title was almost within grasp. Dropping the third set proved no more than a minor delay as Casal again surrendered serve in the third game of the fourth set, and this time Forget and Hlasek completed the kill.

Eight hours of intrigue, attack and counter-attack on semi-finals day, then the contrasting mix of the Forget-Hlasek power against the deft touch and angles of Casal and Sanchez - all underlined the often overlooked appeal of top-class doubles. It became a fitting finale to a year in which the ATP Tour had successfully raised the profile and focus on tandem tennis. Players from 33 countries won doubles titles in 1990 with Australia, the United States, Spain, France, Switzerland, Canada, South Africa and Great Britain represented at the rich Sanctuary Cove championship.

The combinations were split into groups. The Newcombe-Roche Group comprised Pieter Aldrich and Danie Visser, Connell and Michibata, Forget and Hlasek and Darren Cahill and Mark Kratzmann. The Hoad-Rosewall Group was Davis and Pate, Rick Leach and Jim Pugh, Casal and Sanchez, and Neil Broad and Gary Muller. Each player was fêted as a VIP at the 1200-acre resort. A motorised golf cart was assigned to each team to ferry its members around the two champion-ship golf courses, the village, to the marina, or simply from the 4000-seat stadium and two practice courts to the luxury hotel that stands about 300 metres away across two fairways. The on-site conveniences included a pre-championship concert party of 400 guests at the Hyatt Regency Hotel beach pool. Players, officials and guests sipped drinks on the sand as Australia's leading rock singer John Farnham started a national tour from a stage constructed over the water.

The unrelenting sun and afternoon wind proved more of a problem for spectators than for players during the three-day round-robin series which saw the elimination of No. 1 pair Aldrich and Visser and Davis Cup final foes, Leach and Pugh, and Cahill and Kratzmann. At first, it seemed the close shaves of Forget and Hlasek might backfire during an outdoor event on hard court in a sub-tropical climate. But the enterprising 'egg heads' sensibly guarded their unprotected skulls against sunburn by donning ATP Tour caps for practice sessions and matches. Alas, the Kojak look will not stay despite that winning feeling. Forget and Hlasek vowed to be back to normal in 1991 - to be treated with enhanced respect.

Top: Emilio Sanchez (left) and Sergio Casal proving their dexterity at the net. The Spanish duo were runners-up.
Above: Rock and roll aficionados Gary Muller (left) and Neil Broad (right) with Australian singer John Farnham.

Facts and Figures

Results

JANUARY 1-7: BP NATIONALS, WELLINGTON $125,000 Winner: EMILIO SANCHEZ
Rd 32: Emilio Sanchez d Steve Guy 46 61 64; Lars Jonsson d Brett Steven 75 64; Richard Fromberg d Olivier Delaitre 76 61; Paul Chamberlin d Jens Wohrmann 63 67 60; Gilad Bloom d Magnus Gustafsson 61 75; Veli Paloheimo d Markus Zoecke 63 62; Bruce Derlin d Aki Rahunen 63 57 63; Paolo Cane d Ramesh Krishnan 64 57 63; Johan Anderson d Javier Sanchez 63 64; Karel Novacek d Francisco Clavet 62 63; Jeremy Bates d Grant Connell 75 62; Lars Walhgren d Kelly Evernden 36 76 76; Richey Reneberg d Sergio Casal 64 46 75; Christian Bergstrom d Dan Goldie 63 62; Thomas Hogstedt d Shuzo Matsuoka 57 76 62; Andrei Chesnokov d M. Wostenholme 75 26 61. **Rd 16:** E Sanchez d Johnsson 46 63 75; Fromberg d Chamberlin 63 64; Bloom d Paloheimo 64 46 64; Cane d Derlin 76 64; Novacek d Anderson 63 46 63; Wahlgren d Bates 64 67 63; Reneberg d Chesnokov d Hogstedt 76 76. **QF:** E Sanchez d Fromberg 64 63; Cane d Bloom 76 26 63; Novacek d Wahlgren 63 61; Reneberg d Chesnokov 26 60 60. **SF:** E Sanchez d Cane 75 62; Reneberg d Novacek 67 64 60. **F:** E Sanchez d Reneberg 67 64 46 64 61.
DOUBLES: Kelly Evernden/Nicolas Pereira d Sergio Casal/Emilio Sanchez 64 76

JANUARY 1-7: AUSTRALIAN MENS HARDCOURT CHAMPIONSHIP, ADELAIDE $125,000 Winner: THOMAS MUSTER
Rd 32: Sergi Bruguera d Per Henricsson 76 62; Broderick Dyke d Gary Muller 64 64; Michael Stich d Niclas Kroon 64 63; Michiel Schapers d Petr Korda 63 64; Thomas Muster d Claudio Pistolesi 64 46 63; John Fitzgerald d Xavier Daufresne 36 75 63; Mark Kratzmann d Jason Stoltenberg 57 43 Ret; Paul Annacone d Bruno Oresar 61 64; Mark Koevermans d Alexander Mronz 61 64; Patrick Kuhnen d Paul Haarhuis 61 64; Jimmy Arias d Mark Woodforde 76 63; Alexander Volkov d Todd Woodbridge 64 16 64; Marc Rosset d Andrei Cherkasov 62 64; Jerome Potier d Slobodan Zivojinovic 63 64; Jean Fleurian d Tom Nijssen 63 60; Udo Riglweski d Goran Ivanisevic 16 63 61. **Rd 16:** Bruguera d Dyke 67 62 63; Stich d Schapers 64 63; Muster d Fitzgerald 62 76; Kratzmann d Annacone 64 64; Koevermans d Kuhnen 63 36 61; Arias d Volkov 64 76; Potier d Rosset 64 64; Fleurian d Riglewski 63 64. **QF:** Bruguera d Stich 67 60 63; Muster d Kratzmann 75 64; Arias d Koevermans 63 64; Fleurian d Potier 63 36 61. **SF:** Muster d Bruguera 26 62 76; Arias d Fleurian 62 63. **F:** Muster d Arias 36 62 75
DOUBLES: Andrew Castle/Nduka Odizor d Alexander Mronz/Michiel Schapers 76 62

JANUARY 8-14: BENSON AND HEDGES OPEN, AUCKLAND $125,000
Winner: SCOTT DAVIS
Rd 32: Andrei Chesnokov d Markus Zoecke 76 67 75; Richey Reneberg d Gilad Bloom 63 62; Michael Stich d Kelly Jones 75 63; Grant Connell d Paul Chamberlin 75 63; Glenn Layendecker d Kelly Evernden 62 64; Jimmy Arias d Claudio Pistolesi 63 63; Olivier Delaitre d Paul Haarhuis 62 63; Amos Mansdorf d Karel Novacek 64 61; Ramesh Krishnan d Paolo Cane 61 61; Bruce Derlin d Martin Laurendeau 75 62; Jeremy Bates d Jens Wohrmann 26 61 61; Magnus Gustafsson d Johan Anderson 61 62; Scott Davis d Christian Bergstrom 16 64 62; Dan Goldie d Lars Wahlgren 76 60; Brett Steven d Veli Paloheimo 63 60; Steve Guy d Miloslav Mecir 63 63. **Rd 16:** Chesnokov d Reneberg 64 64; Connell d Stich 64 67 62; Arias d Layendecker 26 62 62; Mansdorf d Delaitre 62 75; Krishnan d Derlin 76 75; Gustafsson d Bates 62 60; Davis d Goldie 61 67 62; Guy d Steven 63 67 64. **QF:** Chesnokov d Connell 26 64 63; Mansdorf d Arias 63 76; Krishnan d Gustafsson 76 62; Davis d Guy 62 76. **SF:** Chesnokov d Mansdorf 76 62; Davis d Krishnan 57 63 64. **F:** Davis d Chesnokov 46 63 63.
DOUBLES: Kelly Jones/Robert Van't Hof d Gilad Bloom/Paul Haarhuis 76 60.

JANUARY 8-14: HOLDEN N.S.W. OPEN TOURNAMENT OF CHAMPIONS, SYDNEY $150,000 Winner: YANNICK NOAH
Rd 32: Ivan Lendl d Andrew Sznajder 61 63; Goran Ivanisevic d Sergi Bruguera 75 62; Andrei Cherkasov d Petr Korda 61 46 62; Yannick Noah d Ronald Agenor 64 63; Aaron Krickstein d Jan Gunnarsson 76 62; Paul Annacone d Mark Kratzmann 61 64; Guy Forget d Mark Koevermans 75 63; David Wheaton d Andres Gomez 75 64; Mats Wilander d Marc Rosset 64 62; Niclas Kroon d Christo Van Rensburg 76 62; Omar Camporese d Jordi Arrese 46 64 64; Pete Sampras d Tim Mayotte 76 62; Carl-Uwe Steeb d Leonardo Lavalle 61 64; Jean Fleurian d Goran Prpic 62 62; Wally Masur d Javier Sanchez 26 62 76; Boris Becker d Alexander Volkov 63 62. **Rd 16:** Lendl d Ivanisevic 64 62; Noah d Cherkasov 61 64; Krickstein d Annacone 63 76; Wheaton d Forget 76 61; Wilander d Kroon 61 62; Sampras d Camporese 76 65; Steeb d Fleurian 64 46 62; Becker d Masur 63 63. **QF:** Noah d Lendl 61 64; Krickstein d Wheaton 61 76; Wilander d Sampras 67 75 60; Steeb d Becker 76 63. **SF:** Noah d Krickstein 64 75; Steeb d Wilander 63 62. **F:** Noah d Steeb 57 63 64.
DOUBLES: Pat Cash/Mark Kratzmann d Pieter Aldrich/Danie Visser 64 75.

JANUARY 15-28: FORD AUSTRALIAN OPEN, MELBOURNE $1.5 million
Winner: IVAN LENDL
Rd 128: Ivan Lendl d Jim Pugh 63 62 64; Tomas Carbonell d Cyril Suk 64 75 63; Karel Novacek d Michael Brown 63 61 26 62; Eric Winogradsky d Tim Wilkison 62 76 63; Simon Youl d Martin Laurendeau 46 76 62 62; Brad Drewett d Cedric Pioline 67 63 64 57 63; Christo van Rensburg d Jerome Potier 62 57 75 63; Thomas Muster d Paul Vojtisek 63 62 64; Andres Gomez d Darren Cahill 46 63 16 62 63; Bruno Oresar d Todd Witsken 64 61 64; Michael Stich d Peter Doohan 63 62 62; Leonardo Lavalle d Jeremy Bates 67 61 64 62; Andrei Cherkasov d Shuzo Matsuoka 62 46 46 60 62; Glenn Layendecker d Tarik Benhabiles 62 76 63; Alexander Volkov d Jimmy Brown 63 63 61; Jean Fleurian d Emilio Sanchez 62 64 64; John McEnroe d Thierry Tulasne 62 61 61; Alex Antonitsch d Amos Mansdorf 46 64 64 67 63; Nicolas Pereira d Chris Pridham 64 76 46 63; Dan Goldie d Darren Patten 63 64 64; Petr Korda d Jakob Hlasek 76 60 63; Henri Leconte d Francisco Roig 61 46 75 64; Mikael Pernfors d Slobodan Zivojinovic 62 61 62; Sergi Bruguera d Leif Shiras 61 64 63; Yannick Noah d Goran Prpic 46 76 62 46 75; Ronald Agenor d Richey Reneberg 62 64 36 61; Christian Bergstrom d Pieter Aldrich 62 64 62; Gilad Bloom d John Fitzgerald 76 76 36 62; Claudio Pistolesi d Neil Broad 57 64 64 61; Todd Woodbridge d Michiel Schapers 46 60 63 61; Jordi Arrese d Nick Brown 46 64 61 63; Pete Sampras d Tim Mayotte 76 67 46 75 1210; Aaron Krickstein d Gianluca Pozzi 64 67 64 75; Ramesh Krishnan d Markus Zoecke 46 75 64 57 61; Lars Wahlgren d Horacio de la Pena 63 61 63; Jens Wohrmann d Andres Vysand 63 26 63 61; David Wheaton d Goran Ivanisevic 75 75 60; Magnus Larsson d Marc Rosset 64 61 61; Mark Woodforde d Jose F Altur 26 61 64 64; Andrei Chesnokov d Mark Kratzman 36 67 76 63 62; Jim Courier d Jimmy Arias 63 63 61; Jonas Svensson d Thomas Hogstedt 62 75 75; Magnus Gustafsson d Nicklas Kulti 22 Ret.; Lars Jonsson d Tom Nijssen 63 62 76; Stefano Pescosolido d Jan Gunnarsson 62 67 60 62; P Chamberlin d Shane Barr 60 67 63 64; Patrick Kuhnen d Niclas Kroon 63 67 26 76 62; Stefan Edberg d Johan Anderson 76 63 64; Mats Wilander d Richard Fromberg 76 75 75; Martin Wostenholme d David Macpherson 63 57 76 61; Naduka Odizor d Ian Peter-Budge 62 75 62; Wally Masur d Eric Jelen 62 61 62; Javier Sanchez d Aki Rahunen 60 63 61; Paul Annacone d Gary Muller 63 64 67 26 63; Guy Forget d Grant Connell 26 64 64 62; Veli Paloheimo d Carl-Uwe Steeb 57 63 06 62 62; Miloslav Mecir d Mark Koevermans 62 64 76; Andrew Sznajder d Libor Nemecek 76 67 63 76; Neil Borwick d Kelly Evernden 63 61 61; Udo Riglewski d Paolo Cane 62 63 26 62; Olivier Delaitre d Omar Camporese 26 36 63 64 63; Kelly Jones d Michael Tauson 63 57 26 62 63; Scott Davis d Jamie Morgan 62 62 62; Boris Becker d Paul Haarhuis 61 62 61. **Rd 64:** Lendl d Carbonell 64 62 63; Novacek d Winogradsky 64 61 46 63; Youl d Drewett 64 76 60; Muster d van Rensburg 16 75 75 26 86; Gomez d Oresar 64 36 63 62; Stich d Lavalle 64 64 20 Ret.; Cherkasov d Layendecker 64 57 75 60; Fleurian d Volkov 64 16 75 26 62; McEnroe d Antonitsch 61 62 61; Goldie d Pereira 62 64 63; Leconte d Korda 62 46 63 64; Pernfors d Bruguera 64 63 16 64; Noah d Agenor 76 63 63; Bloom d Bergstrom 26 57 62 64 62; Woodbridge d Pistolesi 63 62 62; Sampras d Arrese 06 62 36 61 63; Krickstein d Krishnan 61 46 63 61; Wahlgren d Wohrmann 46 75 75 63; Wheaton d Larsson 63 62 36 61; Woodforde d Chesnokov 63 62 75; Svensson d Courier 26 62 63 62; Jonsson d Gustafsson 61 62 62; Chamberlin d Pescosolido 67 75 63 64; Edberg d Kuhnen 62 62 64; Wilander d Wostenholme 62 75 63; Masur d Odizor 76 67 63 61; J Sanchez d Annacone 61 76 63; Paloheimo d Forget 64 36 63 63; Mecir d Sznajder 26 61 60 62; Riglewski d Borwick 62 64 62; Delaitre d Jones 63 46 63 64; Becker d Davis 63 76 46 62. **Rd 32:** Lendl d Novacek 64 36 64 61; Youl d Muster 36 64 63 62; Gomez d Stich 64 63 36 76; Cherkasov d Fleurian 64 64 75; McEnroe d Goldie 63 62 62; Pernfors d Leconte 64 61 63; Noah d Bloom 63 63 63; Sampras d Woodbridge 75 64 62; Krickstein d Wahlgren 67 62 63 62; Wheaton d Woodforde 63 45 Ret.; Svensson d Jonsson 64 75 36 46 62; Edberg d Chamberlin 63 64 61; Wilander d Masur 64 57 64 16 63; Paloheimo d J Sanchez 75 64 36 61; Mecir d Riglewski 64 62 60; Becker d Delaitre 63 61 64. **Rd 16:** Lendl d Youl 61 63 61; Cherkasov d Gomez 26 63 76 76; Pernfors d McEnroe 16 64 57 42 Default; Noah d Sampras 63 64 36 62; Wheaton d Krickstein 76 64 63; Edberg d Svensson 62 62 64; Wilander d Paloheimo 75 64 60; Becker d Mecir 46 67 64 61 61. **QF:** Lendl d Cherkasov 63 62 63; Noah d Pernfors 63 75 62; Edberg d Wheaton 75 76 36 62; Wilander d Becker 64 64 62. **SF:** Lendl d Noah 64 61 62; Edberg d Wilander 61 61 62. **F:** Lendl d Edberg 46 76 52 Ret.
DOUBLES: Pieter Aldrich/Danie Visser d Grant Connell/Glenn Michibata 64 46 61 64.

FEBRUARY 5-11: STELLA ARTOIS INDOOR CHAMPIONSHIPS, MILAN $540,000
Winner: IVAN LENDL
Rd 32: Ivan Lendl d Diego Nargiso 63 63; Alexander Volkov d Simone Colombo 61 64; Karel Novacek d Jerome Potier 64 64; Jim Courier d Mark Koevermans 62 61; Aaron Krickstein d Omar Camporese 64 63; Milan Srejber d Stefano Pescosolido 75 62; Pete Sampras d Anders Jarryd 61 63; Markus Zoecke d Jimmy Connors 63 46 76; Tim Mayotte d Martin Strelba 61 61; Thierry Champion d Petr Korda 64 76; Jakob Hlasek d Peter Lundgren 76 75; Jeremy Bates d Yannick Noah 75 64; Horst Skoff d Paolo Pambianco 62 62; Eric Jelen d Paul Haarhuis 64 62; Paolo Cane d Bruno Oresar 76 64; John McEnroe d Andrei Cherkasov 61 46 64. **Rd 16:** Lendl d Volkov 61 26 61; Courier d Novacek 64 64; Srejber d Krickstein 62 63; Sampras d Zoecke 61 76; Mayotte d Champion 62 61; Hlasek d Bates 63 36 63; Jelen d Skoff 76 45 Ret.; McEnroe d Cane 64 61. **QF:** Lendl d Courier 62 64; Sampras d Srejber 67 64 64; Mayotte d Hlasek 75 67 75; McEnroe d Jelen 63 63. **SF:** Lendl d Sampras 36 60 63; Mayotte d McEnroe 64 64. **F:** Lendl d Mayotte 63 62.
DOUBLES: Omar Camporese/Diego Nargiso d Tom Nijssen/Udo Riglewski 64 64.

FEBRUARY 5-11: VOLVO TENNIS, SAN FRANCISCO $225,000
Winner: ANDRE AGASSI
Rd 32: Gary Muller d Brad Gilbert 64 76; Todd Witsken d Robert Seguso 62 64; Chris Garner d Alexis Hombrecher 76 36 63; Richey Reneberg d Leif Shiras 76 63; Joey Rive d Kevin Curren 62 62; Lawson Duncan d Kelly Evernden 75 57 75; Jimmy Arias d Marian Vajda 64 63; Scott Davis d Glenn Layendecker 62 36 63; Jim Grabb d Jimmy Brown 63 76; Derrick Rostagno d Paul Chamberlin 75 30 Ret.; Kelly Jones d David Macpherson 62 64; Christo van Rensburg d Martin Davis 64 67 63; Paul Annacone d Dan Cassidy 76 76; Tim Wilkison d Patrick McEnroe 67 61 76; Dan Goldie d Jonathan Stark 64 57 62; Andre Agassi d Ramesh Krishnan 62 67 60. **Rd 16:** Witsken d Muller 64 63; Reneberg d Garner 61 63; Rive d Duncan 46 63 63; Arias d Davis 63 76; Grabb d Rostagno 62 67 64; van Rensburg d Jones 62 36 75; Annacone d Wilkison 62 62; Agassi d Goldie 26 60 61. **QF:** Witsken d Reneberg 76 64; Rive d Arias 26 64 62; Grabb d van Rensburg 46 62 76; Agassi d Annacone 64 62. **SF:** Witsken d Rive 64 76; Agassi d Grabb 62 62. **F:** Agassi d Witsken 61 63.
DOUBLES: Kelly Jones/Robert Van't Hof d Glenn Layendecker/Richey Reneberg 26 76 63

FEBRUARY 5-11: CHEVROLET CLASSIC, GUARUJA $125,000 Winner: MARTIN JAITE
Rd 32: Jay Berger d Nelson Aerts 64 61; Gabriel Markus d Mauro Menezes 67 61 76; Peter Ballauff d Francisco Yunis 26 64 61; Eduardo Bengoechea d Jaime Oncins 62 64; Luiz Mattar d Fernando Roese 75 63; Herald Rittersbacher d Pedro Rebolledo 64 60; Alejandro Aramburud d Martin Wostenholme 26 64 61; Ivan Kley d Joao Zwetsch 36 64 64; Cassio Motta d Christian Saceanu 36 62 61; Miguel Nido d Danilo Marcelino 64 60; Alexandre Hocevar d Otavio Della 60 64; Mario Tabares d Jaime Yzaga 76 76; Horacio de la Pena d Guillermo Rivas 62 63; Paul Vojtisek d Jeff Tarango 64 63; John Sobel d Roberto Arguello 57 64 64; Martin Jaite d Javier Frana 76 63. **Rd 16:** Berger d Markus 63 60; Bengoechea d Ballauff 64 75; Mattar d Rittersbacher 46 76 64; Kley d Aramburu 63 64; Motta d Nido 64 61; Hocevar d Tabares 57 60 64; Vojtisek d de la Pena 76 31 Ret.; Jaite d Sobel 61 62. **QF:** Bengoechea d Berger 75 60; Mattar d Kley 63 62; Hocevar d Motta 64 61; Jaite d Vojtisek 75 62. **SF:** Mattar d Bengoechea 64 62; Jaite d Hocevar 62 36 63. **F:** Jaite d Mattar 36 64 36.
DOUBLES: Javier Frana/Fernando Luna d Luiz Mattar/Cassio Motta 76 76.

FEBRUARY 12-18: SKYDOME WORLD TENNIS, TORONTO $1,005,000
Winner: IVAN LENDL
Rd 56: Ivan Lendl bye; Jimmy Brown d Malivai Washington 64 67 64; Paul Haarhuis d Patrick McEnroe 63 41 Ret.; Kelly Evernden d Pete Sampras 76 Ret.; Jim Courier d Darren Cahill 60 63; Grant Connell d Dan Goldie 64 26 63; Andrew Sznajder d Ola Jonsson 60 64; Kevin Curren bye; John McEnroe bye; Paul Chamberlin d Derrick

Rostagno 64 75; Richard Matuszewski d Chris Pridham 61 62; Leif Shiras d Scott Davis 63 75; Peter Lundgren d David Wheaton 63 57 62; Richey Reneberg d Tim Wilkison 62 63; Ramesh Krishnan d Glenn Layendecker 61 75; Jay Berger bye; Tim Mayotte bye; Jim Pugh d Jeremy Bates 62 20 Ret.; Jorge Lozano d Robert Seguso 76 10 ret.; Marian Vajda d Jim Grabb 16 76 63; John Fitzgerald d Wally Masur 46 76 63; Martin Wostenholme d Todd Witsken 67 64 75; Tom Nijssen d Lawson Duncan 63 63; Aaron Krickstein bye; Andres Gomez bye; Petr Korda d Martin Laurendeau 62 62; Steve Devries d Jerome Potier 76 76; Jaime Yzaga d Niclas Kroon 64 61; Milan Srejber d Jean Fleurian 36 76 75; Bruno Oresar d Greg van Emburgh 64 57 62; Alex Antonitsch d Jimmy Arias 64 76; Brad Gilbert bye. **Rd 32:** Lendl d Brown 76 61; Haarhuis d Evernden 64 67 61; Connell d Courier 63 75; Curren d Sznajder 60 75; McEnroe d Chamberlin 63 63; Shiras d Matuszewski 76 42 Ret.; Reneberg d Lundgren 75 61; Berger d Krishnan 76 63; Mayotte d Pugh 75 57 63; Lozano d Vajda 75 46 75; Fitzgerald d Wostenholme 61 61; Krickstein d Nijssen 62 62; Korda d Gomez 61 16 64; Yzaga d Devries 64 62; Srejber d Oresar 46 64 62; Gilbert d Antonitsch 63 63. **Rd 16:** Lendl d Haarhuis 75 62; Curren d Connell 76 26 61; McEnroe d Shiras 64 63; Berger d Reneberg 64 76; Mayotte d Lozano 62 46 62; Krickstein d Fitzgerald 62 62; Korda d Yzaga 76 64; Gilbert d Srejber 62 62. **QF:** Lendl d Curren 67 76 63; McEnroe d Berger 64 60; Mayotte d Krickstein 46 64 76; Gilbert d Korda 36 76 62. **SF:** Lendl d McEnroe 63 62; Mayotte d Gilbert 63 76. **F:** Lendl d Mayotte 63 60.
DOUBLES: Patrick Galbraith/David Macpherson d Neil Broad/Kevin Curren 26 64 63

FEBRUARY 12-18: BELGIAN INDOOR CHAMPIONSHIPS, BRUSSELS $465,000
Winner: BORIS BECKER
Rd 32: Boris Becker d Karel Novacek 76 62; Guy Forget d Arnaud Boetsch 63 64; Juan Aguilera d Martin Strelba 62 67; Paolo Cane d Omar Camporese 63 63; Jakob Hlasek d Mark Koevermans 64 61; Jonas Svensson d Alexander Volkov 64 76; Amos Mansdorf d Todd Nelson 63 36 64; Magnus Gustafsson d Jan Gunnarsson 62 62; Ronald Agenor d Michiel Schapers 64 64; Bart Wuyts d Xavier Daufresne 46 62 61; Aki Rahunen d Andrei Cherkasov 46 76 62; Miloslav Mecir d Emilio Sanchez 64 36 64; Goran Ivanisevic d Jens Wohrmann 64 26 63; Goran Prpic d Henri Leconte 63 57 61; Thomas Hogstedt d Marc Rosset 64 62; Carl-Uwe Steeb d Eric Jelen 63 76. **Rd 16:** Becker d Forget 36 63 76; Cane d Aguilera 63 67 64; Svensson d Hlasek 75 26 76; Gustafsson d Mansdorf 64 64; Agenor d Wuyts 64 64; Mecir d Rahunen 76 64; Ivanisevic d Prpic 63 67 62; Steeb d Hogstedt 76 46 62. **QF:** Becker d Cane 64 32 Ret.; Gustafsson d Svensson 67 76 63; Mecir d Agenor 63 62; Steeb d Ivanisevic 63 36 64. **SF:** Becker d Gustafsson 64 76; Steeb d Mecir 62 63. **F:** Becker d Steeb 75 62 62.
DOUBLES: Emilio Sanchez/Slobodan Zivojinovic d Goran Ivanisevic/Balazs Taroczy 75 63

FEBRUARY 19-25: EBEL US PRO INDOOR TENNIS CHAMPIONSHIPS, PHILADELPHIA $825,000 Winner: PETE SAMPRAS
Rd 48: John McEnroe bye; Richey Reneberg d Jim Pugh 63 36 63; Mark Kratzmann d Brad Pearce 75 64; Scott Davis bye; Christo van Rensburg bye; Paul Annacone d Niclas Kroon 67 62 64; Kelly Evernden d Jimmy Brown 63 75; Jim Courier bye; Andre Agassi bye; Jean Fleurian d Ken Flach 76 46 64; Milan Srejber d Jens Wohrmann 36 76 62; Pete Sampras bye; David Wheaton bye; Glenn Layendecker d Peter Lundgren 63 62; Derrick Rostagno d Malivai Washington 76 57 76; Tim Mayotte bye; Andrei Cherkasov bye; Petr Korda d Lawson Duncan 63 61; Chris Garner d Dan Cassidy 75 26 75; Jaime Yzaga bye; Wally Masur bye; Dan Goldie d Paul Chamberlin 26 64 64; Michiel Schapers d Darren Cahill 67 63 76; Jay Berger bye; Andres Gomez bye; Andrew Sznajder d John Fitzgerald 62 46 76; Ramesh Krishnan d Todd Witsken 62 62; Kevin Curren bye; Mikael Pernfors bye; Paul Haarhuis d Jerome Potier 63 64; Tim Wilkison d Rick Leach 64 76; Brad Gilbert bye. **Rd 32:** Reneberg d McEnroe 67 63 63; Kratzmann d Davis 75 46 61; van Rensburg d Annacone 06 76 64; Courier d Evernden 76 64; Agassi d Fleurian 26 60 61; Sampras d Srejber 63 67 61; Layendecker d Wheaton 63 46 64; Mayotte d Rostagno 62 36 76; Korda d Cherkasov 62 64; Yzaga d Garner 60 64; Masur d Goldie 26 76 62; Berger d Schapers 76 67 64; Gomez d Sznajder 75 62; Curren d Krishnan 62 46 63; Haarhuis d Pernfors 46 76 75; Gilbert d Wilkison 62 75. **Rd 16:** Kratzmann d Reneberg 64 64; Courier d van Rensburg 63 57 64; Sampras d Agassi 57 75 Ret.; Mayotte d Layendecker 46 63 76; Korda d Yzaga 26 63 75; Berger d Masur 62 64; Gomez d Curren 67 63 64; Haarhuis d Gilbert 76 57 64. **QF:** Kratzmann d Courier 46 63 76; Sampras d Mayotte 64 46 63; Korda d Berger 76 61; Gomez d Haarhuis 76 67 64. **SF:** Sampras d Kratzmann 46 61 64; Gomez d Korda 62 60. **F:** Sampras d Gomez 76 75 62.
DOUBLES: Rick Leach/Jim Pugh d Grant Connell/Glenn Michibata 36 64 62

FEBRUARY 19-25: STUTTGART CLASSICS, $825,000 Winner: BORIS BECKER
Rd 32: Ivan Lendl d Omar Camporese 64 62; Goran Prpic d Karel Novacek 63 46 64; Martin Strelba d Jordi Arrese 75 63; Patrick Kuhnen d Thomas Muster 46 76 61; Amos Mansdorf d Carl-Uwe Steeb 62 61; Aki Rahunen d Javier Sanchez 76 63; Magnus Gustafsson d Goran Ivanisevic 46 76 64; Emilio Sanchez d Jan Gunnarsson 64 61; Horst Skoff d Markus Zoecke 64 36 63; Thomas Hogstedt d Eric Jelen 64 26 62; Jonas Svensson d Michael Stitch 76 75; Yannick Noah d Guy Forget 64 76; Miloslav Mecir d Ronald Agenor 75 64; Paolo Cane d Jakob Hlasek 64 75; Alexander Volkov d Slobodan Zivojinovic 63 75; Boris Becker d Broderick Dyke 76 64. **Rd 16:** Lendl d Prpic 75 64; Kuhnen d Strelba 61 62; Rahunen d Mansdorf 62 64; Gustafsson d Sanchez 63 60; Skoff d Hogstedt 62 16 63; Svensson d Noah 62 64; Mecir d Cane 60 64; Becker d Volkov 64 36 63. **QF:** Lendl d Kuhnen 63 63; Gustafsson d Rahunen 76 61 62; Svensson d Skoff 64 62; Becker d Mecir 64 62. **SF:** Lendl d Gustafsson 64 67 62; Becker d Svensson 75 62. **F:** Becker d Lendl 62 62.
DOUBLES: Jakob Hlasek/Guy Forget d Michael Mortensen/Magnus Nilsson 63 62.

FEBRUARY 26-MARCH 4: VOLVO TENNIS INDOOR, MEMPHIS $225,000
Winner: MICHAEL STICH
Rd 48: Stefan Edberg bye; Gary Muller d Pieter Aldrich 76 63; Ramesh Krishnan d Cassio Motta 62 61; Jimmy Arias bye; Paul Annacone bye; Danie Visser d Mark Kratzmanna; 64 63; Brian Page d Vijay Amritraj 14 ret.; Marcelo Filippini bye; Andrew Chesnokov bye; Roger Smith d Chris Garner 62 62; Michael Stich d Grant Connell 46 76 64; Kelly Evernden bye; Richey Reneberg bye; Ken Flach d Horacio de la Pena 64 46 76; Malivai Washington d Patrick Kuhnen 36 62 64; Christo van Rensburg bye; Wally Masur bye; Diego Perez d Bryan Shelton 75 76; Niclas Kroon d Udo Riglewski 63 46 61; Jean Fleurian bye; Petr Korda bye; Gilad Bloom d Martin Laurendeau 75 61; Lawson Duncan d K Evans 64 62; Kevin Curren bye; Mikael Pernfors bye; Veli Paloheimo d Derrick Rostagno 76 76; Bruno Oresar d Kelly Jones 76 63; Paul Chamberlin bye; Darren Cahill bye; Tim Wilkison d Leif Shiras 75 63; Glenn Layendecker d Jimmy Brown 62 76; Michael Chang bye. **Rd 32:** Muller d Edberg 61 75; Arias d Krishnan 75 67 63; Visser d Annacone 75 67 64; Filippini d Page 63 76; Chesnokov d Smith 64 64; Stich d Evernden 61 62; Reneberg d Flach 63 62; Washington d van Rensburg 64 64; Masur d Perez 62 63; Fleurian d Kroon 63 46 63; Korda d Bloom 61 64; Curren d Duncan 64 62; Paloheimo d Pernfors 76 63; Chamberlin d Oresar 75 64; Cahill d Wilkison 67 76 75; Layendecker d Chang 64 64. **Rd 16:** Muller d Arias 46 75 63; Visser d Filippini 36 76 64; Stich d Chesnokov 63 61; Washington d Reneberg 46 76 63; Masur d Fleurian 67 61 76; Korda d Curren 76 64; Paloheimo d Chamberlin 75 61; Layendecker d Cahill 64 64. **QF:** Muller d Visser 75 75; Stich d Washington 64 76; Masur d Korda 64 75; Layendecker d Paloheimo 57 76 64. **SF:** Stich d Muller 75 76; Masur d Layendecker 63 62. **F:** Stich d Masur 67 64 76.
DOUBLES: Darren Cahill/Mark Kratzmann d Udo Riglewski/Michael Stich 75 62.

FEBRUARY 26-MARCH 4: ABN WERELD TENNIS TOERNOOI, ROTTERDAM, $450,000 Winner: BRAD GILBERT
Rd 32: Brad Gilbert d Andrei Cherkasov 75 46 64; Omar Camporese d Richard Fromberg 64 62; Christian Bergstrom d John Fitzgerald 76 63; Amos Mansdorf d Anders Jarryd 62 64; Paul Haarhuis d Yannick Noah 62 76; Michael Tauson d Michiel Schapers 76 75; Slobodan Zivojinovic d Jeremy Bates 61 61; Magnus Gustafsson d Jerome Potier 75 62; Jakob Hlasek d Eric Jelen 76 76; Nicolas Pereira d Mark Koevermans 64 62; Alex Antonitsch d L LukeJensen 64 64; Carl-Uwe Steeb d Cedric Pioline 64 64; Jonas Svensson d Tom Nijssen 76 61; Karel Novacek d Peter Nyborg 76 76; Aki Rahunen d Lars Wahlgren 64 61; Thomas Hogstedt d Alberto Mancini 67 64 62. **Rd 16:** Gilbert d Camporese 63 63; Mansdorf 46 61 61; Tauson d Haarhuis 26 63 76; Gustafsson d Zivojinovic 63 63; Hlasek d Pereira 62 63; Antonitsch d Steeb 61 46 63; Svensson d Novacek 76 75; Hogstedt d Rahunen 62 76. **QF:** Gilbert d Mansdorf 61 76; Tauson d Gustafsson 63 16 76; Hlasek d Antonitsch 75 61; Svensson d Hogstedt 63 67 76. **SF:** Gilbert d Tauson 63 63; Svensson d Hlasek 64 75. **F:** Gilbert d Svensson 61 63.
DOUBLES: Jorge Lozano/Leonardo Lavalle d Diego Nargiso/Nicolas Pereira 63 76

MARCH 5-11: NEWSWEEK CHAMPIONS CUP, INDIAN WELLS $750,000
Winner: STEFAN EDBERG
Rd 64: Boris Becker bye; Javier Sanchez d Jim Grabb 61 62; Jean Fleurian d Wally Masur 62 63; Horst Skoff d Rikard Berger 46 63 75; Goran Ivanisevic d Martin Jaite 61 64; Francisco Clavet d Karel Novacek 75 62; Guy Forget d David Pate 62 76; Jay Berger bye; Brad Gilbert bye; Niclas Kroon d Paul Chamberlin 75 62; Shuzo Matsuoka d Marcelo Filippini 16 64 75; Emilio Sanchez d Paul Annacone 63 36 62; Michiel Schapers d Alberto Mancini 64 61; Kevin Curren d Ronald Agenor 63 64; Jimmy Arias d Danie Visser 06 76 64; Andre Agassi bye; Kelly Jones bye; Jim Courier d Steve Bryan 75 61; Christo van Rensburg d Jordi Arrese 61 63; Darren Cahill d Andres Gomez 75 64; Pete Sampras d Ramesh Krishnan 63 62; Richey Reneberg d Miloslav Mecir 57 63 63; Broderick Dyke d Lawson Duncan 46 61 62; Aaron Krickstein bye; Tim Mayotte bye; Jim Pugh d Alexander Volkov 46 62 76; Ken Flach d Todd Witsken 62 63; Jan Gunnarsson d Mats Wilander 76 64; Brad Pearce d Andrew Chesnokov 64 36 64; Sergi Bruguera d Jaime Yzaga 76 62; Scott Davis d Juan Aguilera 62 64; Stefan Edberg bye.
Rd 32: Becker d J Sanchez 76 63; Skoff d Fleurian 63 63; Ivanisevic d Clavet 62 64; Berger d Forget 62 75; Gilbert d Kroon 64 62; E Sanchez d Matsuoka 60 63; Schapers d Curren 76 64; Agassi d Arias 61 76; Courier d Jones 62 63; Cahill d van Rensburg 61 63; Reneberg d Sampras 46 64 62; Krickstein d Dyke 46 63 62; Pugh d Mayotte 62 46 64; Gunnarsson d Flach 46 63 62; Bruguera d Pearce 76 75; Edberg d Davis 63 62. **Rd 16:** Becker d Skoff 64 16 76; Berger d Ivanisevic 64 76; E Sanchez d Gilbert 63 63; Agassi d Schapers 64 75; Courier d Cahill 64 62; Krickstein d Reneberg 62 64; Gunnarsson d Pugh 63 46 60; Edberg d Bruguera 60 63. **QF:** Becker d Berger 61 62; Agassi d E Sanchez 61 76; Courier d Krickstein 62 76; Edberg d Gunnarsson 62 62. **SF:** Agassi d Becker 64 61; Edberg d Courier 64 61. **F:** Edberg d Agassi 64 57 76 76
DOUBLES: Boris Becker/Guy Forget d Jim Grabb/Patrick McEnroe 46 64 63

MARCH 5-11: TROPHEE HASSAN II, CASABLANCA $125,000
Winner: THOMAS MUSTER
Rd 32: Guillermo Perez-Roldan d Todd Woodbridge 76 61; Richard Fromberg d Magnus Larsson 62 46 62; Thierry Tulasne d Niclas Kulti 75 60; Franco Davin d Simon Youl 62 61; Fernando Luna d Martin Strelba 61 60; Roberto Azar d Lars Jonsson 63 75; Martin Wostenholme d Khalid Outaleb 64 64; Tomas Carbonell d Francisco Roig 64 62; Nicklas Utgren d Paul Haarhuis 16 62 63; Johan Anderson d Karim Alami 64 75; Thierry Champion d Jason Stoltenberg 63 62; Goran Prpic d Younef El Ayncoui 62 76; Mark Koevermans d Simone Colombo 61 64; Marian Vajda d Jose F Altur 63 62; Tarik Benhabiles d Leonardo Lavalle 60 62; Thomas Muster d Andres Vysand 62 75. **Rd 16:** Perez-Roldan d Fromberg 36 63 63; Tulasne d Davin 63 76; Carbonell d Wostenholme 61 64; Anderson d Utgren 06 64 63; Prpic d Champion 75 76; Koevermans d Vajda 61 16 63; Muster d Benhabiles 46 61 62. **QF:** Perez-Roldan d Tulasne 62 75; Carbonell d Azar 75 26 63; Prpic d Anderson 63 61; Muster d Koevermans 64 76. **SF:** Perez-Roldan d Carbonell 61 61; Muster d Prpic 61 63. **F:** Muster d Perez-Roldan 61 67 62.
DOUBLES: Todd Woodbridge/Simon Youl d Paul Haarhuis/Mark Koevermans 63 61

MARCH 16-25: LIPTON INTERNATIONAL PLAYERS CHAMPIONSHIPS, KEY BISCAYNE $1,200,000 Winner: ANDRE AGASSI
Rd 96: Ivan Lendl bye; Jens Woehrmann d Richard Matuszewski 46 76 63; Niclas Kroon d Leif Shiras 62 76; Marcelo Filippini bye; Horst Skoff bye; Slobodan Zivojinovic d Tomas Carbonell 63 64; Lawson Duncan d Francesco Cancellotti 61 76; Emilio Sanchez bye; Martin Jaite bye; Karel Novacek d Johan Kriek 46 60 64; Michael Stich d Lars Wahlgren 64 62; Christo van Rensburg bye; Richey Reneberg bye; Ramesh Krishnan d Juan Aguilera 67 62 62; Alexander Volkov d Jimmy Brown 46 76 61; Tim Mayotte bye; Stefan Edberg bye; Roger Smith d Kelly Evernden 75 75; Amos Mansdorf d Derrick Rostagno 76 61; Scott Davis bye; Kevin Curren bye; Peter Lundgren d Jeremy Bates 76 62; Guillaume Raoux d Udo Riglewski 61 60; Car-Uwe Steeb bye; Alberto Mancini bye; Bryan Shelton d Dan Goldie 63 75; Jeff Tarango d Henri Leconte 75 46 63; Sergi Bruguera bye; Jordi Arrese bye; Anders Jarryd d Pieter Aldrich 62 64; Jakob Hlasek d Michiel Schapers 64 67 64; Aaron Krickstein bye; Andre Agassi bye; Kelly Jones d Andrew Sznajder 63 61; Milan Srejber d Tom Nijssen 61 57 76; Jan Gunnarsson bye; Jaime Yzaga bye; Grant Connell d John Fitzgerald 64 64; Bruno Oresar d Pat Cash 62 62; Andres Gomez bye; Jim Courier bye; Kenny Thorne d Glenn Layendecker 75 76; Todd Witsken d Tim Wilkison 75 64; Petr Korda bye; Javier Sanchez bye; Cassio Motta d Andrei Cherkasov 64 63; Gilad Bloom d Nicolas Pereira 26 64 62; Brad Gilbert bye; Jay Berger bye; David Engel d Diego Perez 26 76 62; Markus Zoecke d Jimmy Arias 64 64; Goran Ivanisevic bye; Ronald Agenor bye; Eric Jelen d Jorge Lozano 64 63; Mark Kratzmann d Darren Cahill 63 46 63; Yannick Noah bye; Pete Sampras bye; Paul Chamberlin d Fernando Roese 64 64; Guy Forget d Paul Annacone 63 75; Andrew Chesnokov bye; Jean Fleurian bye; Jim Pugh d Mikael Pernfors 67 63 64; Fabrice Santoro d Marc Rosset 64 61; Boris Becker bye. **Rd 64:** Lendl d Woehrmann 67 62 61; Filippini d Kroon 26 64 76; Skoff d Zivojinovic 62 62; E Sanchez d Duncan 64 61; Jaite d Novacek 64 64; van Rensburg d Stich 63 64; Reneberg d Krishnan 63 75; Volkov d Mayotte 61 64; Edberg d Smith 62 26 64; Mansdorf d Davis 62 62; Curren d Lundgren 60 76(9); Steeb d Raoux 26 64 63; Shelton d Mancini 26 64 63; Tarango d Bruguera 63 64; Arrese d Jarryd 76 62; Hlasek d Krickstein 16 76 63; Agassi d Jones 61 62; Gunnarsson d Srejber 62 76; Yzaga d Connell 76 46 76; Gomez d Oresar 26 62 63; Courier d Thorne 63 63; Witsken d Korda 62 26 64; J Sanchez d Motta 57 76 64; Gilbert d Bloom 63 46 63; Berger d Engel 76 64; Ivanisevic d Zoecke 46 51 Ret.; Agenor d Jelen 76 61; Kratzmann d Noah 64 26 76; Sampras d Chamberlin 26 76 61; Forget d Chesnokov 67 63 63; Fleurian d Pugh 62 75; Becker d Santoro 63 57 62. **Rd 32:** Lendl d Filippini 60 62; E Sanchez d Skoff 36 63 63; Jaite d van Rensburg 46 64 64; Volkov d Reneberg 63 36 63; Edberg d Mansdorf 62 61; Steeb d Curren 36 63 62; Shelton d Tarango 76 36 63; Hlasek d Arrese 76 62; Agassi d Gunnarsson 61 63; Gomez d Yzaga 76 36 76; Courier d Witsken 60 61; J Sanchez d Gilbert 63 67 76; Berger d Ivanisevic 46 63 64; Kratzmann d Agenor 76 75; Sampras d Forget 61 63; Fleurian d Becker 76 61. **Rd 16:** E Sanchez d Lendl 63 67 64; Jaite d Volkov 61 61; Edberg d Steeb 62 46 63; Hlasek d Shelton 63 64; Agassi d Gomez 67 62 63; Courier d Sanchez 76 63; Berger d Kratzmann 60 61; Sampras d Fleurian 57 64 61. **QF:** E Sanchez d Jaite 63 63; Edberg d Hlasek 67 76 76; Agassi d Courier 46 63 61; Berger W/O. **SF:** Edberg d E Sanchez 61 75; Agassi d Berger 57 61 61. **F:** Agassi d Edberg 61 64 06 62.
DOUBLES: Rick Leach/Jim Pugh d Boris Becker/Cassio Motta 64 36 63

APRIL 2-8: PRUDENTIAL-BACHE SECURITIES CLASSIC, ORLANDO $225,000
Winner: BRAD GILBERT
Rd 32: Brad Gilbert d Christian Saceanu 64 64; Jimmy Brown d Lars Wahlgren 75 61; Joey Rive d Jeff Tarango 64 64; Miguel Nido d Veli Paloheimo 64 Ret.; Scott Davis d Thomas Hogstedt 46 76 64; Dan Goldie d Leif Shiras 63 61; Malivai Washington d Kelly Jones 63 62; John Ross d Jimmy Arias 76 16 63; Glenn Layendecker d Jared Palmer 63 61; Jason Stoltenberg d Royce Deppe 61 75; Nicolas Pereira d Robbie Weiss 76 67 76; Christo van Rensburg d Slobodan Zivojinovic 76 36 63; Ramesh Krishnan d Derrick Rostagno 67 62 75; David Pate d Alexander Mronz 64 64; Alexis Hombrecher d David Engel 75 63; Aaron Krickstein d Markus Zoecke 61 62. **Rd 16:** Gilbert d Brown 62 61; Rive d Nido 36 75 64; Davis d Goldie 16 64 62; Washington d Ross 61 75; Stoltenberg d Layendecker 64 67 64; van Rensburg d Pereira 63 76; Pate d Krishnan 62 36 63; Hombrecher d Krickstein W/O. **QF:** Gilbert d Rive 63 63; Washington d Davis 63 75; van Rensburg d Stoltenberg 64 46 61; Pate d Hombrecher 64 76. **SF:** Gilbert d Washington 62 75; van Rensburg d Pate 67 63 75. **F:** Gilbert d van Rensburg 62 61.
DOUBLES: Scott Davis and David Pate d Alfonso Mora and Brian Page 63 76.

APRIL 2-8: BANESPA OPEN, RIO DE JANEIRO $225,000 Winner: LUIZ MATTAR
Rd 32: Luiz Mattar d Jaime Oncins 16 75 61; Roberto Arguello d Pablo Albano 63 60; Paul Vojtisek d Nduka Odizor 63 67 75; Brad Pearce d Olivier Delaitre 64 61; Cassio Motta d Dan Cassidy 64 64; Simone Colombo d Marcelo Ingaramo 64 75; Nick Brown d Alexandre Hocevar 61 57 64; Martin Wostenholme d Ricki Osterthun 36 75 64; Martin Laurendeau d Bryan Shelton 62 36 75; Leonardo Lavalle d Gabriel Markus 64 67 76; Chris Pridham d Danilo Marcelino 63 61; Brian Garrow d Eduardo Bengoechea 60 46 63; Patrick Baur d Horacio de la Pena 63 63; Gianluca Pozzi d Jose Daher 62 76; Fernando Roese d Peter Ballauff 62 61; Andrew Sznajder d Javier Frana 63 61. **Rd 16:** Mattar d Arguello 63 63; Vojtisek d Pearce 63 57 61; Colombo d Motta 76 63; Wostenholme d Brown 76 62; Laurendeau d Lavalle 61 36 62; Garrow d Laurendeau 26 75 61; Baur d Pozzi 62 26 63; Sznajder d Baur 63 63. **QF:** Mattar d Vojtisek 46 61 63; Wostenholme d Colombo 62 62; Garrow d Laurendeau 63 63; Sznajder d Baur 75 61. **SF:** Mattar d Wostenholme 63 61; Sznajder d Garrow 64 16 64. **F:** Mattar d Sznajder 64 64.
DOUBLES: Brian Garrow/Sven Salumaa d Nelson Aerts/Fernando Roese 75 63.

APRIL 2-8: ESTORIL OPEN, $225,000 Winner: EMILIO SANCHEZ
Rd 32: Jay Berger d Joao Cunha-Silva 61 63; Ronald Agenor d Javier Sanchez 76 76; Jordi Arrese d Francisco Clavet 61 63; Andrei Cherkasov d Guillermo Perez-Roldan 75 63; Emilio Sanchez d Richard Fromberg 64 75; Tomas Carbonell d Jean Fleurian 62 76; Omar Camporese d Udo Riglewski 64 63; Karel Novacek d Jaime Yzaga 63 36 62; Thomas Muster d Mark Koevermans 46 63 75; Fabrice Santoro d Marian Vajda 75 64; Paolo Cane d Nuno Marques 64 63; Juan Aguilera d Andres Gomez 46 76 61; Sergi Bruguera d Martin Strelba 63 63; Franco Davin d Mark Ozer 61 64; Goran Prpic d Jerome Potier 61 16 76; Paul Haarhuis d Martin Jaite 60 63. **Rd 16:** Berger d Agenor 75 76; Arrese d Cherkasov 62 62; Emilio Sanchez d Carbonell 64 63; Camporese d Novacek 76 46 61; Muster d Santoro 76 62; Aguilera d Cane 62 67 64; Davin d Bruguera 75 64; Haarhuis d Prpic 62 61. **QF:** Arrese d Berger 46 63 75; E Sanchez d Camporese 63 63; Aguilera d Muster 63 60; Davin d Haarhuis 64 75. **SF:** Emilio Sanchez d Arrese 61 61; Davin d Aguilera 64 63. **F:** Emilio Sanchez d Davin 63 61.
DOUBLES: Sergio Casal/Emilio Sanchez d Omar Camporese/Paolo Cane 75 46 75.

APRIL 9-15: SUNTORY JAPAN OPEN TENNIS, TOKYO $825,000
Winner: STEFAN EDBERG
Rd 64: Ivan Lendl bye; Shuzo Matsuoka d Andrew Castle 62 63; Joseph Russell d Tom Nijssen 75 Ret.; Dan Goldie d Bruce Derlin 64 61; Amos Mansdorf d Chris Garner 62 62; David Lewis d Simon Youl 63 64; Slobodan Zivojinovic d Brad Drewett 61 61; Scott Davis bye; Aaron Krickstein bye; David Pate d Toshihisa Tsuchihashi 62 63; Grant Connell d Hidehiko Tanizawa 63 62; Thomas Hogstedt d Paul Vojtisek 75 63; Patrick Kuhnen d Kelly Evernden 76 63; Todd Woodbridge d Richard Matuszewski 64 46 75; Kelly Jones d Christian Saceanu 62 76; Michael Chang bye; Wally Masur bye; Johan Carlsson d Jeff Tarango 62 63; Patrick McEnroe d Nicolas Pereira 62 76; Paul Chamberlin d Gilad Bloom 76 75; Milan Srejber d Kenta Masuda 62 64; Alexander Mronz d Martin Laurendeau 63 75; Brad Pearce d Lars Wahlgren 61 60; Brad Gilbert bye; Jim Grabb bye; Joey Rive d Miguel Nido 16 63 64; Jonathan Canter d Danny Sapsford 46 76 64; Mark Kratzmanna d Pat Cash 64 67 64; Alex Antonitsch d Jason Stoltenberg 76 57 62; Anders Jarryd d Dan Cassidy 60 63; Leif Shiras d Bret Garnett 67 64 61; Stefan Edberg bye. **Rd 32:** Lendl d Matsuoka 64 62; Russell d Goldie 64 63; Mansdorf d Lewis 63 75; Davis d Zivojinovic 63 76; Krickstein d Pate 64 76; Connell d Hogstedt 64 76; Kuhnen d Woodbridge 36 62 63; Chang d Jones 16 60 61; Masur d Carlsson 61 60; McEnroe d Chamberlin 36 63 75; Mronz d Srejber 46 63 63; Gilbert d Pearce 16 61 60; Grabb d Rive 61 64; Kratzmann d Canter 16 62 64; Antonitsch d Jarryd 62 76; Edberg d Shiras 60 62. **Rd 16:** Lendl d Russell 76 62; Mansdorf d Davis 76 67 62; Krickstein d Connell 63 62; Chang d Kuhnen 75 62; Masur d McEnroe 62 76; Gilbert d Mronz 46 75 61; Grabb d Kratzmann 64 62; Edberg d Antonitsch 62 67 61. **QF:** Lendl d Mansdorf 64 62; Krickstein d Chang 76 61; Gilbert d Masur 61 76; Edberg d Grabb 63 63 **SF:** Krickstein d Lendl 63 57 64; Edberg d Gilbert 61 76. **F:** Edberg d Krickstein 64 75.
DOUBLES: Mark Kratzmann/Wally Masur d Kent Kinnear/Brad Pearce 36 63 64

APRIL 9-15: TROFEO CONDE DE GODO, BARCELONA $375,000
Winner: ANDRES GOMEZ
Rd 64: Jay Berger bye; Omar Camporese d Udo Riglewski 62 63; Michael Stitch d Richard Fromberg 46 76 76; Jordi Arrese d Sergio Casal 64 76; Carlos Costa d Petr Korda 63 26 62; Andrei Cherkasov d Francisco Roig 63 63; Roberto Azar d Lawson Duncan 62 64; Andrei Chesnokov bye; Andres Gomez bye; Michiel Schapers d Bruno Oresar 62 46 75; Marian Vajda d JensWoehrmann 61 62; German Lopez d Ronald Agenor 62 36 75; Paolo Cane d Claudio Pistolesi 62 67 63; Diego Perez d Dirk Leppen 64 64; Aki Rahunen d David de Miguel 75 76; Alberto Mancini bye; Horst Skoff bye; Martin Strelba d Henri Leconte 67 64 64; Marcelo Filippini d Juan Avendano 57 63 64; Sergi Bruguera d Tomas Carbonell 75 64; Jean Fleurian d Paul Haarhuis 31 Ret.; Veli Paloheimo d Juan Aguilera 76 46 63; Franco Davin d Eduardo Bengoechea 61 62; Emilio Sanchez bye; Thomas Muster bye; Goran Prpic d Vincente Solves 64 64; Mark Koevermans d Johan Anderson 63 63; Guillermo Perez-Roldan d Alexander Volkov 64 62; Javier Sanchez d Jerome Potier 64 62; Karel Novacek d Marc Rosset 63 62; Markus Zoecke d Jose Clavet 76 64; Martin Jaite bye. **Rd 32:** Berger d Camporese 57 63 76; Arrese d Stich 63 36 75; Costa d Cherkasov 63 62; Chesnokov d Azar 64 16 63; Gomez d Schapers 46 76 76; Lopez d Vajda 64 76; Perez d Cane 62 20 Ret.; Mancini d Rahunen 76 06 64; Skoff d Strelba 63 46 61; Bruguera d Filippini 75 63; Paloheimo d Fleurian 62 62; E Sanchez d Davin 63 61; Prpic d Muster 36 61 62; Perez-Roldan d Koevermans 63 64; J Sanchez d Novacek 76 62; Jaite d Zoecke 62 76. **Rd 16:** Berger d Arrese 36 63 63; Chesnokov d Costa 64 60; Gomez d Lopez 61 64; Perez d Mancini 64 61; Bruguera d Skoff 62 63; E Sanchez d Paloheimo W/O; Perez-Roldan d Prpic 62 75; Jaite d J Sanchez 63 36 63. **QF:** Chesnokov d Berger 62 64; Gomez d Perez 36 63 76; E Sanchez d Bruguera 57 64 64; Perez-Roldan d Jaite 64 64. **SF:** Gomez d Chesnokov 63 75; Perez-Roldan d E Sanchez 75 76. **F:** Gomez d Perez-Roldan 60 76 36 06 62
DOUBLES: Andres Gomez/Javier Sanchez d Emilio Sanchez/Sergio Casal 76 75

APRIL 16-22: PHILIPS OPEN, NICE $225,000 Winner: JUAN AGUILERA
Rd 32: Jay Berger d Olivier Soules 76 63; Henri Leconte d Marcelo Filippini 76 63; Michael Stich d Jimmy Arias 63 36 63; Andrei Cherkasov d Petr Korda 06 75 75; Niclas Kroon d Horst Skoff 26 64 61; Guy Forget d Veli Paloheimo 62 75; Goran Prpic d Jan Gunnarsson 76 75; Guillermo Perez-Roldan d Ronald Agenor 16 63 64; Marc Rosset d Yannick Noah 57 63 63; Tomas Carbonell d Martin Strelba 63 61; Fabrice Santoro d Jean Fleurian 76 62; Andrei Chesnokov d Karel Novacek 76 61; Aki Rahunen d Jordi Arrese 36 63 64; Juan Aguilera d Javier Sanchez 64 26 61; Jakob Hlasek d Thierry Tulasne 36 64 64; Claudio Pistolesi d Alberto Mancini 64 63. **Rd 16:** Berger d Leconte 63 16 76; Cherkasov d Stich 64 64; Forget d Kroon 76 61; Prpic d Perez-Roldan 75 67 20 Ret.; Rosset d Carbonell 76 46 64; Santoro d Chesnokov 63 64; Aguilera d Rahunen 62 26 64; Hlasek d Pistolesi 64 64. **QF:** Cherkasov d Berger 26 62 63; Forget d Prpic 76 62; Rosset d Santoro 60 57 62; Aguilera d Hlasek 64 64. **SF:** Forget d Cherkasov 46 76 64; Aguilera d Rosset 63 60. **F:** Aguilera d Forget 26 63 64.
DOUBLES: Alberto Mancini/Yannick Noah d Marcelo Filippini/Horst Skoff 64 76.

APRIL 16-22: KAL CUP KOREA, SEOUL $140,000 Winner: ALEX ANTONITSCH
Rd 32: Wally Masur d Christian Saceanu 62 62; Richard Matuszewski d Jason Stoltenberg 62 67 62; Miguel Nido d Slobodan Zivojinovic 60 20 Ret.; Gilad Bloom d Simon Youl 63 61; Grant Connell d Paul Chamberlin 75 62; Pat Cash d Martin Laurendeau 64 63; Johan Carlsson d Nick Brown 64 63; Milan Srejber d Tom Nijssen 63 61; Dan Goldie d Todd Woodbridge 64 26 64; Joey Rive d Jae-Sik Kim 75 64; Shuzo Matsuoka d Nicolas Pereira 61 63; Kelly Evernden d Jin-Ho Lee 63 61; Leif Shiras d Thomas Hogstedt 75 46 64; Alex Antonitsch d Kelly Jones 64 64; Patrick Kuhnen d Bong-Soo Kim 75 26 76; Lars Wahlgren d Amos Mansdorf 64 75. **Rd 16:** Matuszewski d Masur 67 76 64; Bloom d Nido 64 63; Cash d Connell 67 75 62; Srejber d Carlsson 60 64; Goldie d Rive 46 63 64; Matsuoka d Evernden 63 61; Antonitsch d Shiras 61 60; Kuhnen d Wahlgren 60 61. **QF:** Bloom d Matuszewski 62 62; Cash d Srejber 62 63; Goldie d Matsuoka 75 62; Antonitsch d Kuhnen 64 64. **SF:** Cash d Bloom 63 63; Antonitsch d Goldie 46 63 76. **F:** Antonitsch d Cash 76 63.
DOUBLES: Grant Connell/Glenn Michibata d Jason Stoltenberg/Todd Woodbridge 76 64.

APRIL 23-29: VOLVO MONTE CARLOOPEN $750,000 Winner: ANDREI CHESNOKOV
Rd 64: Stefan Edberg bye; Jimmy Arias d Gary Muller 61 63; Juan Aguilera d Diego Nargiso 61 63; Sergi Bruguera d Jean Fleurian 64 64; Jim Courier d Michael Stich 63 46 64; Goran Ivanisevic d Christian Bergstrom 46 62 64; Thomas Muster d Marcelo Filippini 62 62; Martin Jaite bye; Aaron Krickstein bye; Jordi Arrese d Paolo Cane 76 75; Karel Novacek d Luiz Mattar 64 61; Horst Skoff d Niclas Kroon 60 64; Alberto Mancini d Christo van Rensburg 62 64; Henri Leconte d Todd Witsken 61 64; Javier Sanchez d Fabrice Santoro 62 64; Andres Gomez bye; Jay Berger bye; Jaime Yzaga d Lars Jonsson 63 61; Tomas Carbonell d Jakob Hlasek 64 64; Andrei Chesnokov d Goran Prpic 75 63; Guillermo Perez-Roldan d Diego Perez 62 63; Marc Rosset d Sergio Cortes 64 64; David Engel d Jan Gunnarsson 60 30 Ret.; Gabriel Markus bye; Emilio Sanchez bye; Marian Vajda d Martin Strelba 64 62; Guy Forget d Paul Haarhuis 63 75; Jonas Svensson d Carl-Uwe Steeb 76 63; Ronald Agenor d Magnus Gustafsson 62 62; Petr Korda d Yannick Noah 61 36 62; Cedric Pioline d Milan Srejber 61 61; Boris Becker bye. **Rd 32:** Edberg d Arias 76 63; Aguilera d Bruguera 67 64 Ret.; Courier d Ivanisevic 63 61; Muster d Jaite 63 62; Arrese d Krickstein 75 62; Skoff d Novacek 63 67 64; Leconte d Mancini 64 64; Gomez d Javier Sanchez 76 64; Yzaga d Berger 16 64 61; Chesnokov d Carbonell 41 Ret.; Rosset d Perez-Roldan 61 76; Engel d Markus 75 64; E Sanchez d Vajda 61 61; Forget d Svensson 64 57 61; Agenor d Korda 63 62; Becker d Pioline 75 64. **Rd 16:** Aguilera d Edberg 76 76; Muster d Courier 64 64; Skoff d Arrese 67 64 75; Leconte d Gomez 63 64; Chesnokov d Yzaga 62 61; Rosset d Engel 60 64; E Sanchez d Forget 62 62; Becker d Agenor 62 46 64. **QF:** Muster d Aguilera 63 64; Leconte d Skoff 62 67 64; Chesnokov d Rosset 63 62; Emilio Sanchez d Becker 46 75 76. **SF:** Muster d Leconte 62 63; Chesnokov d Emilio Sanchez 46 61 76. **F:** Chesnokov d Muster 75 63 63.
DOUBLES: Petr Korda/Thomas Smid d Andres Gomez/Javier Sanchez 64 76

APRIL 23-29: SALEM OPEN, HONG KONG $185,000 Winner: PAT CASH
Rd 32: Wally Masur d Thomas Hogstedt 63 60; Tom Nijssen d Lars Wahlgren 62 76; Jonathan Canter d Larry Stefanki 61 64; Markus Zoecke d Kelly Evernden 57 63 64; Jason Stoltenberg d Scott Davis 57 63 64; Alex Antonitsch d Richard Matuszewski 62 64; Patrick McEnroe d Vijay Amritraj 36 62 60; Paul Chamberlin d Kelly Jones 64 63; Richard Fromberg d Mark Kratzmanna 76 63; Patrick Kuhnen d Joey Rive 61 64; Brad Pearce d Bong-Soo Kim 62 63; Amos Mansdorf d Nicolas Pereira 76 60; Dan Goldie d Gilad Bloom 63 63; Grant Connell d Leif Shiras 61 62; Eric Jelen d Simon Youl 10 Ret.; Pat Cash d Kevin Curren 61 64. **Rd 16:** Nijssen d Masur 06 63 63; Canter d Zoecke 46 64 63; Antonitsch d Stoltenberg 76 61; McEnroe d Chamberlin 64 64; Kuhnen d Fromberg 75 75; Pearce d Mansdorf 62 26 63; Connell d Goldie 63 64; Cash d Jelen 62 76. **QF:** Canter d Nijssen 61 64; Antonitsch d McEnroe 67 61 76; Kuhnen d Pearce 62 62; Cash d Connell 62 76. **SF:** Antonitsch d Canter 36 63 64; Cash d Kuhnen 67 75 61. **F:** Cash d Antonitsch 63 64.
DOUBLES: Pat Cash/Wally Masur d Kevin Curren/Joey Rive 63 63.

APRIL 30-MAY 6: XIX GRAND PRIX VILLA DE MADRID, MADRID $279,000
Winner: ANDRES GOMEZ
Rd 32: Marian Vajda d Jay Berger 63 63; Juan Carlos Baguena d Juan Rascon 62 64; Carlos Costa d Lars Jonsson 61 64; Javier Sanchez d Jordi Arrese 46 63 75; Emilio Sanchez d David de Miguel 62 62; Marc Rosset d Omar Camporese 46 76 63; Jerome Potier d Marcelo Filippini 46 62 61; Marco Gorriz d Thierry Tulasne 64 62; Alberto Mancini d Luiz Mattar 64 26 63; Cassio Motta d Jose F Altur 76 63; Franco Davin d Francisco Roig 75 46 75; Martin Jaite d Paul Haarhuis 57 60 63; Mark Koevermans d Juan Aguilera 06 62 63; Jimmy Arias d Francisco Clavet 57 62 75; Diego Perez d Eduardo Bengoechea 63 75; Andres Gomez d Andrew Sznajder 61 63. **Rd 16:** Baguena d Vajda 64 67 64; J Sanchez d Costa 75 62; Rosset d E Sanchez 46 64 64; Gorriz d Potier 46 54 Ret.; Mancini d Motta 63 64; Jaite d Davin 63 76; Koevermans d Arias 76 64; Gomez d Perez 36 76 60. **QF:** J Sanchez d Baguena 63 61; Rosset d Gorriz 62 26 75; Jaite d Mancini 63 36 62; Gomez d Koevermans 75 36 63. **SF:** Rosset d J Sanchez 75 26 62; Gomez d Jaite 63 64. **F:** Gomez d Rosset 63 76
DOUBLES: Juan Carlos Baguena/Omar Camporese d Andres Gomez/Javier Sanchez 64 36 63

APRIL 30-MAY 6: BMW OPEN, MUNICH $225,000 Winner: KAREL NOVACEK
Rd 32: Stefan Edberg d Christo van Rensburg 61 60; Martin Strelba d Stefano Pescosolido 63 62; Magnus Gustafsson d Todd Witsken 63 63; Thomas Muster d Guillermo Perez-Roldan 64 64; Petr Korda d Michael Chang 67 75 76; Kevin Curren d Jorge Lozano 63 46 64; Jens Woehrmann d Yannick Noah 62 64; Carl-Uwe Steeb d Jan Gunnarsson 62 64; Jonas Svensson d Pete Sampras 60 61; Milan Srejber d Goran Prpic 76 63; Bruno Oresar d Michael Stich 76 67 64; Jim Courier d Paolo Cane 76 62; Christian Bergstrom d Horst Skoff 62 46 63; Udo Riglewski d Peter Lundgren 64 67 63; Karel Novacek d Hans Schwaier 63 64; Aaron Krickstein d Horacio de la Pena 26 76 63. **Rd 16:** Strelba d Edberg 64 61; Muster d Gustafsson 75 62; Korda d Curren 75 61; Woehrmann d Steeb 75 64; Svensson d Srejber 61 10 Ret.; Courier d Oresar 62 61; Bergstrom d Riglewski 61 46 60; Novacek d Krickstein 62 76. **QF:** Muster d Strelba 43 Ret.; Korda d Woehrmann 63 75; Svensson d Courier 36 63 64; Novacek d Bergstrom 61 61. **SF:** Muster d Korda 63 61; Novacek d Svensson 61 26 61. **F:** Novacek d Muster 64 62.
DOUBLES: Udo Riglewski/Michael Stich d Petr Korda/Tomas Smid 61 64.

APRIL 30-MAY 6: EPSON SINGAPORE SUPER TENNIS, $225,000
Winner: KELLY JONES
Rd 32: Wally Masur d Peter Nyborg 63 64; Eric Jelen d Joey Rive 64 46 64; Chris Pridham d Brad Drewett 76 26 76; Richard Fromberg d Christian Saceanu 63 76; Patrick

McEnroe d Paul Chamberlin 16 62 62; Mark Petchey d Shuzo Matsuoka 63 57 61; Todd Woodbridge d Woody Hunt 76 64; Dan Goldie d Brian Garrow 62 64; Kelly Evernden d Jonathan Canter 64 63; Patrick Kuhnen d Tom Nijssen 76 64; J Siemerink d Leif Shiras 64 75; Martin Laurendeau d Alex Antonitsch 46 61 10 Ret.Jason Stoltenberg d Grant Connell 63 61; Thomas Hogstedt d Dan Cassidy 63 61; Kelly Jones d Markus Zoecke 64 62; Mark Kratzmanna d Lars Wahlgren 61 67 62. **Rd 16:** Masur d Jelen 64 62; Fromberg d Pridham 67 76 75; McEnroe d Petchey 75 61; Goldie d Woodbridge 64 57 60; Evernden d Kuhnen 63 64; Siemerink d Laurendeau 64 64; Hogstedt d Stoltenberg 36 63 75; Jones d Kratzmann 76 61. **QF:** Fromberg d Masur 64 64; Goldie d McEnroe 36 61 76; Siemerink d Evernden 62 61; Jones d Hogstedt 76 26 62. **SF:** Fromberg d Goldie 64 76; Jones d Siemerink 61 64. **F:** Jones d Fromberg 64 26 76.
DOUBLES: Mark Kratzmann/Jason Stoltenberg d Brad Drewett/Todd Woodbridge 61 60.

MAY 7-13: BMW GERMAN OPEN, HAMBURG $750,000 Winner: JUAN AGUILERA
Rd 64: Boris Becker bye; Paolo Cane d Kevin Curren 76 64; Andrei Cherkasov d Markus Zoecke 62 62; Jens Woehrmann d Alberto Mancini 60 62; Jimmy Arias d Martin Jaite 36 75 63; Jakob Hlasek d Michael Stich 76 64; Udo Riglewski d Jan Apell 61 62; Lars Jonsson bye; Aaron Krickstein bye; Jaime Yzaga d Milan Srejber 62 63; Henri Leconte d Todd Witsken 76 26 62; Jordi Arrese d Horst Skoff 31 Ret.; Franco Davin d Christian Bergstrom 75 62; Ronald Agenor d Eric Jelen 75 64; Luiz Mattar d Claudio Pistolesi 64 75; Andres Gomez bye; Jay Berger bye; Patrick Kuhnen d Thierry Champion 67 62 64; Roberto Azar d Jean Fleurian 76 16 64; Carl-Uwe Steeb d Javier Sanchez 64 26 64; Goran Prpic d Guillermo Perez-Roldan 60 63; Guy Forget d Karel Novacek 64 75; Fabrice Santoro d Petr Korda 62 36 76; Emilio Sanchez bye; Michael Chang bye; Juan Aguilera d Goran Ivanisevic 64 61; Paul Haarhuis d Amos Mansdorf 60 63; Jim Courier d Jan Gunnarsson 67 64 62; Magnus Gustafsson d Sergi Bruguera 62 64; Marcelo Filippini d Alexander Volkov 62 75; Diego Perez d Jonas Svensson 63 36 76; Andre Agassi bye. **Rd 32:** Becker d Cane 75 61; Cherkasov d Woehrmann 64 61; Arias d Hlasek 64 26 62; Jonsson d Riglewski 60 64; Krickstein d Yzaga 76 62; Leconte d Arrese 64 16 62; Davin d Agenor 63 26 62; Mattar d Gomez 67 76 63.Berger d Kuhnen 62 62; Azar d Steeb 62 46 75; Forget d Prpic 76 36 64; E Sanchez d Santoro 46 61 61; Aguilera d Chang 63 62; Courier d Haarhuis 61 61; Gustafsson d Filippini 63 57 63; Agassi d Perez 61 10 Ret. **Rd 16:** Becker d Cherkasov 62 63; Arias d Jonsson 61 62; Leconte d Krickstein 64 64; Davin d Mattar 60 62; Berger d Azar 36 62 63; Forget d E Sanchez 76 64; Aguilera d Courier 16 64 64; Gustafsson d Agassi 76 76. **QF:** Becker d Arias 63 61; Leconte d Davin 63 63; Forget d Berger 63 36 64; Aguilera d Gustafsson 61 64. **SF:** Becker d Leconte 63 36 63; Aguilera d Forget 75 76. **F:** Aguilera d Becker 61 60 76.
DOUBLES: Sergi Bruguera/Jim Courier d Udo Riglewski/Michael Stich 76 62

MAY 7-13: US MEN'S CLAY COURT CHAMPIONSHIPS, KIAWAH ISLAND $197,000 Winner: DAVID WHEATON
Rd 32: Richey Reneberg d Tom Mercer 64 76; Alexander Mronz d Robert Van't Hof 63 63; Robbie Weiss d Alejandro Aramburu 60 62; Derrick Rostagno d Miguel Nido 61 61; David Wheaton d Richard Matuszewski 36 61 75; Craig Campbell d Bryan Shelton 60 63; Chris Garner d Dan Goldberg 64 76; Jeff Tarango d Lawson Duncan 63 64; Mark Kaplana d Dan Goldie 63 36 63; David Pate d Jimmy Brown 61 62; Joey Rive d John Ross 63 63; Tim Wilkison d Scott Davis 63 62; Malivai Washington d Leif Shiras 62 61; Leonardo Lavalle d Broderick Dyke 63 61; Martin Wostenholme d Dan Cassidy 62 61; Brad Pearce d Jim Grabb 61 64. **Rd 16:** Mronz d Reneberg 64 62; Rostagno d Weiss 75 63; Wheaton d Campbell 16 63 75; Tarango d Garner 64 75; Kaplan d Pate 63 63; Wilkison d Rive 61 63; Washington d Lavalle 26 63 62; Wostenholme d Pearce 62 63. **QF:** Mronz d Rostagno 63 62; Wheaton d Tarango 62 67 76; Kaplan d Wilkison 64 62; Washington d Wostenholme 64 46 63. **SF:** Wheaton d Mronz 26 75 62; Kaplan d Washington 62 63. **F:** Wheaton d Kaplan 64 64.
DOUBLES: Scott Davis/ David Pate d Jim Grabb/Leonardo Lavalle 62 63.

MAY 14-20: XI VII CAMPIONATI INTERZIONALI I D'ITALIE, ROME $1002,000 Winner: THOMAS MUSTER
Rd 64: Brad Gilbert d Jim Pugh 16 64 64; Luiz Mattar d David Wheaton 62 63; Henri Leconte d Thierry Champion 62 64; Alberto Mancini d Christian Miniussi 46 76 64; Jim Courier d Franco Davin 61 16 64; Jaime Yzaga d Javier Sanchez 64 46 64; Paolo Cane d Federico Mordegan 46 75 62; Andrew Chesnokov d Jimmy Arias 76 63; Emilio Sanchez d Andrew Sznajder 62 61; Marcelo Filippini d Todd Witsken 64 36 64; Tomas Carbonell d Gianluca Pozzi 61 63; Jonas Svensson d Luke Jensen 62 36 62; Guillermo Perez-Roldan d Ronald Agenor 67 62 64; Jean Fleurian d Richey Reneberg 46 63 75; Renzo Furlan d Martin Strelba 63 63; Martin Jaite d Dirk Leppen 63 61; Jay Berger d Amos Mansdorf 36 61 60; Omar Camporese d Arnaud Boetsch 64 64; Massimo Cierro d Claudio Pistolesi 63 76; Paul Haarhuis d Sergio Casal 61 64; Magnus Gustafsson d Jordi Arrese 36 64 63; Stefano Pescosolido d Lawson Duncan 62 63; Diego Nargiso d Cassio Motta 63 62; Andres Gomez d Yannick Noah 61 67 63; Jan Gunnarsson d Michael Chang 63 63; Sergi Bruguera d Milan Srejber 76 67 63; Anders Jarryd d Niclas Kroon 63 63; Thomas Muster d Jakob Hlasek 63 64; Guy Forget d Petr Korda 63 62; Alexander Volkov d Juan Aguilera 63 16 64; Karel Novacek d Torben Theine 64 16 64; Aaron Krickstein d Jim Grabb 61 63. **Rd 32:** Gilbert d Mattar 76 64; Mancini d Leconte 64 64; Courier d Yzaga 63 64; Chesnokov d Cane 46 63 63; E Sanchez d Filippini 46 61 62; Svensson d Carbonell 63 61; Perez-Roldan d Fleurian 63 64; Jaite d Furlan 64 64; Camporese d Berger 64 64; Haarhuis d Cierro 64 64; Gustafsson d Pescosolido 64 67 62; Gomez d Nargiso 76 64; Gunnarsson d Bruguera 64 62; Muster d Jarryd 51 Ret.; Forget d Volkov 61 36 62; Krickstein d Novacek 62 62. **Rd 16:** Mancini d Gilbert 62 61; Chesnokov d Courier 46 76 63; E Sanchez d Svensson 63 62; Perez-Roldan d Jaite 64 63; Camporese d Haarhuis 64 61; Gomez d Gustafsson 64 75; Muster d Gunnarsson 63 62; Forget d Krickstein 64 76. **QF:** Chesnokov d Mancini 76 60; E Sanchez d Perez-Roldan 76 62; Gomez d Camporese 61 62; Muster d Forget 62 36 63. **SF:** Chesnokov d E Sanchez 67 64 76; Muster d Gomez 57 64 76. **F:** Muster d Chesnokov 61 63 61.
DOUBLES: Emilio Sanchez/Sergio Casal d Jim Courier/Scott Davis 76 75

MAY 14-20: YUGOSLAV OPEN, UMAG $147,000 Winner: GORAN PRPIC
Rd 32: Goran Prpic d Eduardo Masso 67 64 60; Diego Perez d Michael Tauson 76 64; Roberto Azar d Paul Dogger 62 63; Marian Vajda d Francesco Cancellotti 64 61; Mark Koevermans d Sasa Hirszon 76 63; Horacio de la Pena d Eduardo Bengoechea 75 26 60; Nuno Marques d Lars Jonsson 46 75 63; Aki Rahunen d Gilad Bloom 75 64; Andrei Cherkasov d Jose Clavet 62 64; Francisco Roig d Olivier Delaitre 76 64; Damir Buljevic d Johan Anderson 63 64; Eric Jelen d Jens Woehrmann 63 16 60; Jerome Potier d Thierry Tulasne 36 63 61; Tarik Benhabiles d Christian Saceanu 62 62; Fernando Luna d Mario Tabares 64 64; Goran Ivanisevic d Nicolas Pereira 61 64. **Rd 16:** Prpic d Perez 62 60; Azar d Vajda 06 76 63; de la Pena d Koevermans 76 63; Rahunen d Marques 76 64; Cherkasov d Roig 63 64; Jelen d Buljevic 26 63 76; Benhabiles d Potier 62 36 76; Ivanisevic d Luna 62 63. **QF:** Prpic d Azar 64 64; de la Pena d Rahunen 57 76 61; Cherkasov d Jelen 62 60; Ivanisevic d Benhabiles 64 76. **SF:** Prpic d de la Pena 76 76; Ivanisevic d Cherkasov 63 57 64. **F:** Prpic d Ivanisevic 63 46 64.
DOUBLES: Vojtech Flegl/Daniel Vacek d Andrei Cherkasov/Andrei Olhovskiy 64 64.

MAY 21-27: PEUGEOT ATP WORLD TEAM CUP, DUSSELDORF. $900,000. Winner: YUGOSLAVIA
Red Group: **USA v Spain**: Jordi Arrese d Brad Gilbert 75 75; Jim Courier d Sergi Brugerua 75 61; Ken Flach/Courier d Bruguera/Thomas Carbonell 75 61; **Germany v USSR**; Carl-Uwe Steeb d Alexander Volkov 75 75; Boris Becker d Andrei Cherkasov 64 63; Michael Stich/Eric Jelen d Cherkasov/Gabrichidze 64 67 62; **USA v Germany** ; Becker d Gilbert 61 61; Courier d Steeb 63 16 63; Flach/Courier d Becker/Jelen 62 62; **Spain v USSR**; Bruguera d Volkov 75 63; Arrese d Cherkasov 62 46 76; Vokov/Andrei Olhovisky d Flach/Courier 63 16 76; **Germany v Spain**; Bruguera d Steeb 62 46 36; Arrese d Becker 62 61; Michael Stich/Jelen dBruguera/ Carbonell; 63 62. **Blue Group**: **Sweden v Austria**; Jonas Svensson d Alex Antonitsch 64 63; Stefan Edberg d Thomas Muster 62 64; Edberg/Magnus Gustafsson d Thomas Buchmayer/Oliver Fuchs 64 61; **Argentina v Yugoslavia**; Goran Ivanisevic d Alberto Mancini 64 60; Goran Prpic d Martin Jaite 76 46 76; Javier Frana/Christian Miniussi d Ivanisevic/Slobodan Zivojinovic 63 ret; **Sweden v Argentina**; Jaite d Edberg 36 62 64; Mancini d Svensson 64 62; Frana/Miniussi d Edberg/ Gustafsson 63 76; **Austria v Yugoslavia**; Ivanisevic d Fuchs 64 62; Prpic d Antonitsch 61 61; Prpic/Zivojinovic d Fuchs/Buchmayer 76 63; **Sweden v Yugoslavia**; Gustafsson d Ivanisevic 64 62; Prpic d Edberg 61 64; Prpic/ Ivanisevic d Edberg/Gustafsson 64 62; **Argentina v Austria**; Mancini d Buchmayer 62 64; Antonitsch d Jaite 64 76; Frana/Miniussi d Antonitsch/Buchmayer 63 63. **F: Yugoslavia d USA**; Prpic d Gilbert 64 64; Ivanisevic d Courier 36 75 61; Flach/Robert Seguso d Prpic/Zivojinovic 75 76.

MAY 21-27: MURRATI-TIME INTERNAZIONALI DI TENNIS, BOLOGNA $234,000 Winner: RICHARD FROMBERG
Rd 32: Guillermo Pere-Roldan d Aki Rahunen 60 75; Xavier Daufresne d Lars Jonsson 26 61 63; Claudio Pistolesi d Stefano Pescosolido 64 64; Richard Fromberg d Luiz Mattar 61 63; Jaime Yzaga d Udo Riglewski 63 60 Ret.; Thierry Tulasne d Francesco Cancellotti 61 76; Jim Pugh d Martin Wostenholme 57 76 75; Jerome Potier d Jimmy Arias 75 76; Martin Strelba d Jim Grabb 26 63 64; Todd Witsken d Nicolas Pereira 63 75; Omar Camporese d Cassio Motta 60 62; Franco Davin d Diego Nargiso 64 64; Paolo Cane d Renzo Furlan 62 36 63; Lawson Duncan d Jose F Altur 63 60; Horacio de la Pena d Federico Mordegan 63 63; Marc Rosset d Gilad Bloom 62 36 61. **Rd 16:** Perez-Roldan d Daufresne 60 60; Fromberg d Pistolesi 36 60 63; Tulasne d Yzaga 62 64; Potier d Pugh 63 76; Witsken d Strelba 76 61; Davin d Camporese 75 63; Duncan d Cane 75 63; Rosset d de la Pena 76 36 64. **QF:** Fromberg d Perez-Roldan 60 16 64; Potier d Tulasne 75 10 Ret.; Davin d Witsken 64 60; Rosset d Duncan 62 63. **SF:** Fromberg d Potier 76 63; Rosset d Davin 62 64. **F:** Fromberg d Rosset 46 64 76.
DOUBLES: Gustavo Luza/Udo Riglewski d Jerome Potier/Jim Pugh 74 46 6l.

MAY 28-JUNE 10: FRENCH OPEN, PARIS $2,700,000 Winner: ANDRES GOMEZ
Rd 128: Sergi Bruguera d Stefan Edberg 64 62 61; Jonas Svensson d Jerome Potier 64 36 61 62; Roberto Azar d Lawson Duncan 63 61 61; Martin Strelba d Kelly Jones 61 63 46 63; Andrew Sznajder d Cedric Pioline 76 63 61; Yannick Noah d Francisco Clavet 64 46 64 16 75; Andrei Cherkasov d Fredric Vitoux 60 64 64; Guillermo Perez-Roldan d Olivier Soules 67 61 63 62; Alberto Mancini d Jay Berger 64 62 62; Franco Davin d Francisco Maciel 62 61 62; Bruno Oresar d Eric Jelen 76 46 26 61 64; Henri Leconte d Ronald Agenor 64 62 64; Jordi Arrese d Markus Zoecke 64 36 63 61; Fabrice Santoro d Guillaume Raoux 61 64 64; Jean Fleurian d Marian Vajda 62 64 61; Andre Chesnokov d Udo Riglewski 61 61 63; Andre Agassi d Martin Wostenholme 46 76 60 61; Todd Woodbridge d Mansour Bahrami 26 61 46 63 86; Gilad Bloom d Richard Fromberg 57 75 16 63 62; Arnaud Boetsch d Mark Kratzmann 64 60 63; Nuno Marques d Christian Miniussi 61 76 62; Johan Anderson d Oliver Delaitre 64 75 61; Milan Srejber d David Wheaton 36 57 63 76 63; Jim Courier d Jose F Altur 61 46 63 64; Michael Chang d Cassio Motta 62 76 61; Marc Rosset d Francisco Roig 36 63 64 64; Christian Bergstrom d Todd Witsken 61 62 60; Tim Wilkison d Miloslav Mecir 64 61 46 64; Javier Sanchez d Marcelo Ingaramo 61 36 62 76; Pedro Rebolledo d Simon Youl 75 63 61; Jakob Hlasek d Peter Lundgren 36 76 26 75 62; Nicklas Kulti d Emilio Sanchez 46 64 67 62 61; Aaron Krickstein d Jaime Yzaga 60 26 63 63; Stephane Grenier d Jeremy Bates 62 64 62; Luiz Mattar d Richard Matuszewski 64 61 64; Karel Novacek d Scott Davis 63 62 62; Alex Antonitsch d Derrick Rostagno 63 76 63; Guy Forget d Richey Reneberg 36 64 64 64; Thierry Champion d Goran Prpic 64 36 63 63; Juan Aguilera d Malivai Washington 75 46 61 62; Magnus Gustafsson d Thomas Carbonell 64 57 64 62; Petr Korda d Veli Paloheimo 64 61 26 63; Omar Camporese d Tarik Benhabiles 62 63 64; Diego Perez d Thomas Hogstedt 61 64 10 Ret.; Alexander Volkov d Nicolas Pereira 64 60 46 64; Jimmy Arias d David Rikl 62 61 36 62; Marcelo Filippini d Lars Wahlgren 46 60 61 60; Andres Gomez d Fernando Luna 76 61 76; Thomas Muster d Lars Jonsson 75 63 62; Eric Winogradsky d Hans Schwaier 64 61 63; Paul Haarhuis d Jim Grabb 63 61 62; Jim Pugh d Thierry Tulasne 64 61 10 Ret.; Aki Rahunen d Grant Connell 16 61 64 60; Leif Shiras d Slobodan Zivojinovic 76 64 36 36 64; Michael Stich d Joey Rive 64 61 61; Martin Jaite d Claudio Pistolesi 62 76 62; Amos Mansdorf d Mario Tabares 63 46 64 64; Francesco Cancellotti d Ramesh Krishnan 64 64 36 76; Niclas Kroon d Dan Goldie 76 63 61; Jason Stoltenberg d Michiel Schapers 64 63 61; Mark Koevermans d Jan Gunnarsson 63 62 67 63 75; Patrick Kuhnen d David Engel 63 61 62; Anders Jarryd d Darren Cahill 62 46 61 67 63; Goran Ivanisevic d Boris Becker 57 64 75 62. **Rd 64:** Svensson d Bruguera 26 26 64 64 60; Azar d Strelba 36 64 46 63 64; Noah d Sznajder 64 57 64 64; Perez-Roldan d Cherkasov 75 64 63; Davin d Mancini 63 57 75 61; Leconte d Oresar 64 62 61; Arrese d Santoro 46 63 62 62; Chesnokov d Fleurian 76 62 60; Agassi d Woodbridge 75 61 63; Boetsch d Bloom 62 61 60; Anderson d Marques 75 63 61; Courier d Srejber 76 61 26 62; Chang d Rosset 75 46 64 63; Bergstrom d Wilkison 64 62 61; J Sanchez d Rebolledo 64 76 62; Kulti d Hlasek 62 64 64; Krickstein d Grenier 63 64 75; Novacek d Mattar 57 63 62 61; Forget d Antonitsch 61 61 61; Champion d Aguilera 36 63 63 62; Gustafsson d Korda 36 76 16 61 97; Perez d Camporese 36 76 63 46 62; Volkov d Arias 16 63 63 46 61; Gomez d Filippini 76 62 61; Muster d Winogradsky 62 63 61; Haarhuis d Pugh 64 76 67 67 75; Rahunen d Shiras 60 61 61; Jaite d Stich 67 64 67 64 63; Mansdorf d Cancellotti 62 26 61 75; Kroon d Stoltenberg 60 62 63; Kuhnen d Koevermans 63 26 64 62; Ivanisevic d Jarryd 63 60 62. **Rd 32:** Svensson d Azar 57 64 61 76; Perez-Roldan d Noah 76 64 46 63; Leconte d Davin 63 76 64; Chesnokov d Arrese 75 64 62; Agassi d Boetsch 63 62 60; Courier d Anderson 60 62 61; Chang d Bergstrom 26 57 60 62 64; J Sanchez d Kulti 64 64 63; Novacek d Krickstein 62 63 36 76; Champion d Forget 64 67 64 57 63; Gustafsson d Perez 61 46 61 63; Gomez d Volkov 62 75 46 63; Muster d Haarhuis 36 75 62 76; Jaite d Rahunen 76 62 61; Kroon d Mansdorf 64 76 61; Ivanisevic d Kuhnen 76 61 75. **Rd 16:** Svensson d Perez-Roldan 26 64 62 62; Leconte d Chesnokov 64 63 46 26 63; Agassi d Courier 67 61 64 60; Chang d J Sanchez 64 64 62; Champion d Novacek 64 46 36 76 63; Gomez d Gustafsson W/O; Muster d Jaite 76 63 62; Ivanisevic d Kroon 62 64 75. **QF:** Svensson d Leconte 36 75 63 64; Agassi d Chang 61 62 46 62; Gomez d Champion 63 63 64; Muster d Ivanisevic 62 46 64 63. **SF:** Agassi d Svensson 61 64 36 63; Gomez d Muster 75 61. **F:** Gomez d Agassi 63 26 64 64.
DOUBLES: Emilio Sanchez/Sergio Casal d Goran Ivanisevic/Petr Korda 75 63.

JUNE 11-17: STELLA ARTOIS GRASS COURT CHAMPIONSHIPS, LONDON $450,000 Winner: IVAN LENDL
Rd 64: Ivan Lendl bye; Simon Youl d Chris Bailey 76 63; Tim Wilkison d Brian Garrow 75 63; Scott Davis d John Fitzgerald 62 67 61; David Pate d Henri Leconte 61 67 61; Leif Shiras d Joey Rive 75 76; Grant Connell d Nuno Narques 63 64; Guy Forget bye; John McEnroe bye; Ramesh Krishnan d Malivai Washington 61 63; Veli Paloheimo d Johan Anderson 46 76 64; Kevin Curren d Slobodan Zivojinovic 63 76; Richard Fromberg d Mark Petchey 76 63; Brad Pearce d Leonardo Lavalle 61 46 97; Mark Kaplan d Peter Lundgren 64 64; Pete Sampras bye; Tim Mayotte bye; Jason Stoltenberg d Eric Jelen 63 63; Patrick Kuhnen d Anders Jarryd 64 64; David Wheaton d Wayne Ferreira 61 64; Alex Antonitsch d Jeremy Bates 26 63 64; Broderick Dyke d Todd Woodbridge 76 63; Paul Chamberlin d

Pat Cash 64 16 61; Boris Becker bye; Wally Masur bye; Danny Sapsford d Bryan Shelton 64 62; Darren Cahill d Guillaume Raoux 64 76; Christo van Rensburg d Chris Pridham 36 63 63; Niclas Kroon d Mark Kratzmann 57 63 86; Derrick Rostagno d Gary Muller 61 57 62; Markus Zoecke d Paul Annacone 64 36 63; Stefan Edberg bye. **Rd 32:** Lendl d Youl 64 62; Davis d Wilkison 63 75; Pate d Shiras 63 64; Forget d Connell 76 64; McEnroe d Krishnan 46 64 62; Paloheimo d Curren 46 64 97; Fromberg d Pearce 76 62; Sampras d Kaplan 61 64; Stoltenberg d Mayotte 41 Ret.; Wheaton d Kuhnen 46 64 61; Antonitsch d Duke 62 63; Becker d Chamberlin 64 64; Sapsford d Masur 57 64 86; van Rensburg d Cahill 63 76; Kroon d Rostagno 75 76; Edberg d Zoecke 60 63. **Rd 16:** Lendl d Davis 60 63; Pate d Forget 61 63; McEnroe d Paloheimo 60 67 75; Fromberg d Sampras 36 64 108; Wheaton d Stoltenberg 63 64; Becker d Antonitsch 36 61 97; van Rensburg d Sapsford 61 61; Edberg d Kroon 63 60. **QF:** Lendl d Pate 62 64; McEnroe d Fromberg 67 63 75; Becker d Wheaton 63 63; Edberg d van Rensburg 75 63. **SF:** Lendl d McEnroe 62 64; Becker d Edberg 64 64. **F:** Lendl d Becker 63 62.
DOUBLES: Jeremy Bates/Kevin Curren d Henri Leconte/Ivan Lendl 62 76

JUNE 11-17: CONTINENTAL GRASS COURT CHAMPIONSHIPS, ROSMALEN $225,000 Winner: AMOS MANSDORF
Rd 32: Milan Srejber d Yannick Noah 63 63; Henrik Holm d Michiel Schapers 64 75; Amos Mansdorf d Kelly Evernden 64 63; Dan Goldie d Tom Nijssen 75 61; David Engel d Paul Haarhuis 76 76; Jeff Tarango d Miguel Nido 64 62; Michael Stich d Miloslav Mecir 63 62; Richey Reneberg d Mark Woodfordea 62 64; Jim Grabb d Jacco Eltingh 76 46 64; Alexander Volkov d Olivier Delaitre 62 61; Glenn Layendecker d Christian Saceanu 64 64; Jakob Hlasek d Nduka Odizor 64 67 62; Patrick McEnroe d Tom Kempers 60 63; Jan Siemerink d Lars Jonsson 61 64; Bret Garnett d Thomas Hogstedt 76 76; Robbie Weiss d Karel Novacek 63 76. **Rd 16:** Holm d Srejber 64 64; Mansdorf d Goldie 76 16 76; Engel d Engel 61 62; Reneberg d Stich 57 63 63; Volkov d Grabb 63 46 76; Layendecker d Hlasek 75 75; McEnroe d Siemerink 62 63; Weiss d Garnett 76 64. **QF:** Mansdorf d Holm 63 64; Reneberg d Engel 76 64; Volkov d Layendecker 63 64; McEnroe d Weiss 63 64. **SF:** Mansdorf d Reneberg 64 64; Volkov d McEnroe 63 46 63. **F:** Mansdorf d Volkov 63 76.
DOUBLES: Jakob Hlasek/ Michael Stich d Jim Grabb/ Patrick McEnroe 76 63.

JUNE 11-17: TORNEO INTERNAZIONALE CITTA' DI FIRENZE, FLORENCE $225,000 Winner: MAGNUS LARSSON
Rd 32: Guillermo Perez-Roldan d Cedric Pioline 46 75 76; Udo Riglewski d Thierry Tulasne 61 61; Mark Koevermans d Jose F Altur 46 62 76; Magnus Larsson d Luiz Mattar 63 62; Alberto Mancini d Marco Gorriz 62 76; Aki Rahunen d Cassio Motta 64 75; Francisco Clavet d Bruno Oresar 61 76; Javier Sanchez d Roberto Azar 61 36 61; Ronald Agenor d Andrei Cherkasov 76 76; Tomas Carbonell d Andrew Sznajder 62 62; Diego Perez d Claudio Pistolesi 62 57 62; Lawson Duncan d Franco Davin 26 76 62; Fernando Luna d Sergi Bruguera 75 64; Eduardo Bengoechea d Tarik Benhabiles 64 63; Horacio de la Pena d Martin Wostenholme 76 61; Omar Camporese d Horst Skoff 62 60. **Rd 16:** Perez-Roldan d Riglewski 67 61 64; Magnus Larsson d Koevermans 36 63 76; Rahunen d Alberto Mancini 26 62 63; J Sanchez d Clavet 76 60; Carbonell d Agenor 63 60; Duncan d Perez 63 61; Luna d Bengoechea 61 61; Camporese d de la Pena 63 64. **QF:** Larsson d Perez-Roldan 75 64; Rahunen d J Sanchez 64 46 75; Duncan d Carbonell 75 63; Camporese d Luna 61 76. **SF:** Larsson d Rahunen 64 64; Duncan d Camporese 62 63. **F:** Larsson d Duncan 67 75 60.
DOUBLES: Sergi Bruguera/Horacio de la Pena d Luiz Mattar/Diego Perez 36 63 64.

JUNE 18-24: IP CUP, GENOA $225,000 Winner: RONALD AGENOR
Rd 32: Udo Riglewski d Martin Jaite 76 63; Fernando Luna d Duncan Lawson 46 76 61; Francisco Clavet d Bruno Oresar 63 63; Cedric Pioline d Tomas Carbonell 64 67 76; Sergi Bruguera d Eduardo Bengoechea 61 75; Mark Koevermans d Jerome Potier 60 63; Tarik Benhabiles d Jimmy Brown 16 64 63; Claudio Pistolesi d Andrei Cherkasov 60 76; Luiz Mattar d Olivier Delaitre 76 63; Francisco Roig d Juan Carlos Baguena 36 61 64; Omar Camporese d Diego Perez 62 16 62; Renzo Furlan d Jordi Arrese 62 62; Ronald Agenor d Cassio Motta 57 75 64; Jose Francisco Altur d Martin Wostenholme 76 62; Roberto Azar d Marco Gorriz 76 62; Horst Skoff d Michael Tauson 63 60. **Rd 16:** Riglewski d Luna 64 75; Pioline d Clavet 60 46 64; Koevermans d Bruguera 46 64 64; Benhabiles d Pistolesi 57 64 76; Mattar d Roig 63 63; Camporese d Furlan 61 61; Agenor d Altur 75 63; Skoff d Azar 62 57 62. **QF:** Pioline d Riglewski 61 67 63; Benhabiles d Koevermans 63 63; Camporese d Mattar 61 61; Agenor d Skoff 36 61 60. **SF:** Benhabiles d Pioline 64 64; Agenor d Camporese 46 63 62. **F:** Agenor d Benhabiles 36 64 63.
DOUBLES: Tomas Carbonell/Udo Riglewski d Cristiano Caratti/Federico Mordegan 76 76

JUNE 18-24: DIRECT LINE INSURANCE MANCHESTER OPEN $225,000 Winner: PETE SAMPRAS
Rd 32: Aki Rahunen d Aaron Krickstein 64 10 Ret.; Gilad Bloom d Jim Pugh 64 46 76; Kelly Jones d Michiel Schapers 63 76; Alex Antonitsch d Patrick Galbraith 63 06 62; Michael Chang d Malivai Washington 63 64; Mark Kratzmann d Paul Annacone 76 46 64; Nick Brown d Thomas Hogstedt 46 64 63; Richard Fromberg d Peter Nyborg 76 75; Christo van Rensburg d Jeremy Bates 26 64 64; Patrick Kuhnen d Andrew Castle 46 63 75; Eric Jelen d Veli Paloheimo 16 62 63; Gary Muller d Marc Rosset 67 64 76; Dan Goldie d Milan Srejber 76 46 64; Kelly Evernden d Jens Woehrmann 57 64 62; Joey Rive d Ramesh Krishnan 67 61 63; Pete Sampras d Alexander Volkov 46 76 76. **Rd 16:** Bloom d Rahunen 62 75; Jones d Antonitsch 63 76; Kratzmann d Chang 76 76; Brown d Fromberg 76 26 60; van Rensburg d Kuhnen 63 63; Jelen d Muller 76 76; Evernden d Woehrmann 76 67 63; Sampras d Rive 46 63 62. **QF:** Bloom d Jones 36 75 61; Brown d Kratzmann 61 63; Jelen d van Rensburg 62 64; Sampras d Evernden 63 76.
SF: Bloom d Brown 64 76; Sampras d Jelen 67 64 64. **F:** Sampras d Bloom 76 76.
DOUBLES: Mark Kratzmann/Jason Stoltenberg d Nick Brown/Kelly Jones 63 26 64.

JUNE 25-JULY 8: WIMBLEDON $2,670,863 Winner: STEFAN EDBERG
Rd 128: Ivan Lendl d Christian Miniussi 36 64 63 64; Jakob Hlasek d Carlos Costa 63 64 61; Bryan Shelton d Thomas Hogstedt 76 57 76 64; Sergi Bruguera d Andrew Castle 67 64 63 61; David Pate d Claudio Pistolesi 63 64 64; Guillaume Raoux d James Turner 63 64 75; Alex Antonitsch d Michael Robertson 76 64 36 46 64; Henri Leconte d Simon Youl 64 63 63; Jim Courier d Mark Kaplan 61 64 64; Jason Stoltenberg d Todd Woodbridge 63 75 76; Udo Riglewski d Veli Paloheimo 64 75 75; Mark Woodforde d John Fitzgerald 75 62 64; Jens Wohrmann d Brian Garrow 64 64 64; Milan Srejber d Richey Reneberg 67 36 76 63 62; Brad Pearce d Ronnie Bathman 63 36 62 63; Shuzo Matsuoka d Luiz Mattar 76 63 64; Stefan Edberg d Broderick Dyke 46 61 63 61; Miloslav Mecir d Tomas Carbonell 64 64 61; Richard Fromberg d Jean Fleurian 76 57 46 61 64; Amos Mansdorf d Henrik Holm 61 16 57 63 62; Mark Kratzmann d Cassio Motta 62 61 63; Anders Jarryd d Rick Leach 63 36 75 75; Jim Pugh d Jan Gunnarsson 63 16 57 63 64; Michael Chang d Jose F Altur 57 64 63 75; Guy Forget d Lars Wahlgren 62 61 64; Eric Jelen d Patrick Kuhnen 63 63 61; Aki Rahunen d Kelly Evernden 36 46 61 76 63; Michael Stich d Dirk Dier 62 63 62; Neil Broad d Lawson Duncan 64 62 76 86; Christian Bergstrom d Tim Wilkison 64 63 64; Paul Chamberlin d Mark Petchey 36 60 76 63; Jim Grabb d Andres Gomez 64 62 62; Gary Muller d Tim Mayotte 46 76 75 63; Kevin Curren d Jeff Tarango 61 64 61; Karel Novacek d Glenn Layendecker 64 67 06 64 60; Joey Rive d Vijay Amritraj 57 64 64 57 64; Kelly Jones d Danny Sapsford 63 36 64 64; Marc Rosset d Scott Davis 76 75 63; Alexander Volkov d Slobodan Zivojinovic 67 76 76 61; Christo van Rensburg d Pete Sampras 76 75 76; Gilad Bloom d Petr Korda 60 64 46 62; Mark Koevermans d Chris Bailey 64 64 62; Niclas Kroon d Tarik Benhabiles 63 62 57 36 63; Ramesh Krishnan d Diego Perez 64 62 64; Olivier Delaitre d Markus Zoecke 75 64 36 62; Goran Ivanisevic d Andreas Lesch 64 60 64; Jeremy Bates d Peter Lundgren 67 67 64 64 60; Derrick Rostagno d John McEnroe 75 64 64; Brad Gilbert d Bruno Oresar 61 36 46 61 62; Danie Visser d Grant Connell 64 64 64; Darren Cahill d Martin Wostenholme 62 62 60; Paul Haarhuis d Tom Nijssen 76 63 63; David Wheaton d Magnus Larsson 76 64 62; Paul Annacone d Leif Shiras 26 36 63 63 86; Malivai Washington d Lars Jonsson 62 63 61; Jonas Svensson d Fabrice Santoro 64 63 62; Wayne Ferreira d Yannick Noah 64 63 62; Juan Aguilera d Martin Strelba 63 75 63; Pat Cash d Dimitri Poliakov 46 76 57 64 61; Johan Anderson d Nick Brown 64 62 76; Dan Goldie d Ralph Kok 75 61 75; Ken Flach d Michiel Schapers 64 76 63; Wally Masur d Andrei Cherkasov 63 64 62; Boris Becker d Luis Herrera 76 76 75. **Rd 64:** Lendl d Hlasek 61 63 60; Shelton d Bruguera 57 26 64 64 64; Pate d Raoux 36 62 64 63; Antonitsch d Leconte 26 64 76 26 63; Courier d Stoltenberg 62 76 64; Woodforde d Riglewski 67 64 64 75; Srejber d Wohrmann 62 67 63 62; Pearce d Matsuoka 76 75 63; Edberg d Mecir 62 63 62; Mansdorf d Fromberg 64 76 61; Kratzmann d Jarryd W/O; Chang d Pugh 63 62 62; Forget d Jelen 76 67 61 62; Stich d Rahunen 62 75 63; Bergstrom d Broad 46 76 62 62; Grabb d Chamberlin 62 67 76 36 63; Curren d Muller 67 64 76 67 64; Novacek d Rive 61 64 76; Rosset d Jones 36 67 63 75 63; Volkov d van Rensburg 75 64 76; Koevermans d Bloom 75 64 63; Kroon d Krishnan 63 26 63 63; Ivanisevic d Delaitre 62 60 46 67 63; Rostagno d Bates 61 36 64 61; Gilbert d Visser 57 63 62 62; Haarhuis d Cahill 75 57 76 46 63; Wheaton d Annacone 64 16 64 67 64; Svensson d Washington 63 63 64; Aguilera d Ferreira 63 76 75; Cash d Anderson 62 63 76; Goldie d Flach 63 64 64; Becker d Masur 67 62 63 62. **Rd 32:** Lendl d Shelton 76 67 64 64; Antonitsch d Pate 64 64 76(75); Woodforde d Courier 75 57 75 64; Pearce d Srejber 63 63 61; Edberg d Mansdorf 64 57 36 62 97; Chang d Kratzmann 36 46 64 62 62; Forget d Stich 36 75 62 46 63; Bergstrom d Grabb 76 64 62; Curren d Novacek 62 46 16 75 63; Volkov d Rosset 63 64 75; Koevermans d Kroon 67 64 67 64 63; Ivanisevic d Rostagno 62 62 64; Gilbert d Haarhuis 61 36 61 62; Wheaton d Svensson 26 67 61 60 64; Cash d Aguilera 61 61 64; Becker d Goldie 63 64 46 75. **Rd 16:** Lendl d Antonitsch 36 64 63 64; Pearce d Woodforde 64 64 64; Edberg d Chang 63 62 61; Bergstrom d Forget 64 36 63 75; Curren d Volkov 64 76 76; Ivanisevic d Koevermans 46 63 64 76; Gilbert d Wheaton 67 36 61 64 1311; Becker d Cash 76 61 64. **QF:** Lendl d Pearce 64 64 57 64; Edberg d Bergstrom 63 62 64; Ivanisevic d Curren 46 64 64 67 63; Becker d Gilbert 64 64 61. **SF:** Edberg d Lendl 61 76 63; Becker d Ivanisevic 46 76 60 76. **F:** Edberg d Becker 62 62 36 36 64.
DOUBLES: Rick Leach/Jim Pugh d Danie Aldrich/Pieter Visser 76 76 76

JULY 7-15: RADO SWISS OPEN, GSTAAD $275,000 Winner: MARTIN JAITE
Rd 32: Andres Gomez d StefanoPescosolido 16 61 63; Ronald Agenor d Martin Wostenholme 64 67 63; Milan Srejber d Omar Camporese 62 63; Carl-Uwe Steeb d Javier Sanchez 62 64; Martin Jaite d Markus Zoecke 75 64; Cassio Motta d Marko Ostoja 26 64 75; Horst Skoff d Christian Bergstrom 64 63; Jim Courier d Tarik Benhabiles 75 Ret.; Juan Aguilera d Cyril Suk 76 26 75; Sergi Bruguera d Alberto Mancini 63 64; Tomas Carbonell d David Wheaton 62 64; Andrew Chesnokov d Andrei Cherkasov 63 76; Marc Rosset d Karel Novacek 76 57 62; Wally Masur d Horacio de la Pena 76 64; Jordi Arrese d Luiz Mattar 75 64; Emilio Sanchez d Jimmy Arias 63 64. **Rd 16:** Agenor d Gomez 16 75 63; Steeb d Srejber 36 63 64; Jaite d Motta 76 61; Courier d Skoff 63 63; Bruguera d Aguilera 63 64; Chesnokov d Carbonell 75 63; Rosset d Masur 64 57 76; E Sanchez d Arrese 63 72. **QF:** Agenor d Steeb 36 62 62; Jaite d Courier 36 76 64; Bruguera d Chesnokov 62 63; Rosset d E Sanchez 64 36 63. **SF:** Jaite d Agenor 75 61; Bruguera d Rosset 63 75. **F:** Jaite d Bruguera 63 67 62 62.
DOUBLES: Sergio Casal/Emilio Sanchez d Omar Camporese/Javier Sanchez 63 36 75.

JULY 9-15: SWEDISH OPEN, BASTAD $225,000 Winner: RICHARD FROMBERG
Rd 32: Guillermo Perez-Roldan d Thomas Enqvist 64 62; Lars Jonsson d Niclas Kroon 75 36 63; Veli Paloheimo d Jan Apell 61 61; David Engel d Jan Gunnarsson 62 60; Richard Fromberg d Marian Vajda 76 75; Nicklas Utgren d Ronnie Bathman 16 63 64; Magnus Nilsson d Jose F Altur 76 57 76; Diego Perez d Paul Haarhuis 76 16 63; Johan Carlsson d Udo Riglewski 06 63 64; Magnus Larsson d Fabrice Santoro 63 61; Per Henricsson d Thierry Tulasne 64 64; Goran Prpic d Martin Strelba 16 75 76; Aki Rahunen d Lars Wahlgren 61 62; Nicklas Kulti d Ola Kristiansson 61 62; Marcelo Filippini d Bruno Oresar 63 62; Mats Wilander d Johan Anderson 60 63. **Rd 16:** Jonsson d Perez-Roldan 64 57 63; Paloheimo d Engel 62 75; Fromberg d Utgren 67 63 76; Perez d Nilsson 62 63;Larsson d Carlsson 64 64; Prpic d Henricsson 63 46 63; Rahunen d Kulti 64 60; Filippini d Wilander 62 36 76. **QF:** Jonsson d Paloheimo 61 62; Fromberg d Perez 75 63; Larsson d Prpic 63 46 63; Filippini d Rahunen 61 63. **SF:** Fromberg d Jonsson 64 62; Larsson d Filippini 64 61. **F:** Fromberg d Larsson 62 76.
DOUBLES: Rikard Bergh/Ronnie Bathman d Jan Gunnarsson/Udo Riglewski 61 64.

JULY 9-15: VOLVO TENNIS/HALL OF FAME CHAMPIONSHIPS, NEWPORT $150,000 Winner: PIETER ALDRICH
Rd 32: Tim Mayotte d Miguel Nido 62 64; Robbie Weiss d Brad Pearce 72 62; Joey Rive d Alexander Mronz 64 62; Pieter Aldrich d Leif Shiras 63 64; Gary Muller d Jimmy Brown 63 36 76; Patrick Baur d John Fitzgerald 76 36 76; Bryan Shelton d Danie Visser 62 67 62; Jim Pugh d Simon Youl 67 63 64; Darren Cahill d Broderick Dyke 63 63; Todd Martin d Jeff Tarango 16 63 62; Bruce Derlin d Brian Garrow 62 61; Mark Kratzmann d Nuno Marques 64 63; Eric Jelen d Mark Kaplan 61 63; Rick Leach d Gianluca Pozzi 64 64; Richard Matuszewski d Alexis Hombrecher 16 76 60; Peter Lundgren d Christo van Rensburg 61 64. **Rd 16:** Weiss d Mayotte 36 63 76; Aldrich d Rive 26 61 64; Muller d Baur 63 63; Pugh d Shelton 62 46 62; Cahill d Martin W/O;Kratzmann d Derlin 46 63 64; Jelen d Leach 60 62; Lundgren d Matuszewski 67 62 63. **QF:** Aldrich d Weiss 64 61; Muller d Pugh 63 67 63; Cahill d Kratzmann 62 64; Jelen d Lundgren 62 62. **SF:** Aldrich d Muller 64 76; Cahill d Jelen 76 63. **F:** Aldrich d Cahill 76 16 61.
DOUBLES: Darren Cahill/Mark Kratzmann d Todd Nelson/Bryan Shelton 76 62.

JULY 16-22: MERCEDES CUP, STUTTGART $825,000 Winner: GORAN IVANISEVIC
Rd 48: Andres Gomez bye; Luiz Mattar d Martin Sinner 63 67 75; Jimmy Arias d Alberto Mancini 64 63; Horst Skoff bye; Guillermo Perez-Roldan bye; Sergi Bruguera d Udo Riglewski 75 64; Goran Prpic d Francisco Clavet 76 75; Guy Forget bye; Martin Jaite bye; Karel Novacek d Jeremy Bates 61 62; Andrei Cherkasov d Jan Gunnarsson 62 57 64; Petr Korda bye; Henri Leconte bye; Jorgen Windahl d Alex Antonitsch 40 Ret.; Jaime Yzaga d Jean Fleurian 57 64 76; Andrei Chesnokov bye; Jim Courier bye; Marcelo Filippini d Ronald Agenor 64 76; Tomas Carbonell d Hans Schwaier 26 76 63; Carl-Uwe Steeb bye; Marc Rosset bye; Richard Fromberg d Thierry Tulasne 46 62 75; Jens Woehrmann d Paul Haarhuis 64 64; Emilio Sanchez bye; Juan Aguilera bye; Wally Masur d Jordi Arrese 67 64 63; Javier Sanchez d Richard Vogel 76 62; Goran Ivanisevic bye; Mats Wilander bye; Franco Davin d Christian Bergstrom 57 62 64; Eric Jelen d Olivier Delaitre 67 61 75; Thomas Muster bye. **Rd 32:** Gomez d Mattar 75 64; Skoff d Arias 62 64; Perez-Roldan d Bruguera 62 64; Prpic d Forget 62 76; Novacek d Jaite 75 67 61; Cherkasov d Korda 76 61; Leconte d Windahl 64 62; Chesnokov d Yzaga 63 63; Filippini d Courier 62 64; Carbonell d Steeb 63 75; Fromberg d Rosset 61 63; E Sanchez d Woehrmann 46 63 63; Masur d Aguilera 76 75; Ivanisevic d J Sanchez 62 63; Davin d Wilander 61 46 62; Jelen d Muster 46 62 20. **Rd 16:** Skoff d Gomez 75 06 64; Perez-Roldan d Prpic 64 63; Cherkasov d Novacek 75 36 64; Leconte d Chesnokov 75 63; Filippini d Carbonell 62 64; E Sanchez d Fromberg 63 26 62; Ivanisevic d Masur 62 67 64; Jelen d Davin 46 76 63. **QF:** Perez-Roldan d Skoff 26 63 76; Leconte d Cherkasov 46 64 64; E Sanchez d

Filippini 76 62; Ivanisevic d Jelen 62 63. **SF:** Perez-Roldan d Leconte 67 63 76; Ivanisevic d Emilio Sanchez 64 64. **F:** Ivanisevic d Perez-Roldan 67 61 64 76. **DOUBLES:** Pieter Aldrich/Danie Visser d Per Henricsson/Niklas Utgren 63 64

JULY 16-22: SOVRAN BANK CLASSIC, WASHINGTON $420,000
Winner: ANDRE AGASSI
Rd 64: Andre Agassi bye; Brad Pearce d Bryan Shelton 64 36 62; Jared Palmer d Thomas Hogstedt 67 64 64; Gilad Bloom d Luis Herrera 64 63; Darren Cahill d Christo van Rensburg 64 60; Miguel Nido d Martin Laurendeau 64 63; Jason Stoltenburg d Mark Kaplan 57 63 60; Richey Reneberg bye; Tim Mayotte bye; Ramesh Krishnan d Kelly Evernden 63 61; Dan Goldie d Kuhnen 62 62; Todd Witsken d Malivai Washington 75 62; Simon Youl d Mark Kratzmann 63 64; Robbie Weiss d Peter Lundgren 60 62; Steve Bryan d Kelly Jones 63 63; Michael Chang bye; Jim Grabb bye; Mark Woodforde d Paul Annacone 67 63 62; Jimmy Brown d Joey Rive 76 64; Grant Connell d Milan Srejber 63 76; Gary Muller d Sandon Stolle 63 63; Derrick Rostagno d Martin Wostenholme 63 67 61; Paul Chamberlin d David Pate 64 64; John McEnroe bye; Alexander Volkov bye; Michael Stich d Grant Stafford 76 60; Nicolas Pereira d John Ross 76 62; Jakob Hlasek d Alexander Mronz 64 75; Andrew Sznajder d Ken Flach 64 57 64; Marcos Ondruska d Patrick Baur 46 61 60; Eliot Teltscher d Jeff Tarango 64 46 63; Brad Gilbert bye. **Rd 32:** Agassi d Pearce 76 63; Bloom d Palmer 62 64; Cahill d Nido 46 60 62; Reneberg d Stoltenberg 36 62 63; Mayotte d Krishnan 62 61; Witsken d Goldie 63 64; Youl d Weiss 63 36 76; Chang d Bryan 62 76; Grabb d Woodforde 62 62; Connell d Brown 63 76; Rostagno d Muller 46 63 62; McEnroe d Chamberlin 62 63; Stich d Volkov 64 75; Hlasek d Pereira 76 63; Sznajder d Ondruska 63 60; Gilbert d Teltscher 61 75. **Rd 16:** Agassi d Bloom 61 75; Reneberg d Cahill 64 26 75; Witsken d Mayotte 26 64 75; Chang d Youl 61 61; Grabb d Connell 64 64; Rostagno d McEnroe 63 16 61; Stich d Hlasek 76 76; Gilbert d Sznajder 62 63. **QF:** Agassi d Reneberg 76 60; Chang d Witsken 63 64; Grabb d Rostagno 64 63; Gilbert d Stich 63 64. **SF:** Agassi d Chang 63 61; Grabb d Gilbert 75 06 61. **F:** Agassi d Grabb 61 64. **DOUBLES:** Grant Connell/Glenn Michibata d Jorge Lozano/Todd Witsken 63 67 62

JULY 23-29: PLAYER'S LTD INTERNATIONAL CANADIAN OPEN TENNIS CHAMPIONSHIPS, TORONTO $930,000 Winner: MICHAEL CHANG
Rd 64: Andre Agassi bye; Michael Stich d Thomas Hogstedt 64 62; Brad Pearce d Peter Lundgren 76 62; Darren Cahill d Alexander Volkov 57 75 63; David Wheaton d Malivai Washington 64 64; Eduardo Velez d Dan Goldie 64 64; Broderick Dyke d Jeff Tarango 62 62; Michael Chang bye; John McEnroe bye; Grant Connell d Kelly Evernden 61 46 76; Jason Stoltenberg d Mark Woodfordea 46 63 60; Amos Mansdorf d Bryan Shelton 76 46 61; Andrew Sznajder d Kevin Curren 75 67 62; Paul Wekesa d Gianluca Pozzi 62 67 62; Martin Wostenholme d Kelly Jones 46 62 64; Pete Sampras bye; Tim Mayotte bye; Chris Garner d Brian Gyetko 64 64; Paul Chamberlin d Joey Rive 63 76; Richey Reneberg d Gilad Bloom 26 62 61; Jean Fleurian d Glenn Michibata 76 62; Derrick Rostagno d Bruce Derlin 26 60 61; Leif Shiras d Paul Annacone 61 64; Jay Berger bye; Petr Korda bye; Jakob Hlasek d Scott Davis 63 62; Jimmy Arias d Libor Nemecek 61 75; Jim Grabb d Udo Riglewski 64 76; Mark Kratzmann d Simon Youl 36 64 63; Ramesh Krishnan d Chris Pridham 76 64; Todd Witsken d Milan Srejber 36 76 64; Brad Gilbert bye. **Rd 32:** Agassi d Stich 63 67 73; Cahill d Pearce 64 64; Wheaton d Velez 62 64; Chang d Dyke 62 63; McEnroe d Connell 76 61; Mansdorf d Stoltenberg 62 62; Sznajder d Wekesa 76 63; Sampras d Wostenholme 63 62; Mayotte d Garner 63 62; Reneberg d Chamberlin 63 26 62; Rostagno d Fleurian 62 62; Berger d Shiras 62 64; Hlasek d Korda 57 64 64; Arias d Grabb 41 Ret.; Krishnan d Kratzmann 26 75 62; Witsken d Gilbert 75 46 62. **Rd 16:** Agassi d Cahill 62 64; Chang d Wheaton 60 63; McEnroe d Mansdorf 62 64; Sampras d Sznajder 46 63 62; Mayotte d Reneberg 63 46 63; Berger d Rostagno 46 64 61; Hlasek d Arias 75 61; Witsken d Krishnan 64 64. **QF:** Chang d Agassi 46 75 75; Sampras d McEnroe 76 46 63; Berger d Mayotte 76 64; Hlasek d Witsken 64 62. **SF:** Chang d Sampras 36 76 75; Berger d Hlasek 36 62 62. **F:** Chang d Berger 46 63 76. **DOUBLES:** Paul Annacone/David Wheaton d Broderick Dyke/Peter Lundgren 61 76

JULY 23-29: THE INTERNATIONAL TENNIS CHAMPIONSHIPS OF THE NETHERLANDS, HILVERSUM $215,000 Winner: FRANCISCO CLAVET
Rd 32: Emilio Sanchez d Tom Nijssen 63 57 64; Wally Masur d Jaime Yzaga 76 46 62; Olivier Delaitre d Jordi Arrese 61 60; Javier Sanchez d Horst Skoff 76 46 76; Juan Aguilera d Marian Vajda 64 75; Eduardo Masso d Goran Prpic 75 63; Sergio Casal d Diego Perez 61 57 62; Sergi Bruguera d Carl-Uwe Steeb 63 61; Carlos Costa d Marc Rosset 62 31 Ret.; Ronald Agenor d Franco Davin 63 61; Omar Camporese d Fabrice Santoro 63 75; Marcelo Filippini d Guillermo Perez-Roldan 63 64; Francisco Clavet d Karel Novacek 76 76; Paul Haarhuis d Alberto Mancini 62 62; Tomas Carbonell d Roberto Azar 76 36 63; Martin Jaite d Mark Koevermans 16 61 63. **Rd 16:** E Sanchez d Masur 46 76 64; Delaitre d J Sanchez 36 64 64; Masso d Aguilera 63 36 62; Bruguera d Casal 61 63; Agenor d Costa 76 36 61; Camporese d Filippini 67 61 76; Clavet d Haarhuis 75 62; Jaite d Carbonell 46 75 64. **QF:**E Sanchez d Delaitre 62 76; Masso d Bruguera 46 75 70; Camporese d Agenor 75 76; Clavet d Jaite 57 61 62. **SF:** Masso d E Sanchez 64 75; Clavet d Camporese 46 76 76. **F:** Clavet d Masso 36 64 62 60. **DOUBLES:** Sergio Casal/Emilio Sanchez d Paul Haarhuis/Mark Koevermans 75 75

JULY 30-AUGUST 5: SAN REMO OPEN $225,000 Winner: JORDI ARRESE
Rd 32: Guillermo Perez-Roldan d Fabrice Santoro 57 76 62; Aki Rahunen d Olivier Delaitre 64 63; Stefano Pescosolido d Daniele Balducci 76 64; Jordi Arrese d Cedric Pioline 64 62; Marcelo Filippini d Thierry Champion 62 26 76; Thierry Tulasne d Tarik Benhabiles 16 76 75; Nicklas Utgren d Christian Geyer 75 61; Renzo Furlan d Ronald Agenor 46 62 76; Claudio Mezzadri d Franco Davin 16 75 63; Jose F Altur d Stephane Sansoni 62 60; Roberto Azar d Christian Bergstrom 62 62; Goran Prpic dFederico Mordegan 75 62; Omar Camporese d Jerome Potier 63 60; Ctislav Dosedel d Karsten Braasch 60 61; Francisco Yunis d Ola Jonsson 61 62; Juan Aguilera d M Nastase 60 63. **Rd 16:** Perez-Roldan d Rahunen 06 75 61; Arrese d Pescosolido 57 62 62; Filippini d Tulasne 26 64 75; Furlan d Utgren 61 63; Mezzandri d Altur 26 61 62; Azar d Prpic 75 62; Camporese d Dosedel 60 63; Aguilera d Yunis 36 64 60. **QF:** Arrese d Perez-Roldan 64 62; Filippini d Furlan 61 63; Azar d Mezzandri 76 76; Aguilera d Camporese 63 62. **SF:** Arrese d Filippini 62 63; Aguilera d Azar 76 62. **F:** Arrese d Aguilera 62 62. **DOUBLES:** Minhea-Ion Nastase/Goran Prpic d Lars Jonsson /Magnus Nilsson 36 75 63

JULY 30-AUGUST 5: PHILIPS AUSTRIAN OPEN/HEAD CUP, KITZBUHEL $337,500 Winner: HORACIO DE LA PENA
Rd 48: Boris Becker bye; Claudio Pistolesi d Branislav Stankovic 76 36 76; Patrick Baur d Gerald Mandl 64 75; David Engel bye; Alex Antonitsch bye; Simone Colombo d Guillaume Raoux 67 76 76; Massimo Cierro d Christian Miniussi 61 46 63; Karel Novacek bye; Thomas Muster bye; Fernando Luna d Thomas Buchmayer 64 60; Dinu Pescariu d Steve Guy 36 64 61; Marian Vajda bye; Tomas Carbonell bye; Cassio Motta d Francisco Clavet 63 64; Christian Saceanu d Paul Vojtisek 62 57 64; Horst Skoff bye; Marc Rosset bye; Martin Sinner d Marco Gorriz 63 26 61; Alexander Mronz d Marcelo Ingaramo 76 64; Andrei Cherkasov bye; Udo Riglewski bye; Ricki Osterthun d Oliver Fuchs 36 63 64; Francisco Roig d Peter Ballauff 63 62; Emilio Sanchez bye; Sergi Bruguera bye; Michael Tauson d Roberto Arguello 67 64 76; Carlos Costa d Neil Borwick 63 61; Javier Sanchez bye; Martin Strelba bye; German Lopez d Bruno Oresar 76 63; Horacio de la Pena d Francisco Maciel 62 26 61; Brad Gilbert bye. **Rd 32:** Becker d Pistolesi 62 61; Engel d Baur 62 62; Antonitsch d Colombo 46 63 76; Novacek d Cierro 64 64; Muster d Luna 62 64; Vajda d Pescariu 76 63; Carbonell d Motta 62 63; Skoff d Saceanu 46 75 76; Rosset d Sinner 62 61; Cherkasov d Mronz 62 64; Riglewski d Osterthun 63 64; E Sanchez d Roig 62 06 75; Bruguera d Tauson 63 63; J Sanchez d Costa 64 36 60; Strelba d Lopez 76 62; de la Pena d Gilbert 62 64. **Rd 16:** Becker d Engel 64 46 60; Novacek d Antonitsch 63 67 64; Muster d Vajda 63 60; Skoff d Carbonell 62 60; Cherkasov d Rosset 63 63; E Sanchez d Riglewski 63 76; Bruguera d J Sanchez 63 62; de la Pena d Strelba 62 61. **QF:** Novacek d Becker 63 63; Skoff d Muster 64 62; E Sanchez d Cherkasov 61 64; de la Pena d Bruguera 64 61. **SF:** Novacek d Skoff 64 46 64; de la Pena d Emilio Sanchez 75 76. **F:** de la Pena d Novacek 64 76 26 62. **DOUBLES:** Javier Sanchez/Eric Winogradsky d Francisco Clavet/Horst Skoff 76 62

JULY 30-AUGUST 5: VOLVO TENNIS, LOS ANGELES $225,000
Winner: STEFAN EDBERG
Rd 32: Stefan Edberg d Malivai Washington 62 64; Shuzo Matsuoka d Kelly Jones 75 64; David Pate d David Macpherson 63 46 61; Jeff Tarango d Milan Srejber 76 26 62; Pete Sampras d Rick Leach 75 63; Brad Pearce d Jorge Lozano 63 76; Jason Stoltenberg d Nicolas Pereira 64 76; Derrick Rostagno d Richey Reneberg 61 63; Jean Fleurian d Robbie Weiss 61 64; Dan Goldie d Jim Pugh 75 61; Andrew Sznajder d Thomas Hogstedt 63 64; Michael Chang d Scott Davis 75 46 64; Gary Muller d Chuck Adams 64 36 66; Joey Rive d Lundgren 62 64; Brian Garrow d Mark Kaplan 62 64; Todd Witsken d Aaron Krickstein 57 76 64. **Rd 16:** Edberg d Matsuoka 75 64; Tarango d Pate 64 67 64; Sampras d Pearce 62 26 64; Stoltenberg d Rostagno 62 63; Goldie d Fleurian 67 76 62; Chang d Sznajder 62 63; Muller d Rive 26 63 61; Garrow d Witsken 46 60 63. **QF:** Edberg d Tarango 64 64; Sampras d Stoltenberg 63 64; Chang d Goldie 61 75; Muller d Garrow 63 64. **SF:** Edberg d Sampras 62 67 61; Chang d Muller 76 62. **F:** Edberg d Chang 76 26 74. **DOUBLES:** Scott Davis/David Pate d Peter Lundgren/Paul Wekesa 36 61 63

AUGUST 6-12: THRIFTWAY ATP CHAMPIONSHIP, CINCINNATI $1,020,000
Winner: STEFAN EDBERG
Rd 64: Stefan Edberg bye; Milan Srejber d John Ross 64 76; Andrew Sznajder d Robert Seguso 46 64 64; Marcos Ondruska d Petr Korda 63 46 75; Pete Sampras d David Pate 76 64; Jim Pugh d Mark Kratzmanna 36 75 60; Amos Mansdorf d Alex Antonitsch 64 61; Michael Chang bye; Andres Gomez bye; Dan Goldie d Paul Chamberlin 64 64; Mats Wilander d Grant Connell 64 36 63; Darren Cahill d Tim Mayotte 16 64 75; Jim Courier d Kelly Jones 63 67 63; Jason Stoltenberg d Thomas Hogstedt 62 36 64; Nicolas Pereira d Gianluca Pozzi 61 63; Jay Berger bye; Aaron Krickstein bye; Johan Carlsson d Thierry Champion 76 75; Jimmy Arias d Aki Rahunen 76 67 61; Jakob Hlasek d Jonas Svensson 64 46 75; Guy Forget d Kevin Curren 63 64; Todd Witsken d Todd Woodbridge 62 64; David Wheaton d Leif Shiras 64 76; Brad Gilbert bye; John McEnroe bye; Jean Fleurian d Christo van Rensburg 63 36 63; Scott Davis d Gary Muller 26 61 61; Andrei Chesnokov d Ramesh Krishnan 64 67 62; Richard Fromberg d Karel Novacek 36 64 64; Joey Rive d Jeremy Bates 75 36 64; Richey Reneberg d Glenn Layendecker 63 62; Andre Agassi bye. **Rd 32:** Edberg d Srejber 64 67 64; Sznajder d Ondruska 63 46 64; Sampras d Pugh 61 16 76; Chang d Mansdorf 60 64; Gomez d Goldie 63 76; Cahill d Wilander 63 62; Courier d Stoltenberg 62 26 76; Berger d Pereira 62 67 64; Krickstein d Carlsson 62 76; Hlasek d Arias 36 62 63; Forget d Witsken 46 63 63; Gilbert d Wheaton 63 62; McEnroe d Fleurian 76 62; Davis d Chesnokov 63 62; Fromberg d Rive 63 62; Agassi d Reneberg 64 63. **Rd 16:** Edberg d Sznajder 61 60; Chang d Sampras 75 64; Gomez d Cahill 76 63; Courier d Berger 62 62; Hlasek d Krickstein 64 62; Gilbert d Forget 62 61; Davis d McEnroe 63 57 64; Fromberg d Agassi 64 36 63. **QF:** Edberg d Chang 36 63 64; Gomez d Courier 61 64; Gilbert d Hlasek 26 61 75; Davis d Fromberg 46 64 76. **SF:** Edberg d Gomez 75 63; Gilbert d Davis 63 64. **F:** Edberg d Gilbert 61 61. **DOUBLES:** Darren Cahill/Mark Kratzmann d Neil Broad/Gary Muller 76 62

AUGUST 6-12: CZECHOSLOVAK OPEN TENNIS CHAMPIONSHIPS, PRAGUE $176,000 Winner: JORDI ARRESE
Rd 32: Claudio Pistolesi d Thomas Muster 10 Ret.; Tarik Benhabiles d Fernando Luna 64 36 64; Stefano Pescosolido d Rene Hanak 63 61; Horacio de la Pena 60 62; Marcelo Filippini d Cyril Suk 76 61; Nicklas Kulti d Alexander Mronz 63 62; Bart Wuyts d Roberto Azar 26 63 63; Franco Davin d Jimmy Brown 63 26 63; Goran Prpic d Paul Vojtisek 46 63 61; Veli Paloheimo d Martin Strelba 60 62; Marian Vajda d Francisco Clavet 36 64 62; Horst Skoff d Lawson Duncan 62 61; Jordi Arrese d Ctislav Dosedel 64 64; J Kodes d C Picoline 76 62; Christian Saceanu d M Damm 64 63; S Hirszon d Guillermo Perez-Roldan 61 Ret. **Rd 16:** Benhabiles d Pistolesi 63 63; de la Pena d Pescosolido 63 61; Kulti d Filippini 61 63; Davin d Wuyts 63 62; Prpic d Paloheimo 75 60; Skoff d Vajda 64 61; Arrese d Kodes 26 60 62; Saceanu d Hirszon 62 26 76. **QF:** de la Pena d Benhabiles 62 76; Kulti d Davin 63 16 62; Prpic d Skoff 26 63 76; Arrese d Arrese W/O. **SF:** Kulti d de la Pena 61 10 Ret.; Arrese d Prpic 75 64. **F:** Arrese d Kulti 75 76. **DOUBLES:** Vojtech Flegl/Daniel Vacek d George Cosac/Florin Segarceanu 57 64 63.

AUGUST 13-19: GTE CHAMPIONSHIPS, INDIANAPOLIS $825,000
Winner: BORIS BECKER
Rd 64: Boris Becker bye; Brian Garrow d David Pate 57 62 63; Kent Kinnear d Alex Antonitsch 60 75; Kevin Curren d Jeff Tarango 46 64 76; Jason Stoltenberg d Guy Forget 46 63 62; Kelly Jones d Aki Rahunen 75 67 75; Ramesh Krishnan d Wayne Ferreira 76 67 64; Jim Courier bye; Jay Berger bye; Darren Cahill d Scott Davis 36 64 62; Paul Wekesa d Slobodan Zivojinovic 64 64; Jakob Hlasek d Joey Rive 63 64; Kelly Evernden d Yannick Noah 75 62; Martin Laurendeau d Mark Kaplana 64 76; Grant Connell d Ken Flach 75 16 61; John McEnroe bye; Pete Sampras bye; Alexander Volkov d Olivier Delaitre 46 64 60; Todd Witsken d Patrick Kuhnen 64 61; Broderick Dyke d Carl-Uwe Steeb 67 64 60; Richey Reneberg d Mark Kratzmann 60 63; Leif Shiras d Robbie Weiss 62 64; Marcos Ondruska d Simon Youl 76 63; Aaron Krickstein bye; Martin Jaite bye; Peter Lundgren d Greg Failla 63 61; Shuzo Matsuoka d Jean Fleurian 26 62 64; Thierry Champion d Karel Novacek 62 31 Ret.; Leonardo Lavalle d Gary Muller 64 64; Todd Martin d Steve Bryan 46 64 75; Robert Seguso d Jeremy Bates 64 76; Andre Agassi bye. **Rd 32:** Becker d Garrow 62 64; Curren d Kinnear 64 26 75; Stoltenberg d Jones 75 75; Courier d Krishnan 63 63; Berger d Cahill 61 06 75; Hlasek d Wekesa 64 62; Kelly Evernden d Martin Laurendeau 46 61 75; John McEnroe d Grant Connell 64 64; Sampras d Volkov 62 76; Witsken d Dyke 75 63; Reneberg d Shiras 60 61; Krickstein d Ondruska 61 61; Lundgren d Jaite 46 63 63; Matsuoka d Champion 26 62 61; Martin d Lavalle 61 64; Agassi d Seguso 62 63. **Rd 16:** Becker d Curren 76 64; Courier d Stoltenberg 46 63 62; Berger d Hlasek 64 62; Evernden d McEnroe 62 64; Sampras d Witsken 67 63 64; Reneberg d Krickstein 64 62; Lundgren d Matsuoka 64 16 75; Agassi d Martin 76 64. **QF:** Becker d Courier 46 75 31; Berger d Evernden 57 61 63; Reneberg d Sampras 36 61 76; Lundgren d Agassi 64 60. **SF:** Becker d Berger 64 63; Lundgren d Reneberg 64 64. **F:** Becker d Lundgren 63 64. **DOUBLES:** Scott Davis/David Pate d Grant Connell/Glenn Michibata 76 76.

AUGUST 13-19: VOLVO INTERNATIONAL TENNIS TOURNAMENT, NEW HAVEN $825,000 Winner: DERRICK ROSTAGNO
Rd 64: Ivan Lendl bye; Malivai Washington d Danilo Marcelino 63 75; Bryan Shelton d Claudio Pistolesi 63 76; David Wheaton d Milan Srejber 61 62; Richard Fromberg d Neil Borwick 63 60; Mark Woodforde d John Fitzgerald 64 62; Tommy Ho d Eliot Teltscher 64 46 76; Jonas Svensson bye; Michael Chang bye; Todd Woodbridge d Thomas Hogstedt 61 60; Brad Pearce d Philip Johnson 75 60; Pat Cash d Mats Wilander 16 75 63; Wally Masur d Michiel Schapers 16 63 64; Dan Goldie d Glenn Layendecker 76 64 63; Paul Chamberlin d Tarik Benhabiles 63 36 62; Goran Ivanisevic bye; Andrei Chesnokov bye; Johan Anderson d Shane Barr 75 63; Anders Jarryd d Dan Cassidy 76

57 61; Jim Grabb d Gilad Bloom 63 75; Amos Mansdorf d Miguel Nido 61 61; Carlos Claverie d Chuck Adams 63 76; Christiano Caratti d Tim Wilkison 64 62; Brad Gilbert bye; Tim Mayotte bye; Derrick Rostagno d Paul Annacone 46 76 62; Jimmy Arias d Jaime Yzaga 61 63; Jim Pugh d Petr Korda 36 64 61; Christo van Rensburg d Magnus Zeile 64 61; Martin Wostenholme d Chris Pridham 62 36 61; Luis Herrera d Martin Strelba 63 63; Andres Gomez bye. **Rd 32:** Washington d Lendl 62 63; Shelton d Wheaton 62 64; Woodforde d Fromberg 61 26 64; Svensson d Ho 46 64 76; Woodbridge d Chang 63 16 63; Pearce d Cash 36 76 63; Masur d Goldie 46 76 75; Chamberlin d Ivanisevic 61 76; Chesnokov d Anderson 62 62; Grabb d Jarryd 63 62; Mansdorf d Claverie 63 62; Caratti d Gilbert 64 64; Rostagno d Mayotte 46 64 63; Pugh d Arias 64 62; van Rensburg d Wostenholme 61 64; Gomez d Herrera 75 57 61. **Rd 16:** Shelton d Washington 64 36 76; Woodforde d Svensson 63 36 64; Woodbridge d Pearce 64 64; Masur d Chamberlin 67 63 63; Chesnokov d Grabb 76 63; Caratti d Mansdorf 57 76 63; Rostagno d Pugh 62 62; van Rensburg d Gomez 75 67 76. **QF:** Woodforde d Shelton 75 62; Woodbridge d Masur 76 36 75; Chesnokov d Caratti 62 61; Rostagno d van Rensburg 75 60. **SF:** Woodbridge d Woodforde 16 64 63; Rostagno d Chesnokov 76 63. **F:** Rostagno d Woodbridge 63 63.
DOUBLES: Jeff Brown/Scott Melville d Goran Ivanisevic/Petr Korda 26 75 60

AUGUST 20-26: NORSTAR BANK HAMLET CHALLENGE CUP, LONG ISLAND $225,000 Winner: STEFAN EDBERG
Rd 32: Stefan Edberg bye; David Wheaton d Jimmy Arias 63 36 61; Yannick Noah d Alex Antonitsch 64 63; Jonas Svensson d Olivier Delaitre 63 64; Brad Gilbert bye; Carl-Uwe Steeb d Udo Riglewski 62 46 60; Michael Stich d Sergi Bruguera 36 61 63; John McEnroe d Neil Borwick 64 61; Goran Ivanisevic d Gianluca Pozzi 63 61; Wayne Ferreira d Ronald Agenor 64 63; Francisco Montana d Jean Fleurian 67 62 63; Pete Sampras bye; Guy Forget d Gary Muller 76 76; Paul Haarhuis d Gilad Bloom 61 62; Eric Jelen d Bryan Shelton 76 06 61; Andres Gomez bye. **Rd 16:** Edberg d Wheaton 36 61 62; Svensson d Noah 64 64; Gilbert d Steeb 26 61 75; McEnroe d Stich 63 75; Ivanisevic d Ferreira 62 26 63; Sampras d Montana 63 76; Forget d Haarhuis 63 63; Gomez d Jelen 64 36 63. **QF:** Edberg d Svensson 64 62; McEnroe d Gilbert 63 62; Ivanisevic d Sampras 76 63; Forget d Gomez 67 60 75. **SF:** Edberg d McEnroe 61 64; Ivanisevic d Forget 62 16 63. **F:** Edberg d Ivanisevic 76 63.
DOUBLES: Guy Forget/Jakob Hlasek d Udo Riglewski/Michael Stich 26 63 64

AUGUST 20-26: OTB INTERNATIONAL TENNIS OPEN, SCHENECTADY $125,000 Winner: RAMESH KRISHNAN
Rd 32: Martin Jaite bye; Fabrice Santoro d Johan Anderson 64 64; Andrei Olhovskiy d Tarik Benhabiles 63 63; Grant Connell d Derrick Rostagno 64 Ret.; Alberto Mancini bye; Chuck Adams d Mike Briggs 57 63 64; Ramesh Krishnan d Jan Kodes 60 64; Milan Srejber d Thierry Champion 57 63 76; Steve Guy d Aki Rahunen 64 64; Martin Strelba d Guillaume Raoux 61 64; Brad Pearce d Thomas Hogstedt 62 75; Jaime Yzaga bye; Kelly Evernden d Dan Goldberg 64 46 62; Jeremy Bates d Daniel Montes de Oca 62 75; Mark Woodforde d Patrick Kuhnen 61 76; Amos Mansdorf bye. **Rd 16:** Jaite d Santoro 75 75; Olhovskiy d Connell 26 64 62; Adams d Mancini 61 64; Krishnan d Srejber 63 46 64; Guy d Strelba 57 64 64; Pearce d Yzaga 63 63; Evernden 57 76 76; Mansdorf d Woodforde 76 63. **QF:** Jaite d Olhovskiy 46 75 64; Krishnan d Adams 63 61 64; Pearce d Guy 75 76; Evernden d Mansdorf 75 76. **SF:** Krishnan d Jaite 16 63 75; Evernden d Pearce 62 36 64. **F:** Krishnan d Evernden 61 61.
DOUBLES: Richard Fromberg/Brad Pearce d Brian Garrow/Sven Salumaa 62 36 76

AUGUST 20-26: CAMPIONATI INTERNAZIONALI DI TENNIS DI SAN MARINO $150,000 Winner: GUILLERMO PEREZ-ROLDAN
Rd 32: Guillermo Perez-Roldan d Massimo Cierro 46 63 64; Paolo Pambianco d Jimmy Brown 64 63; Francisco Clavet d Marco Gorriz 62 76; Renzo Furlan d Roberto Azar 64 62; Marcelo Filippini d Joao Cunha-Silva 67 63 60; Jose F Altur d Massimo Boscatto 76 26 76; Pablo Arraya d Claudio Pistolesi 64 61; Goran Prpic d Claudio Mezzadri 63 42 Ret.; Omar Camporese d Nicola Bruno 63 75; Cedric Pioline d Lars Jonsson 57 63 62; Thierry Tulasne d Fernando Luna 63 61; Franco Davin d Francesco Cancellotti 06 75 64; Paolo Cane d Etpore Rossetti 62 62; Paul Vojtisek d Nuno Marques 64 64; Nicklas Kulti d Stefano Pescosolido 52 Ret.; Horst Skoff d F Mordegan 63 60. **Rd 16:** Perez-Roldan d Pambianco 76 61; Furlan d Clavet 36 64 60; Filippini d Altur 62 75; Arraya d Prpic 75 64; Camporese d Pioline 64 36 75; Davin d Tulasne 36 63 75; Vojtisek d Cane 46 63 64; Kulti d Skoff 67 76 62. **QF:** Perez-Roldan d Furlan 62 63; Filippini d Arraya 63 62; Camporese d Davin 62 06 63; Kulti d Vojtisek 64 62. **SF:** Perez-Roldan d Filippini 16 62 64; Camporese d Kulti 63 16 63. **F:** Perez-Roldan d Camporese 63 63.
DOUBLES: Jordi Burillo/Marco Gorriz d Vojtech Flegl/Daniel Vacek 61 46 76

AUGUST 27-SEPTEMBER 9: US OPEN, NEW YORK $2,554,250
Winner: PETE SAMPRAS
Rd 128: Alexander Volkov d Stefan Edberg 63 76 62; Todd Witsken d Diego Nargiso 63 76 76 64; Malivai Washington d Alberto Mancini 62 64 63; Kevin Curren d Shahar Perkiss 64 64 61; Jonas Svensson d Todd Woodbridge 76 62 36 62; David Wheaton d Jordi Arrese 63 61 60; Paul Annacone d Patrick Kuhnen 76 75 64; Martin Jaite d Martin Blackman 63 64 63; Andrei Chesnokov d Olivier Delaitre 64 75 63; Shuzo Matsuoka d David Witt 75 64 62; David Engel d Mario Rincon 64 62 62; John McEnroe d Javier Sanchez 76 76 64; Jim Grabb d Lawson Duncan 64 62 64; Fabrice Santoro d Ivan Baron 62 64 64; Jim Pugh d Richard Fromberg 26 64 75 76; Emilio Sanchez d Brian Garrow 76 64 64; Ivan Lendl d Martin Laurendeau 75 62 62; Michael Stich d Lars Jonsson 64 62 75; Carl Limberger d Marcelo Filippini 63 75 64; Alex Antonitsch d Mark Kaplan 36 62 61 60; Johan Anderson d Jose-Francisco Altur 75 60 75; Gilad Bloom d Brad Pearce 75 67 75 60; Gary Muller d Roberto Azar 63 36 61 62; Jim Courier d Wally Masur 64 60 57 61; Pete Sampras d Dan Goldie 61 75 61; Peter Lundgren d Chris Garner 61 62 62; Tommy Ho d Nduka Odizor 62 46 62 36 75; Jakob Hlasek d Richey Reneberg 36 76 64 60; Thierry Champion d Tim Mayotte 75 36 63 75; Jaime Yzaga d Karel Novacek 75 76 63; Anders Jarryd d Simon Youl 26 75 Ret.; Thomas Muster d Aki Rahunen 57 64 60 30 Ret.; Luiz Mattar d Andres Gomez 63 36 63 63; Veli Paloheimo d Jeremy Bates 63 75 64; Patrick McEnroe d Jeff Tarango 63 64 16 62 75; Christo van Rensburg d Martin Strelba 76 76 62; Henri Leconte d Ramesh Krishnan 64 61 61; Andrei Cherkasov d Robert Seguso 60 67 62 63; Jimmy Arias d Guy Forget 76 64 36 64; Michael Chang d Mikael Pernfors 60 62 63; Jay Berger d Ronald Agenor 64 64 36 64; Johan Carlsson d Richard Matuszewski 36 62 61 62; Christiano Caratti d Steve Bryan 62 75 26 62; Derrick Rostagno d Tarik Benhabiles 64 62 62; Glenn Layendecker d Dick Bosse 36 63 63 76; Franco Davin d Joey Rive 64 64 76; Petr Korda d Eric Jelen 26 63 60 63; Andre Agassi d Grant Connell 64 62 62; Brad Gilbert d Mats Wilander 64 36 63 75; Rick Leach d Paul Chamberlin 64 76 61; Sergi Bruguera d Thomas Hogstedt 63 62 62; Amos Mansdorf d Broderick Dyke 36 36 63 63 60; Pat Cash d Marc Rosset 26 26 63 63 63; Mark Kratzmann d Bryan Shelton 67 63 63 64; Jason Stoltenberg d Udo Riglewski 46 61 60 21 Ret.; Aaron Krickstein d Andrew Sznajder 61 46 67 61 61; Goran Ivanisevic d Omar Camporese 16 64 61 76; Jean-Philippe Fleurian d Todd Martin 76 63 76; Darren Cahill d Kelly Jones 63 36 62 60; Milan Srejber d Carl-Uwe Steeb 75 76 63; Tomas Carbonell d Paul Haarhuis 67 76 64 60; Scott Davis d Kelly Evernden 75 61 63; Yannick Noah d David Pate 76 64 67 46 62; Boris Becker d Juan Aguilera 75 63 62. **Rd 64:** Witsken d Volkov 62 62 63; Curren d Washington 75 76 64; Wheaton d Svensson 64 75 75; Annacone d Jaite 76 62 62; Chesnokov d Matsuoka 67 63 61 63; J McEnroe d Engel 62 63 75; Santoro d Grabb 76 64 76; E Sanchez d Pugh 61 62 62; Lendl d Stich 64 57 63 63; Antonitsch d Limberger 61 57 64 63; Bloom d Anderson 63 63 46 16 76; Muller d Courier 46 64 76 76; Sampras d Lundgren 64 63 63; Hlasek d Ho 63 62 76; Yzaga d Champion 61 36 63 62; Muster d Jarryd 64 63 46 61; Mattar d Paloheimo 64 60 36 26 63; van Rensburg d P McEnroe 64 64 75; Cherkasov d Leconte 16 61 64 63; Chang d Arias 76 63 62; Berger d Carlsson 36 61 64 62; Caratti d Rostagno 36 76 64 16 76; Davin d Layendecker 67 63 62 64; Agassi d Korda 75 57 60 64; Gilbert d Leach 76 64 62; Mansdorf d Bruguera 76 62 26 63; Cash d Kratzmann 64 26 26 61 64; Krickstein d Stoltenberg 64 62 64; Ivanisevic d Fleurian 64 62 36 61; Cahill d Srejber 63 20 Ret.; Carbonell d Davis 64 64 62; Becker d Noah 64 62 76. **Rd 32:** Curren d Witsken 64 63 63; Wheaton d Annacone 62 76 63; J McEnroe d Chesnokov 63 75 64; E Sanchez d Santoro 63 64 57 36 75; Lendl d Antonitsch 76 61 62; Bloom d Muller 62 63 64; Sampras d Hlasek 63 64 61; Muster d Yzaga 62 62 46 57 76; van Rensburg d Mattar 61 64 57 64; Cherkasov d Chang 64 64 63; Berger d Caratti 46 26 64 63 64; Agassi d Davin 75 64 60; Mansdorf d Gilbert 57 57 63 75 61; Krickstein d Cash 64 76 76; Cahill d Ivanisevic 46 46 62 76 60; Becker d Carbonell 64 62 62. **Rd 16:** Wheaton d Curren 75 76 46 64; J McEnroe d Sanchez 76 36 46 64 63; Lendl d Bloom 60 63 64; Sampras d Muster 67 76 64 63; Cherkasov d van Rensburg 64 64 75; Agassi d Berger 75 60 62; Krickstein d Mansdorf 63 64 64; Becker d Cahill 26 62 63 36 64. **QF:** J McEnroe d Wheaton 61 64 64; Sampras d Lendl 64 76 36 46 62; Agassi d Cherkasov 62 62 63; Becker d Krickstein 36 63 62 63. **SF:** Sampras d J McEnroe 62 64 36 63; Agassi d Becker 67 63 62 63. **F:** Sampras d Agassi 64 63 62.
DOUBLES: Pieter Aldrich/Danie Visser d Paul Annacone/David Wheaton 62 76 62

SEPTEMBER 10-16: GRAND PRIX PASSING SHOT, BORDEAUX $270,000 Winner: GUY FORGET
Rd 32: Thomas Muster d Tom Nijssen 62 62; Tomas Nydahl d Claudio Pistolesi 36 76 64; Tarik Benhabiles d Eduardo Masso 62 61; Ronald Agenor d Arnaud Boetsch 64 75; Guy Forget d Jean Fleurian 75 36 62; Carlos Costa d Jens Woehrmann 63 75; Lawson Duncan d Cedric Pioline 63 32 Ret.; Marcelo Ingaramo d Jordi Arrese 67 62 64; Thierry Champion d Juan Aguilera 62 57 76; Jose F Altur d Jerome Potier 76 62; Tomas Carbonell d Bart Wuyts 61 61; Guillermo Perez-Roldan d Mansour Bahrami 76 62; Yannick Noah d Thierry Tulasne 64 62; Fabrice Santoro d Jimmy Brown 61 62; Fernando Luna d Jordi Burillo 63 36 63; Goran Ivanisevic d Jose-Luis Aparisi 67 61 63. **Rd 16:** Nydahl d Muster 26 64 64; Agenor d Benhabiles 46 63 62; Forget d Costa 64 36 64; Duncan d Ingaramo 63 62; Champion d Altur 51 Ret.; Perez-Roldan d Carbonell 46 64 62; Santoro d Noah 62 76; Ivanisevic d Luna 36 76 60. **QF:** Agenor d Nydahl 60 61; Forget d Duncan 61 67 60; Perez-Roldan d Champion 46 62 61; Ivanisevic d Santoro 62 63. **SF:** Forget d Agenor 63 64; Ivanisevic d Perez-Roldan 64 64. **F:** Forget d Ivanisevic 64 63.
DOUBLES: Tomas Carbonell/Libor Pimek d Mansour Bahrami/Yannick Noah 63 67 62

SEPTEMBER 10-16: BARCLAY OPEN, GENEVA $225,000 Winner: HORST SKOFF
Rd 32: Henri Leconte d Joao Cunha-Silva 63 64; Lars Jonsson d David Engel 57 63 62; Michael Tauson d Nicklas Kulti 64 63; Franco Davin d Claudio Mezzadri 57 76 61; Jakob Hlasek d Martin Strelba 64 63; Horacio de la Pena d Daniel Orsanic 75 26 62; Jan Gunnarsson d Cassio Motta 63 36 64; Sergi Bruguera d Roberto Azar 61 63; Omar Camporese d Bruno Oresar 64 64; Marian Vajda d Udo Riglewski 76 63; Alexander Mronz d Roberto Arguello 75 63; Marc Rosset d Pablo Albano 64 62; Renzo Furlan d Goran Prpic 64 67 64; Jose Conde d Mark Kaplan 64 61; Paolo Cane d Francisco Clavet 63 61; Horst Skoff d Christian Bergstrom 64 64. **Rd 16:** Leconte d Jonsson 61 62; Tauson d Davin 63 64; de la Pena d Hlasek 64 62; Bruguera d Gunnarsson 75 62; Camporese d Vajda 64 64; Rosset d Mronz 64 62; Furlan d Conde 62 64; Skoff d Cane 64 62. **QF:** Tauson d Leconte 64 63; Bruguera d de la Pena 60 62; Rosset d Camporese 76 76; Skoff d Furlan 76 76. **SF:** Bruguera d Tauson 61 62; Skoff d Rosset 46 63 62. **F:** Skoff d Bruguera 76 76.
DOUBLES: Pablo Albano/David Engel d Neil Borwick/David Lewis 63 67 72.

SEPTEMBER 24-30: SWISS INDOORS, BASEL $450,000 Winner: JOHN MCENROE
Rd 32: Jean Fleurian d Andres Gomez 76 76; Scott Melville d Frank Dennhardt 75 64; Yannick Noah d Aki Rahunen 46 76 64; Mansour Bahrami d Marc Rosset 61 57 76; John McEnroe d Milan Srejber 64 63; Nicklas Kulti d Christian Bergstrom 64 64; Andrei Cherkasov d Magnus Larsson 64 61; Jim Courier d Amos Mansdorf 76 60; Magnus Gustafsson d Ronald Agenor 61 46 63; Luiz Mattar d Jan Gunnarsson 64 46 64; Veli Paloheimo d Marcelo Filippini 62 57 63; Andrei Chesnokov d Gary Muller 64 76; Karel Novacek d Christo van Rensburg 60 75; Michael Stich d Jimmy Connors 76 63; Petr Korda d Jaime Yzaga 76 36 63; Goran Ivanisevic d Alexander Volkov 76 61. **Rd 16:** Melville d Fleurian 64 76; Noah d Bahrami 63 63; McEnroe d Kulti 61 62; Cherkasov d Courier 36 62 63; Gustafsson d Mattar 67 76 64; Paloheimo d Chesnokov 26 62 75; Stich d Novacek 62 63; Ivanisevic d Volkov 76 61. **QF:** Melville d Noah 76 67 64; McEnroe d Cherkasov 63 75; Paloheimo d Gustafsson 76 64; Ivanisevic d Stich 61 62. **SF:** McEnroe d Melville 62 26 63; Ivanisevic d Paloheimo 62 64. **F:** McEnroe d Ivanisevic 67 46 76 63 64.
DOUBLES: Stefan Kruger/Christo van Rensburg d Neil Broad/Gary Muller 46 76 63

SEPTEMBER 24-30: 39TH INTERNATIONAL CHAMPIONSHIPS OF SICILY, PALERMO $300,000 Winner: FRANCO DAVIN
Rd 32: Tarik Benhabiles d Emilio Sanchez 76 64; Martin Strelba d Sergio Casal 64 61; Paolo Cane d Diego Perez 36 64 62; Franco Davin d Alessandro de Minicis 64 61; Francisco Clavet d Horst Skoff 36 76 61; Thierry Champion d Roberto Azar 63 63; Horacio de la Pena d Eduardo Masso 63 30 Ret.; Omar Camporese d Marco Gorriz 64 64; Claudio Pistolesi d Sergi Bruguera 57 62 64; Renzo Furlan d Andrea Gaudenzi 76 64; Javier Sanchez d Jens Woehrmann 63 64; Juan Aguilera d Stefano Pescosolido 63 46 31 Ret; Goran Prpic d Federico Mordegan 60 63; Marian Vajda d Christer Allgardh 61 63; Tomas Carbonell d Lawson Duncan 63 62; Guillermo Perez-Roldan d Jeff Tarango 61 62. **Rd 16:** Strelba d Benhabiles 62 46 65; Davin d Cane 63 64; Champion d Clavet 64 62; de la Pena d Camporese 64 64; Pistolesi d Furlan 62 64; Aguilera d Sanchez 76 64; Vajda d Prpic 76 36 62; Perez-Roldan d Carbonell 76 64. **QF:** Davin d Strelba 62 64; Champion d de la Pena 67 61 63; Aguilera d Pistolesi 63 64; Perez-Roldan d vajda 64 76. **SF:** Davin d Champion 61 46 75; Aguilera d Perez-Roldan 62 63. **F:** Davin d Aguilera 61 61.
DOUBLES: Sergio Casal/Emilio Sanchez d Carlos Costa/Horacio de la Pena 63 64

SEPTEMBER 24-30: QUEENSLAND OPEN, BRISBANE $250,000
Winner: BRAD GILBERT
Rd 32: Brad Gilbert d Peter Doohan 60 61; Patrick Kuhnen d Shuzo Matsuoka 64 75; Thomas Hogstedt d Joey Rive 57 63 61; Carl Limberger d Martin Davis 76 36 64; Carl-Uwe Steeb d Mats Wilander 62 63; Sandon Stolle d Jason Stoltenberg 76 62; Brian Garrow d Bryan Shelton 63 64; Niclas Kroon d Mark Kratzmann 63 62; Robbie Weiss d Kelly Evernden 57 64 61; David Pate d Lars Wahlgren 62 61; John Fitzgerald d Johan Anderson 64 46 75; Todd Woodbridge d Richard Fromberg 67 76 64; Eric Jelen d Mark Woodforde 61 62; David Engel d Paul Chamberlin 64 64; Dan Goldie d Brett Steven 64 64; Aaron Krickstein d Anders Jarryd 21 Ret. **Rd 16:** Gilbert d Kuhnen 63 62; Limberger d Hogstedt 62 61; Steeb d Stolle 61 46 60; Kroon d Garrow 76 75; Weiss d Pate 62 63; Fitzgerald d Woodbridge 64 26 64; Jelen d Engel 63 26 62; Krickstein d Goldie 62 63. **QF:** Gilbert d Limberger 62 64; Steeb d Kroon 75 75; Fitzgerald d Weiss 26 63 64; Krickstein d Jelen 62 61
SF: Gilbert d Steeb 57 63 64; Krickstein d Fitzgerald 62 60. **F:** Gilbert d Krickstein 63 61.
DOUBLES: Jason Stoltenberg/Todd Woodbridge d Brian Garrow/Mark Woodforde 26 64 64

OCTOBER 1-7: AUSTRALIAN INDOOR TENNIS CHAMPIONSHIP, SYDNEY $750,000 Winner: BORIS BECKER
Rd 48: Stefan Edberg bye; Niclas Kroon d Lars Wahlgren 63 63; Simon Youl d Thomas Hogstedt 61 64; Mark Kratzmann bye; David Wheaton bye; Sandon Stolle d Paul

Chamberlin 63 63; Patrick Kuhnen d Eric Jelen 63 60; Richard Fromberg bye; Ivan Lendl bye; Aki Rahunen d Jason Stoltenberg 64 64; Scott Davis d Shuzo Matsuoka 67 63 64; Jim Grabb bye; Carl-Uwe Steeb bye; Peter Lundgren d Dan Goldie 62 64; Todd Witsken d Todd Nelson 63 26 64; Michael Chang bye; Aaron Krickstein bye; Grant Connell d Charlton Eagle 76 64; Paul Haarhuis d Anders Jarryd 67 62 63; Derrick Rostagno bye; Darren Cahill bye; Brad Pearce d David Engel 26 61 75; Todd Woodbridge d Kelly Jones 64 60; Brad Gilbert bye; Richey Reneberg bye; David Pate d Bryan Shelton 62 63; Pat Cash d John Fitzgerald 67 76 62; Wally Masur bye; Kelly Evernden bye; Joey Rive d Johan Anderson 76 63; Mats Wilander d Mark Woodforde 63 64; Boris Becker bye. **Rd 32:** Edberg d Kroon 63 62; Kratzmann d Youl 63 36 63; Wheaton d Stolle 46 60 62; Kuhnen d Fromberg 76 62; Lendl d Rahunen 60 36 63; Davis d Grabb 36 63 63; Lundgren d Steeb 75 63; Chang d Witsken 46 61 64; Connell d Krickstein 76 60; Haarhuis d Rostagno 76 64; Pearce d Cahill 64 61; Woodbridge d Gilbert 76 63; Reneberg d Pate 62 63; Masur d Cash 46 64 63; Evernden d Rive 63 26 76; Becker d Wilander 62 75. **Rd 16:** Edberg d Kratzmann 62 76; Wheaton d Kuhnen 75 36 63; Lendl d Davis 76 46 62; Lundgren d Chang 62 64; Connell d Haarhuis 57 75 64; Woodbridge d Pearce 63 46 63; Reneberg d Masur 75 63; Becker d Evernden 64 63. **QF:** Edberg d Wheaton 62 76; Lendl d Lundgren 62 76; Woodbridge d Connell 76 26 61; Becker d Reneberg 64 64. **SF:** Edberg d Lendl 36 76 63; Becker d Woodbridge 75 64. **F:** Becker d Edberg 76 64 64.
DOUBLES: Broderick Dyke/Peter Lundgren d Stefan Edberg/Ivan Lendl 62 64.

OCTOBER 1-7: GRAND PRIX DE TOULOUSE, TOULOUSE $260,000
Winner: JONAS SVENSSON
Rd 32: Fabrice Santoro d Andres Gomez 62 36 63; Jaime Yzaga d Mansour Bahrami 64 36 63; Christian Bergstrom d Patrick McEnroe 36 61 61; Jean Fleurian d Marcelo Filippini 36 62 63; Jim Courier d Alex Antonitsch 63 62; Alexander Volkov d Gary Muller 64 75; Guillaume Raoux d Olivier Soules 63 62; Ronald Agenor d Jimmy Connors 64 62; Henri Leconte d Christo van Rensburg 46 63 63; Magnus Larsson d Rodolph Gilbert 76 36 63; Veli Paloheimo d Tarik Benhabiles 76 62; Jonas Svensson d Luiz Mattar 62 36 64; Amos Mansdorf d Nicklas Kulti 60 63; Jimmy Arias d Thierry Guardiola 46 64 62; Yannick Noah d Milan Srejber 64 67 76; Andrei Chesnokov d Michael Stich 26 76 64. **Rd 16:** Santoro d Yzaga 62 62; Bergstrom d Fleurian 76 64; Volkov d Courier 65 62; Agenor d Raoux 36 63 62; Larsson d Leconte 76 26 63; Svensson d Paloheimo 75 60; Mansdorf d Arias 62 60; Noah d Chesnokov W/O. **QF:** Santoro d Bergstrom 75 64; Agenor d Volkov 64 64; Svensson d Larsson 64 67 63; Mansdorf d Noah 64 64. **SF:** Santoro d Agenor 76 63; Svensson d Mansdorf 67 64 63. **F:** Svensson d Santoro 76 62.
DOUBLES: Neil Broad/Thomas Muller d Michael Mortensen/Michiel Schapers 76 64

OCTOBER 1-7: ATHENS GRAND PRIX, ATHENS $125,000
Winner: MARK KOEVERMANS
Rd 32: Thomas Muster d Martin Wostenholme 76 63; Marian Vajda d Jens Woehrmann 62 76; Tomas Carbonell d Marco Gorriz 76 63; Horacio de la Pena d Diego Perez 64 64; Guillermo Perez-Roldan d Carlos Costa 76 67 61; Jeff Tarango d Sergio Casal 63 46 64; Fernando Luna d Martin Strelba 62 62; Franco Davin d Renzo Furlan 63 61; Javier Sanchez d Ctislav Dosedel 67 62 63; Lawson Duncan d Jose F Altur 63 76; Jimmy Brown d George Kalovelonis 62 62; Jordi Arrese d German Lopez 62 61; Mark Koevermans d Joao Cunha-Silva 64 62; Tasos Bavelas d Roberto Azar 64 36 62; Francisco Clavet d Tomas Nydahl 26 63 62; Francisco Roig d Emilio Sanchez 62 76. **Rd 16:** Vajda d Muster 36 76 63; Carbonell d de la Pena 61 64; Perez-Roldan d Tarango 62 63; Davin d Luna 75 73; J Sanchez d Duncan 64 60; Arrese d Brown 63 76; Koevermans d Bavelas 63 46 62; Roig d Clavet 62 67 64. **QF:** Vajda d Carbonell 63 63; Davin d Perez-Roldan 62 61; Arrese d J Sanchez 62 63; Koevermans d Roig 36 61 62. **SF:** Davin d Vajda 76 26 63; Koevermans d Arrese 62 76. **F:** Koevermans d Davin 57 64 61.
DOUBLES: Sergio Casal/Javier Sanchez d Tom Kempers/Richard Krajicek 64 63

OCTOBER 8-14: SEIKO SUPER TENNIS, TOKYO $750,000 Winner: IVAN LENDL
Rd 48: Stefan Edberg bye; Todd Woodbridge d Daijirou Furusho 63 76; Patrick Kuhnen d Simon Youl 63 76; Darren Cahill bye; Jakob Hlasek bye; Paul Haarhuis d Jim Grabb 63 64; Brian Garrow d Kelly Evernden 63 64; Richard Fromberg bye; Ivan Lendl bye; Mark Woodforde d Shuzo Matsuoka 67 76 Ret.; Derrick Rostagno d Grant Connell 76 64; Wally Masur bye; David Wheaton bye; Aki Rahunen d Paul Chamberlin 75 62; Scott Davis d Mark Kratzmanna 75 76; Aaron Krickstein bye; Guy Forget bye; Brad Pearce d Dan Goldie 67 64 63; Jason Stoltenberg d Peter Lundgren 43 Ret.; Richey Reneberg bye; Carl-Uwe Steeb bye; Eric Jelen d Kelly Jones 64 64; Thomas Hogstedt d Bryan Shelton 76 76; Andres Gomez bye; Michael Chang bye; Pat Cash d Niclas Kroon 62 76; Rick Leach d David Pate 76 76; Andrei Cherkasov bye; Tim Mayotte bye; Todd Witsken d Kentaro Masuda 62 63; Ryuso Tsujino d Joey Rive 26 76 64; Boris Becker bye. **Rd 32:** Edberg d Woodbridge 63 61; Cahill d Kuhnen 64 63; Hlasek d Haarhuis 46 60 63; Garrow d Fromberg 36 63 76; Lendl d Woodforde 62 76; Masur d Rostagno 64 64; Wheaton d Rahunen 75 64; Davis d Krickstein 63 61; Forget d Pearce 67 63 63; Reneberg d Stoltenberg 61 64; Jelen d Steeb 63 36 75; Hogstedt d Jelen 64 64; Cash d Chang 36 76 64; Cherkasov d Leach 61 64; Witsken d Mayotte 26 76 64; Becker d Witsken 64 76. **Rd 16:** Edberg d Cahill 64 62; Hlasek d Garrow 64 64; Lendl d Masur 64 36 63; Davis d Wheaton 64 76; Reneberg d Forget 76 76; Hogstedt d Jelen 46 64 62; Cherkasov d Cash 76 63; Becker d Witsken 62 63. **QF:** Edberg d Hlasek 64 36 76; Lendl d Davis 76 62; Reneberg d Hogstedt 63 62; Becker d Cherkasov 64 64. **SF:** Lendl d Edberg 75 63; Becker d Reneberg 76 62. **F:** Lendl d Becker 46 63 76.
DOUBLES: Guy Forget/Jakob Hlasek d Scott Davis/David Pate 76 75.

OCTOBER 8-14: BERLIN OPEN, BERLIN $260,000 Winner: RONALD AGENOR
Rd 32: Goran Ivanisevic d Leonardo Lavalle 76 75; Martin Sinner d Luke Jensen 62 62; Milan Srejber d Gary Muller 67 75 61; Danie Visser d Franco Davin 64 64; Kevin Curren d Magnus Gustafsson 64 46 62; Pieter Aldrich d Paul Annacone 62 62; Jens Woehrmann d Malivai Washington 75 63; Ronald Agenor d Thierry Champion 62 63; Petr Korda d Michael Stich 16 64 76; Jean Fleurian d Veli Paloheimo 62 62; Luiz Mattar d Jan Kodes 63 61; Horst Skoff d Diego Perez 62 60; Alexander Volkov d Jimmy Arias 63 64; Udo Riglewski d Christian Bergstrom 67 76 64; Markus Zoecke d Jan Gunnarsson 64 67 61; Jonas Svensson d Andrei Olhovskiy 60 36 62. **Rd 16:** Sinner d Ivanisevic 76 64; Srejber d Visser 64 64; Curren d Aldrich 64 62; Agenor d Woehrmann 61 62; Fleurian d Korda 64 61; Mattar d Skoff 61 46 63; Volkov d Riglewski 63 63; Svensson d Zoecke 62 57 62. **QF:** Sinner d Srejber 64 57 62; Agenor d Curren 76 64; Mattar d Fleurian 76 64; Volkov d Svensson 63 60. **SF:** Agenor d Sinner 61 76; Volkov d Mattar 63 62. **F:** Agenor d Volkov 46 64 76.
DOUBLES: Peter Aldrich/Danie Visser d Kevin Curren/Patrick Galbraith 76 76.

OCTOBER 8-14: RIKLIS ISRAEL TENNIS CENTER CLASSIC, TEL AVIV $125,000
Winner: ANDREI CHESNOKOV
Rd 32: Andrei Chesnokov d Nicolas Pereira 63 62; Michael Robertson d Eyal Ran 61 63; Lars Jonsson d Marco Gorriz 64 64; David Engel d Ohad Weinberg 63 60; Christo van Rensburg d Jan Siemerink 61 63; Amit Naor d Noam Behr 61 60; Piet Norval d M Daniel 62 76; Gilad Bloom d Gianluca Pozzi 62 61; Tomas Carbonell d Shai Friedman 62 61; Jeff Tarango d Paul Vojtisek 63 62; Alexis Hombrecher d Boaz Merenstein 64 64; Mark Koevermans d Oren Motevassel 63 16 62; Gill Kovalski d Yuval Karutzi 75 26 63; Nduka Odizor d Yuval Hirsch 60 61; Shahar Perkis d Wayne Ferreira 63 64; Amos Mansdorf d Raviv Weidenfeld 63 61. **Rd 16:** Chesnokov d Robertson 75 64; Jonsson d Engel 06 64 62; van Rensburg d Naor 64 62; Bloom d Norval 61 64; Tarango d Carbonell 62 75; Koevermans d Hombrecher 64 64; Odizor d Kovalski 61 64; Mansdorf d Perkis 76 64. **QF:** Chesnokov d Jonsson 63 61; Bloom d van Rensburg 26 76 75. Tarango d Koevermans 76 61; Mansdorf d Odizor 75 61. **SF:** Chesnokov d Bloom 63 63; Mansdorf d Tarango 61 62. **F:** Chesnokov d Mansdorf 64 63.
DOUBLES: Nduka Odizor /Christo van Rensburg d Ronnie Bathman/Rikard Bergh 63 64.

OCTOBER 15-21: CA TENNIS TROPHY, VIENNA $225,000 Winner: ANDERS JARRYD
Rd 32: Thomas Muster d Martin Strelba 76 64; Paul Annacone d Jeff Tarango 75 76; Andrei Olhovskiy d Olivier Delaitre 60 63; Jimmy Arias d Jeremy Bates 75 64; Horst Skoff d Alexander Antonitsch 36 75 62; Dimitri Poliakov d Reinhardt Wawra 62 64; Lars Jonsson d Martin Sinner 62 76; Carl-Uwe Steeb d Roberto Azar 63 63; Alexander Volkov d Thomas Hogstedt 76 64; Jens Wohrmann d Harold Mair 75 61; Jan Siemerink d Patrick McEnroe 46 75 63; Martin Jaite d Tomas Carbonell 76 64; Anders Jarryd d Michael Stich 75 62; Patrick Kuhnen d Joao Cunha-Silva 76 63; Udo Riglewski d Jan Gunnarsson 76 36 76; John McEnroe d Brian Garrow 46 76 64. **Rd 16:** Muster d Annacone 36 76 76; Olhovskiy d Arias 75 64; Skoff d Poliakov 67 64 62; Jonsson d Steeb 63 63; Volkov d Wohrmann 75 63; Jaite d Siemerink 63 63; Jarryd d Kuhnen 63 64; J McEnroe d Riglewski 67 64 63. **QF:** Muster d Olhovskiy 06 64 76; Skoff d Jonsson 63 64; Volkov d Jaite 62 61; Jarryd d J McEnroe 76 63. **SF:** Skoff d Muster 62 76; Jarryd d Volkov 76 75. **F:** Jarryd d Skoff 63 63 61.
DOUBLES: Udo Riglewski/Michael Stich d Jorge Lozano/Todd Witsken 64 64.

OCTOBER 15-21: GRAND PRIX DE TENNIS DE LYON, LYON $225,000
Winner: MARC ROSSET
Rd 32: Aaron Krickstein d Yahiya Doumbia 76 64; Christian Bergstrom d Cyril Suk 61 62; Eric Winogradsky d Luke Jensen 63 76; Alexander Mronz d Jean Fleurian 36 63 60; Jonas Svensson d Tarik Benhabiles 62 63; Eduardo Masso d Pier Gauthier 76 62; Gilad Bloom d Diego Perez 61 06 60; Mats Wilander d Andrei Cherkasov 62 36 63; Marc Rosset d Milan Srejber 76 67 76; Eric Jelen d Malivai Washington 57 60 75; Ramesh Krishnan d Fabrice Santoro 61 46 63; Ronald Agenor d Bryan Shelton 67 63 61; Yannick Noah d Kelly Jones 36 75 63; Gary Muller d Guillaume Raoux 63 64; Thierry Champion d Cedric Pioline 64 63; David Pate d Guy Forget 76 46 76. **Rd 16:** Krickstein d Bergstrom 64 63; Mronz d Winogradsky 67 64 64; Svensson d Masso 64 76; Wilander d Bloom 62 62; Rosset d Jelen 61 36 63; Agenor d Krishnan 16 76 75; Muller d Noah 63 64; Pate d Champion 63 36 63. **QF:** Mronz d Krickstein 64 26 64; Wilander d Svensson 46 64 63; Rosset d Agenor 76 75; Pate d Muller 76 46 63. **SF:** Wilander d Mronz 62 76; Rosset d Pate 64 16 64. **F:** Rosset d Wilander 63 62.
DOUBLES: Patrick Galbraith/Kelly Jones d Jim Grabb/David Pate 76 64.

OCTOBER 22-28: STOCKHOLM OPEN $840,000 Winner: BORIS BECKER
Rd 48: Stefan Edberg bye; Mats Wilander d Todd Woodbridge 75 67 60; Marc Rosset d Derrick Rostagno 26 62 62; Jonas Svensson bye; Andrei Chesnokov bye; Jim Courier d Broderick Dyke 61 63; Jakob Hlasek d Andrei Cherkasov 63 64; Brad Gilbert bye; Andre Agassi bye; Nicklas Kulti d Tim Mayotte 64 76; Magnus Larsson d David Engel 63 64; Guy Forget bye; Aaron Krickstein bye; Magnus Gustafsson d Richard Fromberg 76 61; Alexander Volkov d Carl-Uwe Steeb 46 64 63; Emilio Sanchez bye; Andres Gomez bye; David Wheaton d Christer Wedenby 76 63; Martin Jaite d Marcelo Filippini 64 63; Michael Chang bye; Guillermo Perez-Roldan bye; Petr Korda d Jan Gunnarsson 46 64 75; Rikard Berger d Peter Lundgren 64 76; Pete Sampras bye; John McEnroe bye; Karel Novacek d Wally Masur 76 36 63; Leonardo Lavalle d Henrik Holm 62 36 63; Goran Ivanisevic bye; Jay Berger bye; Richey Reneberg d Sergi Bruguera 61 64; Darren Cahill d Kevin Curren 63 63; Boris Becker bye. **Rd 32:** Edberg d Wilander 64 63; Rosset d Svensson 67 76 76; Courier d Chesnokov 36 63 75; Gilbert d Hlasek 63 76; Kulti d Agassi 63 75; Forget d Larsson 63 36 63; Gustafsson d Krickstein 62 63; Volkov d Sanchez 75 63; Wheaton d Gomez 67 63 61; Chang d Jaite 64 63; Korda d Perez-Roldan 63 64; Sampras d Bergh 76 67 63; McEnroe d Novacek 62 67 75; Ivanisevic d Lavalle 76 63; Reneberg d Berger 63 63; Becker d Cahill 62 60. **Rd 16:** Edberg d Rosset 64 64; Gilbert d Courier 63 64; Kulti d Forget 64 62; Volkov d Gustafsson 63 76; Wheaton d Chang 67 62 63; Sampras d Korda 63 36 76; Ivanisevic d McEnroe 64 64; Becker d Reneberg 64 63. **QF:** Edberg d Gilbert 64 36 61; Volkov d Kulti 62 61; Sampras d Wheaton 76 57 64; Becker d Ivanisevic 64 62. **SF:** Edberg d Volkov 76 62; Becker d Sampras 64 64. **F:** Becker d Edberg 64 60 63.
DOUBLES: Guy Forget/Jakob Hlasek d John Fitzgerald/Anders Jarryd 64 62.

OCTOBER 22-28: PHILIPS OPEN, SAO PAULO $125,000 Winner: ROBBIE WEISS
Rd 32: Jonathan Canter d Franco Davin 62 36 61; Miguel Nido d German Lopez 63 67 61; Eduardo Bengoechea d Martin Wostenholme 60 61; Robbie Weiss d Xavier Daufresne 60 46 64; Mark Koevermans d Jaime Oncins 64 75; Jacco Eltingh d Bart Wuyts 63 63; Pedro Rebolledo d Andrew Sznajder 61 62; Joao Cunha-Silva d Roberto Azar 63 76; Cassio Motta d Fernando Roese 63 36 62; Chris Garner d Mikael Pernfors 63 60; Marcelo Saliola d Paul Vojtisek 46 61 62; Jaime Yzaga d Marco Gorriz 62 62; Javier Frana d Nuno Marques 76 63; Danilo Marcelino d Tim Wilkison 63 64; Bruno Oresar d Stefano Pescosolido 64 62; Luiz Mattar d Pablo Arraya 63 62. **Rd 16:** Nido d Canter 76 06 76; Weiss d Bengoechea 64 64; Eltingh d Koevermans 67 75 75; Cunha-Silva d Rebolledo 64 62; Garner d Motta 75 76; Yzaga d Saliola 62 75; Marcelino d Frana 76 64; Mattar d Oresar 75 26 64. **QF:** Weiss d Nido 64 63; Eltingh d Cunha-Silva 75 76; Yzaga d Garner 75 75; Marcelino d Mattar 67 62 76. **SF:** Weiss d Eltingh 76 64 76; Yzaga d Marcelino 64 36 76. **F:** Weiss d Yzaga 36 76 63.
DOUBLES: Shelby Cannon/Alfonso Mora d Mark Koevermans/Luiz Mattar 67 63 76

OCTOBER 29-NOVEMBER 4: OPEN DE LA VILLE DE PARIS, PARIS $1,650,000
Winner: STEFAN EDBERG
Rd 48: Stefan Edberg bye; Andrei Cherkasov d Fabrice Santoro 36 63 62; Yannick Noah d Karel Novacek 63 36 76; Aaron Krickstein bye; Goran Ivanisevic bye; Magnus Gustafsson d David Wheaton 76 76; Jakob Hlasek d Mats Wilander 63 62; John McEnroe bye; Pete Sampras bye; Cark-Uwe Steeb d Wally Masur 62 76; Guillaume Raoux d Marcelo Filippini 26 64 63; Guillermo Perez-Roldan bye; Michael Chang bye; Marc Rosset d Jordi Arrese 63 61; Sergi Bruguera d Henri Leconte 16 62 52 Ret.; Andres Gomez bye; Emilio Sanchez bye; Patrick McEnroe d Richard Fromberg 76 67 75; Ronald Agenor d Alexander Volkov 26 75 75; Guy Forget bye; Jonas Svensson bye; Thierry Champion d Tim Mayotte 46 63 64; Kevin Curren d Petr Korda 62 62; Ivan Lendl bye; Brad Gilbert bye; Amos Mansdorf d Martin Jaite 67 63 60; Michael Stich d Horst Skoff 61 10 Ret.; Andrei Chesnokov bye; Juan Aguilera bye; Jim Courier d Jim Grabb 75 67 63; Richey Reneberg d Eric Winogradsky 76 63; Boris Becker bye. **Rd 32:** Edberg d Cherkasov 62 63; Krickstein d Noah 63 62; Ivanisevic d Gustafsson 62 64; Hlasek d J McEnroe 36 63 76; Sampras d Steeb 76 36 76; Raoux d Perez-Roldan 75 64; Rosset d Chang 76 64; Bruguera d Gomez 46 61 63; E Sanchez d P McEnroe 64 76; Forget d Agenor 76 62; Svensson d Champion 62 62; Lendl d Curren 63 64; Gilbert d Mansdorf 63 76; Stich d Chesnokov 76 64; Courier d Aguilera 62 62; Becker d Reneberg 46 63 62. **Rd 16:** Edberg d Krickstein 63 62; Hlasek d Ivanisevic 63 61; Raoux d Sampras 63 36 63; Bruguera 46 61 63; E Sanchez d Forget 75 63; Svensson d Lendl 36 64 62; Stich d Gilbert 64 64; Becker d Courier 61 75. **QF:** Edberg d Hlasek 63 64; Bruguera d Raoux 46 61 63; Svensson d E Sanchez 75 64; Becker d Stich 61 62. **SF:** Edberg d Bruguera 63 63; Becker d Svensson 46 76 61. **F:** Edberg d Becker 33 Ret.
DOUBLES: Scott Davis/David Pate d Darren Cahill/Mark Kratzmann 67 63 64.

NOVEMBER 5-11: DIET PEPSI INDOOR CHALLENGE, LONDON $297,000
Winner: JAKOB HLASEK
Rd 32: Pete Sampras d Cedric Pioline 62 46 63; Christian Bergstrom d Eduardo Masso 64 64; Patrick McEnroe d Jim Grabb 62 75; Scott Davis d Alex Antonitsch 63 46 64; Michael Chang d Mark Kratzmann 60 60; Jeremy Bates d Ramesh Krishnan 76 76; Peter Lundgren d Nicolas Pereira 67 63 64; Aaron Krickstein d Rick Leach 62 64; Patrick Baur d Horst Skoff 36 64 62; Diego Nargiso d Aki Rahunen 62 64; Darren Cahill d Pat Cash 76 64; Magnus Larsson d Guy Forget 62 76; Jakob Hlasek d Todd Woodbridge 61 67 63; Gary Muller d Goran Prpic 64 64; Niclas Kulti d Mark Woodforde 62 61; Ivanisevic d Thierry Champion 64 62. **Rd 16:** Bergstrom d Sampras W/O; Patrick McEnroe d Davis 75 36 64; Lundgren d Krickstein 75 64; Nargiso d Baur 36 76 76; Larsson d Cahill 76 36 76; Hlasek d Muller 75 75; Ivanisevic d Kulti 76 64. **QF:** Bergstrom d Patrick McEnroe 62 64; Chang d Lundgren 63 64; Hlasek d Larsson 63 36 63; Hlasek d Ivanisevic 41 Ret. **SF:** Chang d Bergstrom 63 36 76; Hlasek d Nargiso 76 62. **F:** Hlasek d Chang 76 63.
DOUBLES: Jim Grabb/Patrick McEnroe d Rick Leach /Jim Pugh 76 46 63.

NOVEMBER 5-11: KREMLIN CUP, MOSCOW $297,000 Winner: ANDREI CHERKASOV
Rd 32: Jan Gunnarsson d Andres Gomez 62 64; Petr Korda d Wally Masur 75 64; Anders Jarryd d Michael Stich 62 60; David Wheaton d Eric Jelen 63 60; Tim Mayotte d Magnus Gustafsson 46 76 75; Patrick Kuhnen d Glenn Layendecker 76 61; Alexander Mronz d Milan Srejber 63 64; Alexander Volkov d Andrei Medvedev 64 63; Marc Rosset d Javier Sanchez 76 64; Sergio Casal d Thomas Hogstedt 46 75 76; Udo Riglewski d Bryan Shelton 76 67 62; Richey Reneberg d John Fitzgerald 75 62; Andrei Cherkasov d Amos Mansdorf 62 60; Gilad Bloom d Andrei Olhovskiy 62 62; Veli Paloheimo d Paul Haarhuis 62 64; Emilio Sanchez d Francisco Clavet 57 62 76. **Rd 16:** Korda d Gunnarsson 61 67 62; Jarryd d Wheaton 63 75; Mayotte d Kuhnen 63 76; Volkov d Mronz 62 36 64; Casal d Rosset 64 63; Riglewski d Reneberg 16 63 62; Cherkasov d Bloom 63 63; E Sanchez d Paloheimo 26 75 62. **QF:** Korda d Jarryd 75 76; Mayotte d Volkov 63 62; Riglewski d Casal 46 76 63; Cherkasov d E Sanchez 63 63. **SF:** Mayotte d Korda 76 36 63; Cherkasov d Riglewski 61 76. **F:** Cherkasov d Mayotte 62 61.
DOUBLES: Henrik Jan Davids/Paul Haarhuis d Anders Jarryd/John Fitzgerald 64 76

NOVEMBER 5-11: CITIBANK OPEN, ITAPARICA $225,000 Winner: MATS WILANDER
Rd 32: Danila Marcelino d Juan Aguilera 76 63; Nuno Marques d Alberto Mancini 60 67 64; Jaime Yzaga d Martin Wostenholme 62 62; Marcelo Filippini d Tomas Zdrazila 62 63; Thomas Carbonell d Franco Davin 76 60; Jose Francisco Altur d Pablo Arraya 67 63 75; Cassio Motta d Fernando Roese 36 76 64; Luiz Mattar d Roberto Azar 63 46 75; Mats Wilander d Tim Wilkison 62 62; Joao Cunha-Silva d Horacio de la Pena 26 63 64; Andrew Sznajder d Diego Perez 67 63 76; Karel Novacek d Chris Garner 61 64; Jean Philippe Fleurian d Jaime Oncins 61 61 64; Maurice Ruah d Todd Martin 75 76; Bart Wuyts d Carlos Costa 26 63 62; Mark Koevermans d Martin Jaite 63 67 62. **Rd 16:** Marques d Marcelino 36 61 61; Filippini d Yzaga 62 62; Carbonell d Altur 46 61 62; Motta d Mattar 61 26 75; Wilander d Cunha-Silva 62 62; Sznajder d Novacek 64 63; Ruah d Fleurian 76 63; Koevermans d Wuyts 36 63 75. **QF:** Filippini d Marques 63 36 76.Carbonell d Motta 63 75; Wilander d Sznajder 61 60; Koevermans d Ruah 76 63. **SF:** Filippini d Carbonell 76 64; Wilander d Koevermans 64 63. **F:** Wilander d Filippini 61 62.
DOUBLES: Mauro Menezes/Fernando Roese d Thomas Carbonell/Marco Gorriz 76 75.

NOVEMBER 13-18: ATP TOUR WORLD CHAMPIONSHIP, FRANKFURT $2,000,000 Winner: ANDRE AGASSI
Arthur Ashe Group: Stefan Edberg, Andre Agassi, Pete Sampras, Emilio Sanchez. **Cliff Drysdale Group**:Boris Becker, Ivan Lendl, Andres Gomez, Thomas Muster. **Round Robin**: Edberg d Sampras 67 63 61; Agassi d Sampras 64 62; Lendl d Muster 63 63; Sampras d Sanchez 62 64; Becker d Gomez 46 63 63; Edberg d Agassi 76 46 76; Lendl d Gomez 64 61; Becker d Muster 75 64; Agassi d Sanchez 60 63; Becker d Lendl 16 76 64; Edberg d Sampras 75 57 64; Muster d Gomez 75 57 64. **SF:** Edberg d Lendl 64 62; Agassi d Becker 62 64. **F:** Agassi d Edberg 57 76 75 62.

NOVEMBER 21-25: ATP TOUR DOUBLES CHAMPIONSHIP, SANCTUARY COVE $1,000,000 Winners: GUY FORGET AND JAKOB HLASEK
Newcombe-Roche Group: Pieter Aldrich/Danie Visser, Grant Connell/Glenn Michibata, Guy Forget/Jakob Hlasek, Darren Cahill/Mark Kratzmann. **Hoad-Rosewall Group**: Scott Davis/David Pate, Rick Leach/Jim Pugh, Sergio Casal/Emilio Sanchez, Neil Broad/Gary Muller. **Round Robin**: Forget/Hlasek d Connell/Michibata 63 76; Aldrich/Visser d Cahill/Kratzmann 64 62; Davis/Pate d Leach/Pugh 76 36 64; Connell/Michibata d Cahill/Kratzmann 64 57 64; Forget/Hlasek d Aldrich/Visser 63 75; Broad/Muller d Leach/Pugh 67 64 76; Casal/Sanchez d Davis/Pate 63 76; Conell/Michibata d Aldrich/Visser 62 76; Forget/Hlasek d Cahill/Kratzmann 62 76. **SF:** Casal/Sanchez d Connell/Michibata 64 67 64 63; Forget/Hlasek d Davis/Pate 36 46 64 76 64. **F:** Forget/Hlasek d Casal/Sanchez 64 76 57 64.

Singles Rankings

Singles rankings based on the best 14 tournaments at 26 November 1990

RANK	NAME	TOTAL PTS	TOURS PLAYED
1	EDBERG, STEFAN	3889	19
2	BECKER, BORIS	3528	19
3	LENDL, IVAN	2581	15
4	AGASSI, ANDRE	2398	13
5	SAMPRAS, PETE	1888	21
6	GOMEZ, ANDRES	1680	26
7	MUSTER, THOMAS	1654	20
8	SANCHEZ, EMILIO	1564	23
9	IVANISEVIC, GORAN	1514	22
10	GILBERT, BRAD	1451	21
11	SVENSSON, JONAS	1365	19
12	CHESNOKOV, ANDREI	1361	22
13	MCENROE, JOHN	1210	15
14	PEREZ-ROLDAN, GUILLERMO	1190	23
15	CHANG, MICHAEL	1119	19
16	FORGET, GUY	1101	24
17	HLASEK, JAKOB	1089	23
18	BERGER, JAY	1066	18
19	AGUILERA, JUAN	1048	22
20	KRICKSTEIN, AARON	1025	25
21	CHERKASOV, ANDREI	1003	26
22	ROSSET, MARC	977	26
23	RENEBERG, RICHEY	967	25
24	VOLKOV, ALEXANDER	929	26
25	COURIER, JIM	923	21
26	SKOFF, HORST	899	25
27	WHEATON, DAVID	893	20
28	BRUGUERA, SERGI	886	24
29	AGENOR, RONALD	864	29
30	LECONTE, HENRI	860	16
31	GUSTAFSSON, MAGNUS	810	17
32	FROMBERG, RICHARD	809	26
33	MANSDORF, AMOS	800	24
34	NOVACEK, KAREL	792	31
35	DAVIN, FRANCO	774	25
36	JAITE, MARTIN	747	21
37	MAYOTTE, TIM	737	19
38	KORDA, PETR	706	26
39	ARRESE, JORDI	691	27
40	NOAH, YANNICK	676	21
41	WILANDER, MATS	669	14
42	STICH, MICHAEL	652	24
43	MATTAR, LUIZ	645	23
44	FILIPPINI, MARCELO	640	25
45	DAVIS, SCOTT	638	23
46	CAMPORESE, OMAR	613	24
47	STEEB, CARL-UWE	611	21
48	ROSTAGNO, DERRICK	604	19
49	KOEVERMANS, MARK	601	28
50	WOODBRIDGE, TODD	569	30
51	KULTI, NICKLAS	563	18
52	HAARHUIS, PAUL	563	29
53	MULLER, GARY	557	22
54	MASUR, WALLY	555	21
55	PRPIC, GORAN	553	22
56	LARSSON, MAGNUS	551	17
57	CAHILL, DARREN	541	20
58	WITSKEN, TODD	535	20
59	CHAMPION, THIERRY	534	23
60	ARIAS, JIMMY	529	28
61	VAN RENSBURG, CHRISTO	527	21
62	SANTORO, FABRICE	526	23
63	DE LA PENA, HORACIO	518	19
64	ANTONITSCH, ALEX	516	22
65	FLEURIAN, JEAN-PHILIPPE	516	32
66	LUNDGREN, PETER	510	18
67	BLOOM, GILAD	508	26
68	JELEN, ERIC	502	23
69	PALOHEIMO, VELI	502	23
70	SANCHEZ, JAVIER	499	24
71	CURREN, KEVIN	491	18
72	GRABB, JIM	490	19
73	RAHUNEN, AKI	480	30
74	KRATZMANN, MARK	479	23
75	CARBONELL, TOMAS	474	25
76	FURLAN, RENZO	459	20
77	PEARCE, BRAD	453	20
78	KRISHNAN, RAMESH	450	25
79	BERGSTROM, CHRISTIAN	440	20
80	CASH, PAT	432	12
81	KUHNEN, PATRIK	430	26
82	JARRYD, ANDERS	429	16
83	VAJDA, MARIAN	428	23
84	SREJBER, MILAN	425	28
85	RAOUZ, GUILLAUME	423	18
86	MRONZ, ALEXANDER	418	22
87	YZAGA, JAIME	406	21
88	RIGLEWSKI, UDO	394	28
89	WEISS, ROBBIE	393	19
90	CLAVET, FRANCISCO	391	25
91	WASHINGTON, MALIVAI	390	22
92	HOGSTEDT, THOMAS	380	30
93	CONNELL, GRANT	376	21
94	PATE, DAVID	364	16
95	GARROW, BRIAN	364	22
96	GOLDIE, DAN	356	26
97	EVERNDEN, KELLY	348	23
98	GUNNARSSON, JAN	342	24
99	JONSSON, LARS	342	25
100	WOODFORDE, MARK	340	13
101	MARQUES, NUNO	339	25
102	HERRERA, LUIS	335	12
103	SZNAJDER, ANDREW	333	23
104	MOTTA, CASSIO	331	29
105	AZAR, ROBERTO	328	25
106	BENHABILES, TARIK	324	29
107	STOLTENBERG, JASON	315	20
108	CANE, PAOLO	313	17
109	ONCINS, JAIME	310	20
110	LUNA, FERNANDO	310	24
111	ALTUR, JOSE FRANCISCO	309	26
112	PISTOLESI, CLAUDIO	301	29
113	CUNHA-SILVA, JOAO	299	23
114	MERCIR, MILOSLAV	297	8
115	SINNER, MARTIN	296	19
116	TARANGO, JEFF	296	24
117	CARATTI, CRISTIANO	293	12
118	ENGEL, DAVID	291	17
119	MCENROE, PATRICK	289	12
120	PUGH, JIM	285	15
121	ROIG, FRANCISCO	284	20
122	SHELTON, BRYAN	282	24
123	REBOLLEDO, PEDRO	280	16
124	PIOLINE, CEDRIC	279	17
125	KROON, NICLAS	279	18
126	MASSO, EDUARDO	277	14
127	MANCINI, ALBERTO	274	18

128	BATES, JEREMY	271	23
129	PEREZ, DIEGO	269	20
130	ELTINGH, JACCO	267	18
131	JONES, KELLY	262	23
132	LAYENDECKER, GLENN	260	14
133	BAUR, PATRICK	257	15
134	HOLM, HENRIK	257	16
135	RIVE, JOEY	255	22
136	STRELBA, MARTIN	255	28
137	WOEHRMANN, JENS	251	23
138	PESCOSOLIDO, STEFANO	248	25
139	MATSUOKA, SHUZO	247	14
140	TAUSON, MICHAEL	247	17
141	GARNER, CHRIS	247	20
142	DUNCAN, LAWSON	246	21
143	SIEMERINK, JAN	245	13
144	WUYTS, BART	241	20
145	DOSEDEL, CTISLAV	239	14
146	CHAMBERLIN, PAUL	232	24
147	OLHOVSKIY, ANDREI	230	10
148	KRAJICEK, RICHARD	227	6
149	MARCELINO, DANILO	226	19
150	COSTA, CARLOS	224	16
151	DELAITRE, OLIVIER	223	23
152	ARRAYA, PABLO	221	19
153	GORRIZ, MARCO AURELIO	220	21
154	YOUL, SIMON	217	21
155	PRIDHAM, CHRIS	215	14
156	WOSTENHOLME, MARTIN	215	25
157	TULASNE, THIERRY	214	20
158	ORESAR, BRUNO	211	21
159	MINIUSSI, CHRISTIAN	210	19
160	NARGISO, DIEGO	206	16
161	BROWN, JIMMY	198	20
162	GILBERT, RODOLPHE	194	7
163	GEYER, CHRISTIAN	194	19
164	FERREIRA, WAYNE	189	13
165	ANNACONE, PAUL	187	18
166	LOPEZ, GERMAN	186	11
167	ORSANIC, DANIEL	177	16
168	DYKE, BRODERICK	174	14
169	SACEANU, CHRISTIAN	170	16
170	POLIAKOV, DIMITRI	168	14
171	FRANA, JAVIER	167	14
172	WILKISON, TIM	165	16
173	ANDERSON, JOHAN	165	23
174	PERNFORS, MIKAEL	162	6
175	NIDO, MIGUEL	162	17
176	BOETSCH, ARNAUD	161	9
177	BENGOECHEA, EDUARDO	161	15
178	STANKOVIC, BRANISLAV	157	9
179	ZOECKE, MARKUS	157	16
180	KAPLAN, MARK	156	20
181	HO, TOMMY	154	11
182	LAVALLE, LEONARDO	154	11
183	CARLSSON, JOHAN	152	13
184	ODIZOR, NDUKA	150	13
185	POTIER, JEROME	149	16
186	FITZGERALD, JOHN	148	14
187	SHIRAS, LEIF	147	20
188	MELVILLE, SCOTT	145	7
189	BORWICK, NEIL	144	17
190	ALDRICH, PIETER	142	6
191	SCHAPERS, MICHIEL	142	14
192	DAHER, JOSE	141	14
193	CANTER, JONATHAN	140	11
194	VISSER, DANIE	138	6
195	PAMBIANCO, PAOLO	138	9
196	TABARES, MARIO	137	14
197	YUNIS, FRANCISCO	136	18
198	NIJSSEN, TOM	134	18
199	OOSTING, MENNO	133	18
200	GRENIER, STEPHANE	132	9

Doubles Rankings

Doubles rankings based on best 14 tournaments at 26 November 1990.

RANK	NAME	TOTAL PTS	TOURNS PLAYED
1T	ALDRICH, PIETER	2192	18
1T	VISSER, DANIE	2192	18
3	PUGH, JIM	2134	20
4	FORGET, GUY	2112	21
5	LEACH, RICK	2069	19
6	PATE, DAVID	2053	24
7	KRATZMANN, MARK	2031	25
8	DAVIS, SCOTT	2013	24
9	SANCHEZ, EMILIO	1936	22
10T	CONNELL, GRANT	1925	25
10T	MICHIBATA, GLENN	1925	25
12	HLASEK, JAKOB	1910	23
13	CASAL, SERGIO	1825	21
14	BROAD, NEIL	1692	27
15	KORDA, PETR	1505	26
16	MULLER, GARY	1498	27
17	LOZANO, JORGE	1496	25
18	CAHILL, DARREN	1467	19
19	RIGLEWSKI, UDO	1400	36
20	GALBRAITH, PATRICK	1382	28
21	WITSKEN, TODD	1380	23
22	JONES, KELLY	1373	24
23	MCENROE, PATRICK	1246	20
24	GRABB, JIM	1235	16
25	WOODBRIDGE, TODD	1219	21
26	CURREN, KEVIN	1172	16
27	STICH, MICHAEL	1166	22
28	BECKER, BORIS	1136	11
29	ANNACONE, PAUL	1121	18
30	SANCHEZ, JAVIER	1115	24
31	IVANISEVIC, GORAN	1113	22
32	DYKE, BRODERICK	1106	29
33	STOLTENBERG, JASON	1074	18
34	HAARHUIS, PAUL	1059	28
35	SMID, TOMAS	1021	25
36	LUNDGREN, PETER	998	15
37	MOTTA, CASSIO	977	23
38	MACPHERSON, DAVID	968	33
39	MASUR, WALLY	964	19
40	COURIER, JIM	937	17
41	CAMPORESE, OMAR	932	18
42	FITZGERALD, JOHN	903	17
43	KOEVERMANS, MARK	865	25
44	PEREIRA, NICOLAS	862	28
45	SCHAPERS, MICHIEL	854	21
46	WHEATON, DAVID	853	12
47	SALUMAA, SVEN	838	26
48	WINOGRADSKY, ERIC	837	23
49	KRUGER, STEFAN	837	25
50	BATES, JEREMY	836	17
51	CARBONELL, TOMAS	829	22
52	JARRYD, ANDERS	827	14
53	NIJSSEN, TOM	810	23
54	LUZA, GUSTAVO	803	21
55	EVERNDEN, KELLY	797	22
56	GOMEZ, ANDRES	787	16
57	RENEBERG, RICHEY	781	23
58	MELVILLE, SCOTT	772	15
59	BRUGUERA, SERGI	758	13
60	VAN'T HOF, ROBERT	755	21
61	VAN RENSBURG, CHRISTO	749	21
62	BAHRAMI, MANSOUR	748	28
63	BECKMAN, CHARLES	744	34
64	BROWN, JEFF	737	13
65	FRANA, JAVIER	726	16
66	JENSEN, LUKE	725	33
67	MATTAR, LUIZ	721	25
68	ODIZOR, NDUKA	707	24
69	CASTLE, ANDREW	201	19
70	GARROW, BRIAN	699	22
71	UTGREN, NICKLAS	690	17
72	KINNEAR, KENT	687	24
73	PEARCE, BRAD	686	20
74	SUK, CYRIL	684	32
75	DEVRIES, STEVE	683	30
76	FLACH, KEN	664	18
77	DE LA PENA, HORACIO	654	22
78	LAVALLE, LEONARDO	632	18
79	MORTENSEN, MICHAEL	628	20
80	ROIG, FRANCISCO	616	22
81	NOVACEK, KAREL	615	27
82	ROESE, FERNANDO	609	23
83	SMITH, ROGER	599	24
84	WARDER, LAURIE	599	26
85	SHELTON, BRYAN	596	22
86	NARGISO, DIEGO	594	21
87	JELEN, ERIC	592	13
88	AERTS, NELSON	591	22
89	FERREIRA, WAYNE	589	15
90	NORVAL, PIET	580	14
91	CIHAK, JOSEF	570	21
92	HENRICSSON, PER	567	15
93	NELSON, TODD	553	26
94	LAYENDECKER, GLENN	551	13
95	BROWN, NICK	550	20
96	GORRIZ, MARCO AURELIO	550	25
97	SEGUSO, ROBERT	546	11
98	CANNON, SHELBY	538	29
99	DERLIN, BRUCE	523	23
100	CASH, PAT	521	11
101	MORDEGAN, FEDERICO	521	21
102	MORA, ALFONSO	514	32
103	VACEK, DANIEL	513	17
104	SVANTESSON, TOBIAS	508	20
105	BATHMAN, RONNIE	507	18
106	VAN EMBURGH, GREG	505	20
107	FLEGL, VOJTECH	498	17
108	MINIUSSI, CHRISTIAN	487	19
109	CANTER, JONATHAN	480	25
110	MARCELINO, DANILO	479	20
111	POUL, SIMON	478	24
112	SREJBER, MILAN	476	19
113	ALBANO, PABLO	471	25
114	NOAH, YANNICK	467	11
115	ANTONITSCH, ALEX	466	19
116	COSTA, CARLOS	465	19
117	LENDL, IVAN	455	5
118	WOODFORDE, MARK	452	11
119	MENEZES, MAURO	452	22
120	ZIVOJINOVIC, SLOBODAN	451	9
121	BERGH, RIKARD	448	14
122	PEREZ, DIEGO	441	15
123	WILKISON, TIM	440	20
124	BAGUENA, JUAN CARLOS	439	24
125	RIKL, DAVID	436	21
126	ZDRAZILA, TOMAS	435	23
127	PIMEK, LIBOR	435	27

128	COLOMBO, SIMONE	430	20
129	EDBERG, STEFAN	428	7
130	GARNETT, BRET	428	19
131	DAVIS, MARTIN	417	10
132	DAVIDS, HENRIK JAN	398	12
133	RIVE, JOEY	382	21
134	MASSO, EDUARDO	380	15
135	OLHOVSKIY, ANDREI	377	13
136	BORWICK, NEIL	376	21
137	PEREZ-ROLDAN, GUILLERMO	374	14
138	DOOHAN, PETER	370	18
139	WEKESA, PAUL	361	19
140	TALBOT, BYRON	361	21
141	CLAVET, FRANCISCO	361	24
142	SKOFF, HORST	360	14
143	DEPPE, ROYCE	360	23
144	GUNNARSSON, JAN	358	17
145	LEWIS, DAVID	350	17
146	FLEURIAN, JEAN-PHILIPPE	338	26
147	PATRIDGE, SCOTT	334	23
148	PRPIC, GORAN	332	8
149	BRANDI, CRISTIAN	331	17
150	DREWETT, BRAD	328	7

Prize Money

	NAME	TOTAL PRIZE
1	EDBERG, STEFAN	$1,995,901
2	AGASSI, ANDRE	$1,741,382
3	BECKER, BORIS	$1,587,502
4	LENDL, IVAN	$1,145,742
5	SAMPRAS, PETE	$900,057
6	GOMEZ, ANDRES	$874,605
7	SANCHEZ, EMILIO	$734,291
8	IVANISEVIC, GORAN	$720,945
9	HLASEK, JAKOB	$661,671
10	FORGET, GUY	$638,358
11	MUSTER, THOMAS	$605,267
12	GILBERT, BRAD	$555,733
13	SVENSSON, JONAS	$441,745
14	COURIER, JIM	$437,490
15	CHESNOKOV, ANDREI	$423,863
16	DAVIS, SCOTT	$422,390
17	CHANG, MICHAEL	$416,072
18	MCENROE, JOHN	$372,505
19	KRICKSTEIN, AARON	$350,183
20	BERGER, JAY	$349,354
21	KRATZMANN, MARK	$346,366
22	PATE, DAVID	$342,637
23	BRUGUERA, SERGI	$342,423
24	PUGH, JIM	$342,307
25	WHEATON, DAVID	$341,240
26	KORDA, PETR	$331,404
27	ALDRICH, PIETER	$331,272
28	VISSER, DANIE	$322,665
29	PEREZ-ROLDAN, GUILLERMO	$317,538
30	AGUILERA, JUAN	$311,806
31	CONNELL, GRANT	$307,589
32	RENEBERG, RICHEY	$307,341
33	CAHILL, DARREN	$292,899
34	CHERKASOV, ANDREI	$292,171
35	NOVACEK, KAREL	$282,727
36	LEACH, RICK	$282,355
37	ROSSET, MARC	$282,048
38	STICH, MICHAEL	$280,513
39	CASAL, SERGIO	$279,641
40	JAITE, MARTIN	$271,498
41	MAYOTTE, TIM	$263,156
42	MULLER, GARY	$261,675
43	VOLKOV, ALEXANDER	$259,417
44	CURREN, KEVIN	$257,542
45	ROSTAGNO, DERRICK	$257,542
46	PRPIC, GORAN	$251,018
47	WITSKEN, TODD	$250,624
48	WOODBRIDGE, TODD	$247,362
49	SKOFF, HORST	$247,236
50	MANSDORF, AMOS	$246,286
51	AGENOR, RONALD	$243,950
52	MASUR, WALLY	$243,266
53	LUNDGREN, PETER	$241,053
54	HAARHUIS, PAUL	$238,564
55	GRABB, JIM	$237,612
56	LECONTE, HENRI	$235,590
57	FROMBERG, RICHARD	$228,987
58	SANCHEZ, JAVIER	$226,368
59	GUSTAFSSON, MAGNUS	$224,554
60	NOAH, YANNICK	$222,729
61	ARRESE, JORDI	$218,212
62	RIGLEWSKI, UDO	$218,098
63	CAMPORESE, OMAR	$214,402
64	JONES, KELLY	$211,067
65	VAN RENSBURG, CHRISTO	$210,540
66	ANTONITSCH, ALEX	$208,090
67	JELEN, ERIC	$206,631
68	KOEVERMANS, MARK	$202,883
69	MICHIBATA, GLENN	$201,181
70	MATTAR, LUIZ	$200,016
71	DAVIN, FRANCO	$197,163
72	CARBONELL, TOMAS	$195,984
73	ZIVOJINOVIC, SLOBODAN	$191,663
74	SREJBER, MILAN	$191,197
75	WILANDER, MATS	$187,435
76	STEEB, CARL-UWE	$184,050
77	FLEURIAN, JEAN-PHILIPPE	$180,718
78	PEARCE, BRAD	$179,189
79	JARRYD, ANDERS	$176,618
80	BROAD, NEIL	$169,273
81	FILIPPINI, MARCELO	$168,729
82	ANNACONE, PAUL	$168,729
83	STOLTENBERG, JASON	$166,467
84	MCENROE, PATRICK	$159,860
85	ARIAS, JIMMY	$155,994
86	EVERNDEN, KELLY	$155,595
87	KUHNEN, PATRICK	$153,036
88	DYKE, BRODERICK	$151,867
89	DE LA PENA, HORACIO	$149,426
90	RAHUNEN, AKI	$148,458
91	BLOOM, GILAD	$148,399
92	MOTTA, CASSIO	$148,047
93	LOZANO, JORGE	$146,953
94	BATES, JEREMY	$146,433
95	CHAMPION, THIERRY	$145,007
96	BERGSTROM, CHRISTIAN	$144,238
97	GUNNARSSON, JAN	$143,253
98	MANCINI, ALBERTO	$140,732
99	SHELTON, BRYAN	$138,962
100	CASH, PAT	$137,916
101	GOLDIE, DAN	$136,848
102	YZAGA, JAIME	$131,300
103	HOGSTEDT, THOMAS	$130,546
104	KRISHNAN, RAMESH	$128,898
105	SANTORO, FABRICE	$127,027
106	WOODFORDE, MARK	$125,142
107	CHAMBERLIN, PAUL	$124,601
108	GARROW, BRIAN	$123,511
109	RIVE, JOEY	$121,676
110	LARSSON, MAGNUS	$120,972
111	GALBRAITH, PATRICK	$120,347
112	SZNAJDER, ANDREW	$120,150
113	PALOHEIMO, VELI	$119,973
114	FITZGERALD, JOHN	$116,894
115	CLAVET, FRANCISCO	$116,862
116	FLACH, KEN	$116,019
117	KROON, NICLAS	$114,362
118	PEREIRA, NICOLAS	$112,587
119	NARGISO, DIEGO	$110,378
120	NIJSSEN, TOM	$110,372
121	YOUL, SIMON	$109,817
122	BENHABILES, TARIK	$109,328
123	RAOUX, GUILLAUME	$108,245
124	MRONZ, ALEXANDER	$108,082
125	KULTI, NICKLAS	$106,809
126	PEREZ, DIEGO	$105,780
127	MACPHERSON, DAVID	$105,752
128	STRELBA, MARTIN	$105,448
129	WASHINGTON, MALIVAI	$105,246
130	LAYENDECKER, GLENN	$103,776
131	SCHAPERS, MICHIEL	$101,802
132	CANE, PAOLO	$100,765
133	VAJDA, MARIAN	$99,972
134	SEGUSO, ROBERT	$96,989
135	LAVALLE, LEONARDO	$95,858
136	ALTUR, JOSE FRANCISCO	$95,453
137	WINOGRADSKY, ERIC	$95,043
138	DELAITRE, OLIVIER	$94,308
139	ENGEL, DAVID	$94,061
140	JONSSON, LARS	$92,881
141	SHIRAS, LEIF	$91,908
142	FRANA, JAVIER	$91,714
143	AZAR, ROBERTO	$88,299
144	SMID, TOMAS	$87,313
145	DUNCAN, LAWSON	$86,886
146	ROIG, FRANCISCO	$84,263
147	FURLAN, RENZO	$84,061
148	TARANGO, JEFF	$83,521
149	WOSTENHOLME, MARTIN	$82,598
150	MECIR, MILOSLAV	$82,293

Picture Credits

Gala Dinner

of the IBM/ATP Tour

17th November 1990

Hotel Gravenbruch Kempinski